Praise for *Prosecuted but Not Silenced*

This book, *Prosecuted, But Not Silenced: Courtroom Reform for Sexually Abused Children*, is a powerful documentary about one mother and daughter's tragic involvement with the judicial and legal systems when there were allegations of child sexual abuse. I would like to say that this is an unusual situation and rarely happens in our society. Sadly, I can't say that because it happens all too often in all communities around our country. I know this because I have encountered dozens and dozens of such cases just in the last decade alone in which I reviewed the records as a forensic psychologist or testified as an expert witness for people just like Maralee McLean. Her story portrays the failure of various systems when child sexual abuse is reported, and how these cases can get turned against a protective parent in family courts. An abusive parent obtaining custody of a child s/he has abused is the ultimate in re-victimization. The same can be said for an abused women who has her child or children taken away by the courts since that is exactly what the perpetrator has likely threatened to do. If we sometimes wonder why victimized women stay in an abusive relationship, reading this book helps explain what many women are afraid will happen to them if they leave. Unfortunately, many judges, attorneys, and mental health professionals still do not understand the overlapping dynamics of spouse abuse with child abuse, and how nearly half of either type of case likely has the other going on as well. It is easier for many people to believe an allegation of child sexual abuse is false and made up by a parent getting back at the other parent despite substantial research in many countries indicating that this is not accurate. Common logic should make us realize that if there are millions of women and men who are adult survivors of childhood abuse, then they must have been abused as children! However, we would rather blame the victim or the protective parent (who like Maralee would rather wish their child had not really been abused even when they had been) than to think that an adult could do the things we know they do to their children. It is easier to use a label such as "Parental Alienation Syndrome" (there is no such syndrome or disorder, by the way) to blame victims and to sweep away child abuse allegations then to have to follow through with a thorough investigation of the allegations and to prosecute the offenders. This riveting book is a must read for all those working in the fields of domestic violence, child abuse, or child trauma so they can realize what does occur even today. It is important to ensure that all judges, attorneys, mental health professionals, medical personnel, child custody evaluators, and social workers are trained in the dynamics of such maltreatment so that there are no more situations like what happened to Maralee and her daughter.

—**Robert Geffner**, Ph.D., ABPP, ABN Founding President, Family Violence & Sexual Assault Institute (FVSAI) Founding President, Institute on Violence, Abuse, & Trauma (IVAT)
Distinguished Research Professor, CSPP, Alliant International University
Co-Chair, National Partnership to End Interpersonal Violence Across the Lifespan (NPEIV)
Past President, Trauma Psychology Division, American Psychological Association

"In my twenty-five years of experience in child welfare and victim advocacy, I have seen hundreds of cases very similar to Maralee and her daughter's experience. We blame women who stay in abusive relationships for not protecting their children, but when they do leave and try to protect they are deemed "overeacting" or trying to "alienate the children and father." Research has shown that at least 60% of men who are battering their wives are also simultaneously abusing their children. This abuse includes sexual, physical and emotional abuse. How would a mother not do everything in her power to stop this abuse that is occurring to her children? Maralee has shown in her book the need to continue vigilant efforts to train the professionals who oversee these types of cases. Many professionals who make life-altering decisions on these cases have little to no formal training on domestic violence and child abuse. Maralee has shown example after example where the systems that are in place to protect children did not work. May each of us be vigilant in our own way to inform, educate and hold accountable systems and people that are in place to protect children and empower mothers to protect their children also."

—**Lisa O'Dell Davis**, BSW,
MPA, Executive Director of a child-
focused non-profit in Denver, CO

"This book provides what the literature on Parental Alienation Syndrome has lacked: a personal chronicle that explains what individual citizens and our legal system misunderstand: how unsuspecting women become embroiled in relationships that physically and psychologically threaten them and their children and how incompetent, biased and self-serving legal and mental health professionals make bad situations worse. Legal and mental health practitioners and academics have written, of course, about Parental Alienation Syndrome. No unified voice, however, has emerged. More importantly, the literature describes only in general or "scientific" terms the havoc wreaked on the lives of women and children who fall victim to this "junk" science and then are swept into a dysfunctional legal system. This story provides much needed insight into the incomprehensible pain experienced and pitfalls encountered by women in that dysfunctional legal system as they attempt to protect their children from physical and sexual predators. We can only hope that this personal story will open the eyes of a legal system that does not want to see and provide insights and assistance for the many other mothers "trapped"in similar incomprehensible situations."

—**Penelope Bryan** Dean and
Professor of Law Whittier Law School

"Maralee Mclean's story cries out for our attention. The tragedy of abuse suffered by her daughter at the hands of her father and Maralee's abuse at the hands of our court system does not have a fairytale ending. Again and again she trusted the system to provide a measure of justice for her and her daughter, but the system failed them utterly. The disastrous effects of incompetence, personal agendas and individual prejudices are all too common in our system of justice. Sadly, once having made a decision, individuals are often unwilling to admit they were wrong despite overwhelming evidence to the contrary. Today the concept of "Believe the Children" has become more widely accepted, but Maralee and her daughter can never regain what they have irrevocably lost. Maralee left no stone unturned in her fight to protect her daughter. Her thoughtful, well-written account may help others caught up in the same tragedy."

—**C. de Roda,** M.Ed

In this riveting book, protective parent Ms. Mclean calls our hearts and minds to sharp attention. We simply cannot look away from this reality, from this clear-cut example of what can take place in and within all too common poorly informed, flawed, biased, and at times dishonest judicial and legal processes.

—**Dr. Angela Browne-Miller**

"Prosecuted but Not Silenced" is a riveting account of a mother's courageous efforts to protect her child from incest, while battling a dysfunctional, and hostile family court system. Her experience contains key elements of all the worst cases I have ever dealt with or written about, but even for someone who is familiar with how these cases play out, this book still has the power to shock, and to remind the reader that we have a long way to go to fix the problem. Maralee is a skilled writer—able to convey complex, painful information in a clear manner, focusing on what is relevant and at the same time making it emotionally compelling. She has conveyed and captured not only the deficits in our system of child protection—but more subtly—the portrait of an abuser and his seduction of key players in the system to his advantage—a pattern that we find repeatedly in cases involving failure to protect a child from incest.

Above all, what stands out is her strength—to have come through this experience and survived—and to have brilliantly strategized maintaining a relationship with her daughter through all of this horror. It is a must read for protective mothers and their advocates, as well as policy-makers who want to bring about meaningful change.

—**Leora N. Rosen**, Ph.D.
Author of *"The Hostage Child: Sex Abuse Allegations in Custody Disputes"* and *"Beyond the Hostage Child: Towards Empowering Protective Parents."*

Prosecuted But Not Silenced

PROSECUTED BUT NOT SILENCED

Courtroom Reform for Sexually Abused Children

MARALEE MCLEAN

NEW YORK

LONDON • NASHVILLE • MELBOURNE • VANCOUVER

Prosecuted But Not Silenced

Courtroom Reform for Sexually Abused Children

Published in New York, New York, by Morgan James Publishing. Morgan James is a trademark of Morgan James, LLC. www.MorganJamesPublishing.com

ISBN 9781683507802 paperback
ISBN 9781683507819 eBook
Library of Congress Control Number: 2017914837

Cover Design by:
Rachel Lopez
www.r2cdesign.com

Interior Design by:
Chris Treccani
www.3dogcreative.net

DEDICATION

I dedicate this book in loving memory to my precious mom and dad, whose hearts broke seeing this atrocity unfold. For my family and close friends, and the professionals that supported us—my therapists, Duane Mullner and Dr. Cynthia Daugherty, my attorneys who represented my child and me, and several who worked pro bono, Jeanne Elliott, Esq., Michael Scott, Esq. For Joan Pennington, Esq. out of New Jersey for her efforts to educate and make a difference in many mothers' lives. Alliance For the Rights of Children, Glennie Rohelier. My thanks to Ruth Gibbens, Ami's daycare provider. To all the mothers in the grassroots of this nightmare that had the courage to stay in there and fight such as Kitty Kruse (Iowa), Evelyn Hayes (Alabama), Kathryn Andrews (Texas), Dr. Amy Neustein (New York), Debbie Williams (Indiana), Linda Leon (Florida), Paula Oldham (Colorado), in memory of Marcia Rimland, Esq. (New York), and the many, many others I have not mentioned. For the hundreds of thousands of loving protective mothers and their children that are suffering today, you are not alone in this battle. God bless all of you who stood by us. You know who you are.

The most important dedication of all is to my amazing and beautiful daughter.

MARALEE MCLEAN

CONTENT

FOREWORD

This is a very important book that illustrates a very common experience for mothers seeking to protect a child from a sexually abusive father. Recently, a horrified nation was outraged that officials at Penn State University failed to effectively respond to evidence that a football coach was raping young boys. An otherwise reputable football coaching legend and an accomplished university president were summarily tossed out in disgrace, for a strong consensus of the trustees, supported by editorial writers, TV pundits, and water cooler chat nationwide screamed out that "you just don't ignore evidence of child sexual abuse!" The United States Congress and Pennsylvania legislators soon began to schedule hearings to craft new laws to ensure that such sexual abuse is timely, exposed, and stopped, with the perpetrators swiftly hauled away for judgment and punishment.

Indeed, the Pennsylvania scandal, like the pedophile- sheltering Catholic Church hierarchy, deserved every iconoclastic journalistic drop of ink and second of airtime disinfecting these trusted institutions. Yet, the nationwide system most egregiously guilty of routinely ignoring strong proof that the children under its watch are being abused goes much farther in its sins by punishing those who responsibly act on behalf of the child victims. Yes, our country's family courts, where the same mother who stays with an abusive father can face termination of her parental rights for "failure to protect," will likewise lose custody of her child if she leaves the dangerous husband and asks the court for protection, because she is not "supporting the child's relationship" with the father. She is "damned if she does, damned if she doesn't." Yes, our family courts, often where fatally flawed and inherently bogus "evidence" and "experts" which would be rejected outright in any other courtroom following the dictates of constitutional law, the rules of evidence, and routine judicial procedure, are extolled as infallible. Yes, our family courts, where the attorneys typically seem too eager to be a court "team member" striving to "reduce conflict," immobilized against actually representing their clients and fighting for truth and justice by fear of upsetting the judge.

Most sexually abused children are victimized in their own homes. The family court is the gatekeeper of their safety. May Ms. McLean's painful story energize its readers and spark a tsunami of accountability and scrutiny for those judges, custody evaluators, guardians ad litem, and lawyers whose misguided, and often misogynistic, nonsense jeopardizes generations of children and compounds their misery.

—**Richard Ducote**, Esq. of the
Pennsylvania and Louisiana
Bars Ducotelaw.com

Mr. Ducote has devoted his 33-year law practice to protecting domestic violence and child abuse victims in family court litigation. His work has taken him to 44 states.

AUTHOR'S NOTE

To the hundreds of thousands of loving protective mothers and their children that are suffering today, you are not alone in your custody battle, the experiences with your ex-spouse, with professionals in the family law court system, or even in the at times immense emotional toll it takes to keep going and survive this nightmare.

This book is my story, but you will likely find similarities in your own experience. You may be experiencing domestic violence which it is clear there are many different forms. It may be emotional and coercive abuse, physical abuse, and/or child abuse, sexual abuse to you or your children. The type of abuse may differ, but there are parallels in the manipulation and tactics that abusers, with possible narcissistic personalities or sociopaths use, as well as commonalities that survivors go through. My mission is to ensure that you are not as blindsided as I was.

I have been supporting mothers for over 25 years. I want you to know I'm here to help make a difference in your plight.

To the Courageous Law Professionals:

We hear from professionals working in Family Law in different countries with similar challenges who know the system can do better. We hear the cry to have more tools to be made available for lawyers, social workers, judges and evaluators. Our aim is to work with you and help ensure that above all else, children are granted the right to safe childhoods that lead to better adult experiences. Please read this book as a case study that unfortunately mirrors many others of the injustices happening in the family courts and visit www.MaraleeMclean.com for info.

Maralee Mclean, Author, Advocate,
Domestic Violence, and National Speaker

INTRODUCTION

It was the beginning of summer 1989. As I opened the windows to my kitchen, I got a breath of fresh air, and the smell of lilacs plummeted into the room. Ami's tiny bare feet pitter pattered across the hardwood floors as she yelled, "Let's go shopping, Mommy!"

Gosh, was she cute. I know, I know, every little two-year- old is cute, but not one is nearly as cute as my little girl. She had dancing blue eyes, high cheekbones, long, dark hair, and a smile that lit up the room. Oh, she was special, and she had a personality to go with it!

"We can't go shopping today, honey," I said. "Mommy has to go to work."

I was a single mother and a flight attendant. When I first had Ami, I did not want to keep flying, so I had taken leave from Continental Airlines and began selling Yellow Pages advertising. I kept Ami home with me in the mornings and conducted business in the afternoons while she was being taken care of by a wonderful daycare provider named Ruth Gibbens. After that, I either took her back for the evening, or she had limited visitation with her father, who I had divorced due to the domestic violence and emotional abuse I endured throughout my marriage and pregnancy.

I told Ami to come upstairs; we had to get ready to leave. She began counting the stairs: one, two, three, four, and five— all the way up to sixteen. She took her bath, and afterward I smoothed Johnson's baby lotion all over her little body. She looked and smelled so clean. Then I put her long, dark hair into a high ponytail and helped her into her pink dress. As we drove to the daycare provider's, I imagined her father picking her up for his visitation that afternoon for his three hour visit and going nuts over her. She was such a doll.

◆◆◆◆◆◆

That evening when I arrived at her father's house to pick her up, I rang the doorbell, but no one answered. I rang it again and knocked a few times. Still no answer. Finally, he came to the door and told me that Ami was sick. Funny—she hadn't been sick earlier that day. As he went upstairs to get her, I looked around at his place. It was filthy. The vacuum cleaner had been in the same spot for three months, there was food all over the place, the house stunk, and Ami's beautiful clothes were strewn about the living-room floor.

When he brought her down, Ami was wet, nude, and limp in his arms. Her arms dangled at her sides, her ponytail was out of its band, and her hair was matted. She was soaked with sweat. My heart sunk and my gut pulled tight. "What the heck happened to her?"

Her father looked at me with a smirk on his face. "I can't believe what I'm seeing," he said. "She's sick!"

I didn't understand what had happened. All I wanted to do is get her out of there. I began grabbing and collecting her things. "That's funny," I said, "she was fine a few hours ago." I quickly got her dressed and out of that filthy place.

I think that was one of the first times that Derek sexually abused our daughter. That smirk on his face used to wake me up at two in the morning, causing me to sit upright in my bed. He was abusing Ami right in front of my face, and his attitude was like O.J. Simpson's: What are you going to do about it?

I am telling you our story because I want to change a judicial system that is detrimental to sexually abused children. I write this book with the best interest of the child in mind and to acknowledge the pain that is inflicted upon families by our inept and biased judicial system, a system designed to fail the child and protect the abuser. There is an unequivocal need for courtroom reform and more adequate training for judges, lawyers, therapist, social workers and court appointed evaluators.

A mother's first instinct is to protect her child, and when the means and the power to do this are stripped unjustly from a mother, there are no words to describe the constant heartache that is felt as each day passes by.

CHAPTER 1

The Hidden Truth Behind the Fairy Tale

I grew up in a small Wyoming town as the middle child in a family of six. My childhood was uncomplicated and full of spontaneity, love, and care. My parents instilled in each of us high morals, values, and integrity. I was a cheerleader in high school, semifinalist for homecoming queen in college, and runner-up for Miss Wyoming—a wholesome, small-town girl through and through.

After graduating from college, I began working as a flight attendant for Continental Airlines, which was based in LA. California was quite the culture shock, but I loved it and found my life to be quite exciting. I was fulfilling my childhood dream, which was to get a college education and become a flight attendant, so I could travel and meet all kinds of interesting people and to see the world. During my first few months in LA, I lived with several other flight attendants, and I did meet some interesting people. One of them happened to be the man that I would marry. Derek and I met while working out at an athletic club at the facility where we lived. He had a muscular build, curly brown hair, and nice blue eyes—a rather rugged but nice-looking man. We began talking, and he asked me out.

He was different from the other men I had met in LA. He had real values and seemed to appreciate my morals. And he seemed to covet my attention. In fact, in the beginning he was extremely persistent and never seemed to let go of me. While I found him attractive, I didn't feel quite as drawn to him.

For this reason, I tried to break things off several times, but each time he cried and pleaded until I gave him another chance. I could not bear to hurt him. In time, after a lot of persistence on his part, I began to care for him. He had a horrible childhood, and I marveled at how well he had turned out. He was kind, emotional, and caring of others, and he continually professed his deep love for me. Because I had been so loved my whole life, I wanted a man who was going to do the same, and he did. He wined and dined me at LA's most exclusive restaurants, bought me flowers, and treated me like gold. Now how could I not love someone like that? Even though he was, at times, socially inadequate—he had a hard time being comfortable with others—I felt I could help him in this area, and I was inspired by his formidable intellect. We seemed to complement each other. Yet something was holding me back. It took a long time before I could tell him that I loved him. Even after he proposed to me, it took two years before I could say yes.

Our problems began when he became very jealous, and that made me extremely uncomfortable. It got so that I had to harness my outgoing personality when we were out in public, for fear that he would verbally abuse me when he took me home. I reasoned that once he was sure of my love for him, he wouldn't be so easily threatened. But as time went on, things only escalated. He would tell me to button my blouse up to my neck, and one day he cut up one of my bikinis because he thought it was too revealing. Now, I could adjust my behavior to a point, but I wasn't going to let anyone tell me what to wear and how to wear it. So I bought another bikini and continued to dress attractively. I recognized that he was testing me, putting me through trials and tribulations to see if I could handle them. I did, of course, much to my later dismay, because I wanted to prove to him that I would not abandon him as his mother and family had.

However, I finally agreed to marry him—but not to set a wedding date

◆ ◆ ◆ ◆ ◆ ◆

I enjoyed living in California, things went generally good between us until the day he came to my apartment and told me he was getting transferred to

Midland, Texas. I thought he was kidding. I had never heard of Midland until I had become a flight attendant and heard the other attendants complain about having a Midland layover. His father was starting a new company and wanted him to run it. He was to leave in two weeks.

After he moved there, I couldn't get a transfer to Texas and really did not want one. I loved LA, so we would fly to see each other on weekends. On one of those visits he asked me to marry him again, and this time I finally agreed after five years to a date. Since he did not want a big wedding and I did, we eloped in Lake Tahoe without telling anyone but had an official wedding a month later in Wyoming.

It was a beautiful wedding. Friends flew in from all over the country, and I left all the planning to my mom. I was the first girl in the family to get married, and I knew it would be important to both my parents. As for his side of the family, his father refused to come to the wedding because he was Jewish and had decided never to set foot in a Catholic church, however his two step sisters came whom I liked very much.

Before the ceremony, we met with Bishop Wolfrom, who had been my minister since I was a girl. To my surprise, the bishop told me he was against our marriage and did not feel good about my fiancé. He felt that we would have a difficult time together but didn't tell me why.

On our honeymoon, Derek started yelling at me out of the blue about a former boyfriend my friends had talked about at the wedding. I was shocked and wondered where he was coming from. I didn't really know what to say. Suddenly, he reached over and slapped me hard in the head.

I was stunned at first; I couldn't believe he had hit me. Then I began to sob uncontrollably, not because it hurt me so much physically but because no one had ever done such a degrading thing to me. I began to cry out for my dad. Who had I just married?

"Stop this car immediately!" I said as I got out, crossed the road, and stuck out my thumb to hitchhike down off the mountain. We had gone to Winter Park, Colorado, to ski.

I didn't know how I would get home; all I knew was that I wanted to get away from this lunatic. But he jumped out of the car and came after me, apologizing profusely. He said he didn't know what had gotten into him.

Looking back, I should have left him that day. But how could I admit that I had made such a big mistake? How would my family look at me? I reasoned that the wedding— the ultimate social event for someone who hated such gatherings—had been so difficult for him that it had caused him to snap.

◆◆◆◆◆◆

Back home, I managed to get transferred to El Paso, a half-hour flight from Midland. I had reservations about leaving LA, but I was married now, and my place was with my husband. We built a beautiful home in Midland, and I commuted to and from El Paso on a little commuter plane. He was working very hard for the first time in his life. But soon we began to fight because I had to commute and live in a place I could not stand and because he was frustrated with the way his father's company was being run—money was constantly being transferred from Midland to the parent company in New York. Plus, I found out that while I had been living in LA—back when he had quizzed me about my every move and made sure I was home by nine every night—he had been seeing another woman. When I flew in to visit him, he used to meet me at the gate. One day the pilot I was flying with recognized him as someone he had seen with another woman at the gate. Yes, Mr. Conservative, the guy who would jump all over me if a man paid any attention to me, had been having an affair during our engagement. I was devastated. I told him I did not care if it was before we were married; we had every bit as much of a commitment. Once again, he cried, seemingly drawing his tears from nowhere, and told me that I was as pure as snow and that he didn't deserve me.

With all this in mind and believing I really did love this man despite what had happened, I told him we had to leave Midland.

I didn't care if we ever had another dime; I wanted to get out of that place and not be controlled by his dad's money. I did some research on townhouses available in Denver, left Derek with the Midland house, and flew to Denver to buy a townhouse there. In Denver I decided we could start fresh.

◆ ◆ ◆ ◆ ◆ ◆

Derek eventually joined me in Denver, but he couldn't find a job—he had always just worked for his father—so I supported him for quite some time. In the meantime, I flew back to Midland to try to sell our house and to make sure it was in "show" condition. What I found there was shocking. After I had left, Derek hadn't paid any of the bills. (At the time, I didn't know he had a $20,000 IRS debt he had incurred before we were married, nor did I know that all his charge cards had been over extended.) There was water all over the floor; the electricity had been turned off; somebody had come to repossess the television; and the phone line was disconnected.

I left town the next day, and we quickly sold the house at a financial loss.

I was ready for a new start.

◆ ◆ ◆ ◆ ◆ ◆

With my husband out of work, I had to carry the load of his IRS debt and his credit card debt. But I was young and foolish and believed in his intelligence and capabilities, so I used the money I had in my savings account to buy a new car and a townhouse.

For the next eight years, we were—on the surface—a happy couple. And for the most part, we were. We were in love. We did everything together. When I had to fly, I couldn't wait to get home to him, and he would always be waiting at the door for me. We couldn't stand to be apart from each other; we would even talk several times a day while at work. We spent all the pleasurable time together that most young people in love do, except at a faster pace—we traveled all through Europe, rode bikes, worked out, skied, went for walks, and played backgammon for foot massages. We joined an athletic club and made friends with other couples. The owner of the athletic club said that of all the couples who walked through his doors, we seemed to be the happiest. And that's how I saw us, too. Most of the couples we socialized with were successful the wives didn't work, and the husbands were doctors, lawyers, or businessmen. Even though we were not in the same financial situation, we pretended we were and lived on borrowed money and off my savings.

I used to distinguish my life from that of my friends in the airline world. I thought those people were pretty wild, whereas I had a safe, secure life at home, with people who were family oriented, health conscious, and down to earth. I ignored some pretty obvious signs that underneath this surface life of fun and togetherness was a dark, violent element that would eventually ruin everything for me.

CHAPTER 2

Domestic Violence and Coercive Control

About every three months or so, something would set Derek off. One time I had to have jaw surgery and my mouth was wired shut for six weeks. I could only take in liquids through a straw and out of nowhere he slugged me in the gut. I felt his fist penetrate my stomach and it felt like it entered and pierced through to the other side. We were not fighting, and I was so stunned and heartbroken. Being so frail it was like hitting a child. The abuse was way more prevalent emotionally which I feel is even harder to understand. A couple of years later he was in a state handball tournament. I watched him play, and lose, the championship game. When he came out to the car, I told him he had played well. Out of the blue, he slugged me in the head. I was physically stunned. My head was pounding, and I felt dizzy. I got out of the car, walked across the street to find a field, and fell to the ground. When I woke up, I had no idea how much time had elapsed. I saw my friend Cheri's blue Porsche come around the corner and stop. I asked her to take me home. The tournament was out of town, and as we drove back, I kept falling asleep. She drove me to a clinic where the doctor told me I had a concussion. I refused to tell the doctor that Derek had hit me.

For the next three days, Derek didn't show up at home. When he did, he denied ever hitting me. I could not stand him and wanted him to stay away from me.

Another time we were play fighting in bed when all of a sudden it became real. He sadistically began smothering me with a pillow until I panicked, desperately trying to scream and flailing at him to get off me. Feeling that I was going to pass out or stop breathing.

I had always felt that I was an independent woman. I had always prided myself in being a strong woman. But during these first eight years of my marriage, I lived in fear of Derek's mood swings and emotional abuse. Walking on egg shells waiting for his next outrageous anger attack.

◆ ◆ ◆ ◆ ◆ ◆

As I approached thirty, Derek finally had secured a good job, and everything seemed to be right in our lives. He had become financially stable, and I told myself that his mood swings had improved, that the occasional physical and emotional abuse were nothing compared to how much we loved each other and how well we got along. So we discussed having a child.

I wasn't sure I was ready, and I wanted to make absolutely sure he was. The last thing I wanted was for him to resent me and not share in the responsibility of a child. By that time, we had a dog—a pit bull named Rustle—but having a baby was a bigger decision, and it had to be mutual. I did not want the sole responsibility for our baby's care. He assured me that he was certain he wanted a child.

We decided to try to conceive. I applied for a supervisor position for flight attendants and began working in an office.

We figured it would take some time for me to get pregnant, but soon after we began trying, I found out I was carrying our child.

Little did I know what was going on behind my back.

Cheri was one of my best friends. We had met at our athletic club. She had a lovely home with her husband and little boy. She did not work, and she seemed to be very disconnected with her life. She always looked at my life—and my husband—as exciting. However, I never felt threatened by her.

Friends kept telling me how Cheri seemed to covet my life so much that she actually began dressing and acting like me. She wanted to work for Continental, too, so I helped her prepare for her interview. While she didn't qualify as a flight attendant, she was hired in reservations.

As it turns out, she coveted everything about my life, including Derek. This was obvious to me; I knew she had a horrible crush on him. Once when I was playing in a racquetball tournament, they both came to watch one of my games. During time outs, Derek ran down to give me some advice and encouragement. Sometimes, if a particular serve wasn't working or I was worried about how I was playing, I looked up toward him in the stands to see what I should do. When I did, I saw her standing near him, staring as if she could not take her eyes off him. At the time, I felt so sorry for her that she needed the extra attention. I felt certain that he was so in love with me that he would never be tempted to be with her.

One time we all went cross-country skiing together, and afterward we went out for some Mexican food. Derek and I were wearing the same snow boots that I had brought back from New Zealand. All of a sudden, Cheri started rubbing her foot against mine, playing footsies under the table. I tried to decide whether to kick her and say something or to just watch her eyes. I chose the latter and saw her gaze romantically at Derek. I wanted to say something, but Cheri's husband was a nice man, and I couldn't bear to hurt his feelings. So I waited until Derek and I got home and said, "I don't know what's going on with you and Cheri, but she was playing footsie with me under the table tonight. If I so much as see eye contact between the two of you again, so help me I will embarrass the both of you in front of whoever may be around!"

I didn't see anything happen after that, and I believed in my heart that Derek wasn't cheating on me. Derek knew that the one thing I would never stand for was infidelity. He always made me feel like no one else was even close to what I was, and maybe because of my loving upbringing, I felt I had nothing to worry about.

One day, I received a phone call from my sister, Leslie, saying that she was pregnant. I told her I thought I was too, and she just laughed with disbelief. A month or so later, it was my parents' fortieth wedding anniversary. As a present, all six of us (three kids with our spouses) went home to paint the family house for them, and then we took them with us on a trip to England and Scotland. It was my idea. Every time Derek and I had gone to England I would say, "Oh, if my dad could see this!" or, "My mom would love this!" It was important for me to take them there.

While we were in England, I was sick almost every morning, yet my mother still didn't believe that I was pregnant. We had a wonderful time there—sightseeing, driving through the beautiful countryside, and sleeping in quaint little bed-and-breakfasts. My parents loved it. My mother had always been leery of Derek, but on this trip, he won her over. For the first time, my parents liked Derek and believed he truly loved me.

After we returned from England, my doctor confirmed what I had already known: I was indeed pregnant. I still had to work, but I began to worry about pushing myself too hard. On a trip to New York to pick up baby furniture at Derek's father's house, I began spotting. When we returned home, I told him what was going on. I was terrified, but he acted as though it was nothing. Once he left the house, I called my doctor, who told me to come into his office immediately. The doctor sent me to the hospital for an ultrasound and told me I may lose the baby. I began to sob and called Derek, telling him I would not be going into work. When they did the ultrasound, they found a membrane running through the womb and said it could wrap around the baby's neck or a limb. They would watch me closely until my fifth month. I was told to be on bed rest and not to make love.

CHAPTER 3

The Good, the Bad, the Ugly

It was during this time that I felt my greatest separation from Derek. I felt so alone, fighting for this tiny life inside of me. I now wanted this baby more than ever. I began to bond with my baby, talking to him or her every day, and staying happy because he or she could feel when I was unhappy.

In those days, while I was heading out to work before sunrise, Derek would stay in bed until at least eleven. Then he would go to the athletic club, work out until far past lunchtime, and return to the club in the evening. He would call me every day at work, pressuring me about getting a new house in a better neighborhood because he wanted to impress our influential friends. His credit was so terrible that we had to use mine and hope that they didn't find out anything about him. Meanwhile, I was going to work, calling realtors, visiting properties, and trying to secure a mortgage, all the while carrying his baby. To make matters more insulting, he wasn't making love to me. I had long since gotten the okay from my doctor that I could be sexually active again, but Derek never wanted to. He said that it bothered him with the baby inside. I came to the conclusion that he was not attracted to me because I was fat. More people were telling me I was beautiful than in any other time in my life, but I couldn't understand why Derek didn't feel the same way.

I began to feel very alienated from Derek. But despite feeling so alone, I didn't allow myself to get too upset about it because I didn't want to upset the baby. The baby was all that mattered to me.

As for Derek, I hoped that this was another one of his phases that he could not deal with, and I decided to see what he would be like after our baby's birth. I would have to get through this phase with him and be strong. I remembered reading in one of his journals that one of his biggest fears in life was having a family.

Still, it was all beginning to wear on me. I had no support, and we had to really finagle to get the loan on our new house. The townhouse had not sold, so we would be making payments on two homes with a baby coming and without my income once I went on maternity leave.

Finally, I liquidated my retirement fund to use as a down payment on our house, and we were able to move in. Everything seemed fine, except for the fact that Derek could have cared less that I was pregnant and would not involve himself in any part of the process. We started Lamaze classes, but he refused to go to any more classes at a point when we had almost completed the program.

As it turns out, he was having an affair.

◆ ◆ ◆ ◆ ◆ ◆

My car had broken down, and it was going to be very expensive to fix, so he told me not to fix it until after the baby was born—one more way to keep me isolated while he went to the athletic club to meet his lover. He often didn't show up to take me to my doctor's appointments, even up until two weeks before the baby was born. I had to call friends to come and take me to the doctor. This was at the end of my pregnancy, and I was too tired after work to be worried about why he did not want to fix my car. He came home every evening around nine, when I would already be asleep. He carried on his affair during the day while I was at work, because the married woman he was having the affair with had to be home at night also. She never called him at home, and I never saw any evidence of their affair. I was naïve—I never even considered that he was seeing a married woman during the day—and he was extremely careful. He had always told me that he hated people who cheated on their spouses. They were sleazy lowlifes as far as he was concerned. In fact, he couldn't stand a good-looking doctor at the club because we knew he was cheating on his wife. And yet, here he was, acting exactly like that doctor.

Toward the end of my pregnancy, I kept busy decorating the house, wallpapering, and picking out drapes. It turned out beautifully, but I was still feeling the emptiness of my marriage, holding everything inside in my attempt to get through the pregnancy without harming my baby. Once when we got into a fight, he had thrown me to the ground, pregnant! Still, I did not want to battle with him in my condition. I wanted to keep things calm for the baby's sake. I made a vow to myself that I would get through this alone. Then, after my baby was born, I was going to leave him if he did not turn around.

Meanwhile, I became more and more afraid of him. He had done things in the past that I had blocked out for one reason or another, but now I became acutely aware of how often he had gone out of his way to ruin anything that meant a lot to me—our wedding, our honeymoon, Christmas, or any family event. What would he do after our child was born?

Two days before I went into labor, the same night my mom was flying in from Honolulu after being with my sister Leslie for the birth of her baby, Derek and I got into a horrible fight. Money had always been an issue, but that month, after working out with his friends at the club, he had spent three hundred dollars on drinks for himself and his buddies. When he told me he was paying the athletic club bill, it didn't cross my mind that he would pay it with the three hundred dollars I had set aside for after the baby was born to buy groceries and baby necessities. When I found out, I finally reached my limit. I just despised him and we got into a horrible fight.

When my mother arrived, having left a completely wonderful household with my sister to come into my living hell, Derek had left for the athletic club again, and I was extremely ill. I had deep circles under my eyes, had just finished vomiting, and according to my mother, I looked like death. "What happened to you?" she said. "You looked great when I saw you three weeks ago!" She wanted to take me to the hospital, but I told her I just had the flu. "I wish your dad was here!" she said. The next day, I went to the doctor for a stress test because my stomach was very soft and the baby had not moved for a couple of days. My mom thought I may have lost the baby, but the baby was fine. Thank God.

At that point, I had really begun to despise Derek. If I could just get through the delivery, I thought, I will leave him. At around eleven in the evening, my water broke, and I began to experience painful cramping. A few months earlier, my friend Patra had died in labor, so I was extremely afraid of going into labor. I was older than Patra, so if she could die, so could I. And would the baby be okay after the complications he or she had suffered through at the beginning of my pregnancy?

I told my mom that I thought I was going into labor, but she laughed and told me that my sister had, had a similar experience for days before her baby was born. But by midnight, I was having painful contractions and told Derek that I thought the labor had started. I asked my mother if she thought this was the beginning of labor, and she realized that she had been wrong earlier: "No, honey," she said, "you're in it!" The contractions were very close. I could not even make it from the top of the stairs to the bottom of the stairs before I had another one.

A few hours later, on February 22, 1986, I gave birth to a healthy six-pound, seven-ounce baby girl.

As soon as Ami was born, I knew she was the most wonderful thing that had ever happened to me. No one can ever explain the kind of love a mother feels for her child, and I felt it from the moment of her birth—well, before that even. Her father, on the other hand, seemed to feel differently.

He spent time with her only if there were people around that he wanted to impress; otherwise, he had nothing to do with her. He was home at night, but day after day he was absent. He spent all his time at the athletic club or (as I later found out) with other women while I walked Ami around the block in a pram. As the cool air brushed against my face, I wondered why he did not want to be with us.

I asked him to move out, but he refused. Then I begged him to move out. At one point, after a fight, I threw his clothing into his car. His reaction was to throw me over the couch and try to have sex with me, even though it had hurt my back, and I was in excruciating pain. He accused me of overreacting, so I did not go to the doctor for a couple of weeks, even though one of my legs was shorter than the other and I had severe back spasms. When I finally did see a doctor, he couldn't believe that I had waited a week. I lied and said I had hurt myself cleaning. I wound up spending two months in physical therapy.

With Derek gone all the time, I began to feel certain that he was having an affair. I tried to tell myself this was another one of his phases, and I would just have to be strong for the three of us. But I just couldn't do it anymore. I had no motivation left to work on my marriage. He was nothing but a roommate to me. He could not have cared less about his baby, and that was what pushed me over the edge. I wanted him out. So I went to a marriage counselor to help me get out of my marriage. Meanwhile, Derek refused to move out and started going to couples counseling with me. He convinced the counselor that our problems were based on finances and charmed her into thinking he was a wonderful, loving man who would never have an affair. She then told me that Derek should be able to have a $300 athletic club bill, that she was sure he was not having an affair, and that we should move out of our house and cut back on grocery spending. I asked her, "Is that roof not over his head? Do we not need to eat? If your husband wanted a Lear jet to play with, would you give up your home and your food intake?" This is when I began to realize his power to manipulate and control others, something he had acquired at a very early age.

One evening, after he came home late from the club once again, I had had it. I told him I did not know who he was seeing, but I knew he was having an affair with someone, whether it was a guy friend of his, or Pam. She was a woman we had met at the club; I didn't know her, but something told me she was the one. He got up, grabbed all my credit cards, and left. Normally I would just let him go because of the baby, but this time I picked up Ami, buckled her into the car seat of my now-repaired car, and drove by the club to find out who he was having the affair with. He wasn't there, so I went to the house of a woman named Suzie that he had been spending a lot of time with. They were completely taken aback when I arrived. He had his boots off, his feet on the table, and a glass of wine in his hand. I walked in with Ami in my arms and said, "Now, isn't this cozy!"

Suzie retorted, "Maralee, it isn't what you think!"

"Where is your husband then?" I asked. "Suzie," I said, "he spends more time with you and at the athletic club than he does with his own wife and baby!" Derek then jumped up, ran outside, got into his car, and drove away.

I drove to my friend Cheri's house for comfort, but her husband met me at the door, telling me not to come in that my husband was inside. Later I would find out that Derek had been sleeping with both of these women.

Needless to say, that was the last straw. I stuffed all of his things into green garbage bags and forbade him to come back into the house. His reaction was to spread horrible lies about me at the club, telling them I was nuts. Looking back, under the circumstances I would have to say that I behaved rather calmly. But as I would soon learn, reality didn't count for much; Derek could convince and manipulate anyone to take his side.

And I hadn't seen anything yet.

CHAPTER 4

Manipulation, Threats, and Fear: The Charming Psychopath

On December 15, 1987, there was a horrible snow storm, and I had to be at work very early. After my day was over, I was getting ready to lock my office door to go home when out in the crew room I heard the news that there had been an airplane crash at the Denver airport, and it happened to be a Continental plane. Management had just gone through extensive training on what each of us was to do in a crash situation. My position was to notify the base manager, and I was to go out to the crash site and get the flight attendants away from the aircraft—to account for the lives—and to keep everyone away from the media. I was in a dress and heels, not proper attire for a major snow storm, so I asked someone else to go out to the aircraft. Meanwhile, I manned the phones as mothers, fathers, and friends began to call, wondering if their loved ones were on that flight. I received a phone call from a captain from United who said that his daughter was a flight attendant with us; he asked if she had been on the flight. When he mentioned her name, I became very ill, and tears welled up in my eyes because I had just received word that she had been killed. I calmly told him that I did not know her status and would transfer him to a base manager.

I had to stay until almost midnight, speaking with families of the victims, so I had Derek pick up Ami from the daycare provider's and take her to Cheri's house where Derek was living. When I arrived to pick up Ami, who by this time was nine months old, Derek was talking loudly to a friend from New York over the phone, describing how he was going to take her from me because I was crazy. I ignored him and went to get Ami. All of a sudden, she began choking. I found they had given her a bagel, and huge chunks had stuck to the roof of her mouth. I was very upset. She was way too young to have such large bites in her mouth.

From this point on, things got worse. In October, I hired a divorce attorney, Stan Lipkin, and filed for divorce. Derek avoided being served with the papers, and in the meantime, I fled to Billings, Montana, where my parents now lived because I was scared of what he might do. He called me there, devastated, begging me to reconsider.

From October to June, when the divorce was finalized, Derek never let me go. His attorney constantly sent my attorney letters filled with lies about me while Derek continued to act cruel. He would call my office many times a day, neglect to see Ami for weeks at a time, call me at night before bed and in the morning before I woke, write long editorials to newspapers to harass me, and write inflammatory remarks about me on the chalkboard at the club.

Right before Christmas, when my family was planning on coming, I received a Christmas card for Ami and me from acquaintances of mine from the club, part of a group of people from which I now disassociated myself. For some reason, that card gave me the feeling that one of them may have known something that I didn't, so I called her two days before Christmas and asked her point blank, "Is Derek having an affair?"

I hoped she would say no, but she exclaimed, "Yes! He is!" When I asked her who he was having the affair with, she told me Pam.

Sickened by the betrayal, I left work and drove home. When I reached the door, my sister, who was visiting me, was standing there and asked me what was wrong. I told her about the affair, and we both decided to go to the club. He had to be there. It takes a lot to make me angry, but when you do, look out! I grabbed my coat, and I had an air about me that could have set anyone's hair on end.

When we walked into the club, he was doing sit-ups on the floor. When he saw me he asked, "What's with you?"

I placed my foot on his stomach and said, "Move! Now!"

He got up, and I told him to go out by the pool. Once the three of us were alone, I screamed, "You pig. You pig!" I slapped him across the face as I screamed at him for having an affair on me while I had been carrying his child.

He stared at me with his cold, blue eyes and told my sister that he was going to hit me. My sister—a beautiful but slender girl—told him that if he touched me, she would blow him away. He turned and ran away, jumping over the wall of the club to go to Cheri's house.

When I arrived home, my phone was ringing. It was Cheri, yelling at me and asking me what the hell was wrong with me. She said that Derek was trying to be so rational about everything, and I was acting crazy. "Cheri, I just found out that Derek was having an affair while I was carrying his child. How would you react?"

All she could muster was "Do you know that for a fact?"

Duh! She was probably upset because she thought she was next in line after our divorce went through. She had known nothing about Pam. He had told Cheri that I kicked him in the stomach and beat the crap out of him. Mind you, I weighed 118 pounds, and he dead-lifted about 500. I couldn't believe that everyone believed him and not me.

Trying to maintain a large home, handle a stressful job, and take care of my baby with this sociopath became very difficult. My parents lived with me for about three months in order to help keep Derek from harassing me and stalking me. I had previously given him a ticket to go back to New York for Christmas, so I could spend it in peace with my family. Since he was living at his friends' house, I gave him a thousand dollars out of our account; plus, I made his Honda payment, leaving us with eight hundred dollars in our account. When I went to buy diapers, I found out that he had taken that money, too. If my parents hadn't been there, I wouldn't have been able to buy groceries.

On Christmas Eve, I received a phone call from him. He didn't ask about the baby or mention his affair; he just made small talk about the weather. Later, he sent me a telegram telling me not to have any men in our home. I was incredulous. I had never even looked at another man while married; I wasn't the one having multiple affairs. When he returned weeks later for the pre-trial of our divorce, I had lost ten pounds from stress.

His behavior remained erratic; his phone calls became more excessive. My attorney advised me to hold him in contempt for harassment, but at the time, I was more concerned about money than putting out the fire right away. (See Stan Lipkin, esq. letter Appendix D). I was worried about who I was dealing with, so for the first time in my life, I went to a therapist not for marriage counseling but for myself. Once I told her everything, she became alarmed and worried for my life. She asked me if I had a gun. I told her that in order to protect myself I had changed the locks and had my parents living with me. She then called my attorney and told him to get a restraining order for Derek. I then remembered an article I had read in a magazine when I was first married to Derek. I had saved it all these years in a book that I seldom wrote in unless I was upset about something. It defined a type of man called "The Crazy."

> The Crazy. (Who often is a brute as well.) True loonies can be devastatingly appealing, charismatic, kindly, and splendid in bed. Why then should a girl shun a psycho? The problem is that beneath all the fabulous sex and extravagant protestations of love, psychos feel absolutely nothing—but they are geniuses at mimicking normal human emotions like loyalty, compassion, empathy, trust. The crazy will spend enormous amounts of time, effort, and money to win you then suddenly lash out in attack so vicious you're left gasping, "He seemed so normal until..." and then may briefly convince you that whatever horror happened was your fault, and therein lies his strength. The crazy is a supreme manipulator of others. Because his personality was arrested early in life, he can only think of his needs and his desires as an infant does and will stop at nothing to fulfill his desires or needs... However well he plays at being human, the crazy man is basically a shell, a victim of severe mental or emotional disorder who's savagely at odds with other people and society.

I had added at the bottom, "Wouldn't you, Maralee, rather enjoy the company of a man who makes love not war?"

◆ ◆ ◆ ◆ ◆ ◆

Back home, I was very nervous about what could happen to me. I remembered that he had left all of his belongings at my house, including the journals he had written in since he was eighteen. I grabbed the journals and looked through them to find excerpts about me. I found a passage in which he quoted Nietzsche: "I have found my greatest enemy, and she is mine to conquer and destroy." Then he listed actual war strategies and plotted out how he was going to win me and then conquer and destroy me. One day he wrote very intellectually stimulating things about life, and the next day he wrote "Action will stop you, traction will kill you...which will you choose: self-hate!" He wrote about the hideous demons he had clawing and shrieking inside of him—they terrorized him and doled out agonizing blows to his guts as they howl and ride along. He wrote:

> When I was young, I felt wet, cold, and alone. I now stand alone or crawl alone. Why do I take my pain out on others? Why not be hard on yourself, hard on your- self, hard on yourself? How the bullet would feel rushing through my head so much the better to do it in the bath and watch as life's blood seeps away into the warm water. Why not have the courage to inflict the pain on yourself instead of those you envy?

His writing was large and out of control.

After reading through many journals, I copied them and took them to Dr. Laurie Margolis, a psychiatrist that Stan, my attorney, had recommended. I asked Dr. Margolis if she could analyze them and give me a better perspective of what I was dealing with. Dr. Margolis sent me a letter stating that he had in-cognitive behavior and paranoid ideation. It was the writing of what could be a disturbed and conflicted individual. She said that if Ami was to be left in his care, she would be unsafe. I thought that Dr. Margolis might have been overreacting. Ami wasn't in danger. I mean, she wasn't even a year old. He wouldn't hurt her. I was still in denial of who he was. Who had I been married to? The emotional and physical abuse I had endured for years was staring me in the face. It was still hard for me to grasp he would hurt a baby. Due to the excessive phone calls and the harassment I was enduring from the father on a daily basis my attorney suggested we immediately take him into court for contempt. I was afraid that would make things worse. He told me we need to get him under control now, or if we let his behavior continue, it would only get worse.

In the meantime, Derek was constantly bugging me, telling me he was going to get therapy, cut off his arm, commit suicide, and so on. He was living in an apartment with two other guys who smoked pot all the time, even when Ami was there. I felt like I had been married to Charles Manson, and I had to de-program myself.

At this point, he had three-hour visits three times a week. He never had to change a diaper, make a bottle, or perform any responsible duties for Ami. One evening, after a long day at the office, I came home to find that my parents were very upset. Ami had been sick with a high fever all day, but Derek had insisted on taking her out in a terrible snow storm. My mother told him she would get Ami ready to go, but he snuck her out of the house with no blanket, bottle, diaper, or clothing, only a receiving blanket. My parents were shocked, and my normally low-key father had exploded.

When I walked in, the phone was ringing, and he was laughing on the other end about how crazy my parents were. When he arrived at the door, my parents answered, and he ran back to the car, demanding to speak with me. My mom replied that I was no longer his wife and that the baby needed to come into the house. He locked himself and Ami in the car, with Ami wearing only one of his t-shirts and his socks up her legs. My dad came out and ordered him to give me the baby or he was going to call the police. He would not give Ami to me unless I got in the car with him. My mother immediately stood behind his car, in case he tried to leave with us. My father came out and confronted him. What kind of man was he? I found it very odd that he had taken her with no clothes on in below zero weather. He was really starting to give me the creeps. I was now very concerned for Ami that he would take her out with a fever not considering her welfare.

After staying with us for a couple of months, my parents finally decided to leave. Things had calmed down, and they thought I would be safe.

That spring, he begged me to come back to him and to start all over. He wanted us to have more kids, to move away where no one would know us so we could have a fresh start. No matter how many times I told him that I would never go back to him, he kept asking. He asked if we would spend Easter with him, go to brunch together, and fly kites in the park. He wanted us to be a family.

On Sunday, I took Ami to an Easter-egg hunt before his visitation began. Ami looked darling in her little bunny costume, and a part of me wanted him to see her as I did. I figured he would be at the club, so I took Ami there rather than going all the way back home. When I arrived, he was standing outside, talking with the married woman he had been having an affair with. All those lonely times while I was pregnant suddenly became very fresh in my mind. I remembered getting up at five in the morning to go to work to support him and our unborn child while he was having affairs with woman after woman. In an instant, I got the urge to jump out of the car and say something to her, but as I did, he slammed me up against the car and screamed for the other woman to leave.

When I got out of his grip, I got back into my car and tried to drive away, but Derek jumped out in front of it so I couldn't leave. I felt sick. I just wanted to go home. I began to cry and told him to get away from my car. After five minutes of this game, I started to edge the car forward slowly, which finally caused him to move. Thinking I was headed to Pam's, he got in his car and pursued me. Not far down the road, with Ami still in my car, he cut me off and tried to run me off the road into a ditch. He could have killed us!

I drove home in shock, but after a while he showed up at my front door, asking for Ami. After he had just tried to run us off the highway? I told him no. He rang my bell until I decided to call the police. He continued to ring it, and when I finally answered, I told him I had called the police. I know he thought he was in trouble then because he said, "You hit my car," even though I hadn't touched his car and he was the one trying to run us off the road. He then went back to the athletic club to call the police, just as I had just done.

A female police officer met him there. He told her that I had hit him with my car from twenty-five feet away and that I was lying about his role in what had happened. In truth, I hadn't even touched him with my car; he had moved out of the way when I edged it forward. I guess he thought it through and realized he could not use that I hit his car because of no damage on the car. The officer then came to my home and asked for my side of the story. After I told her, she read me my Miranda rights, took out her handcuffs, and said she was going to arrest me. A friend of mine from the club was there with me. She yelled, "You can't have her tell you the whole story and then arrest her!" Well, the officer had just spent three hours with Derek and believed everything he had to say. He was so good at manipulating people that he could even control the police. I was so distraught thinking about how he had just tried to run me off the road with his baby in the car. The police officer moved toward me as I was sitting at the kitchen table and threatened to give my baby to social services and handcuff me. I am wondering why she went to him first when I called the police over two hours ago and what lies has he told her to manipulate her to react like this. I started to cry and raise my voice. I was not a criminal. I did not deserve this. I couldn't believe what was happening. She was a rookie and rethought her position, and then she handed me a ticket to show up to court on Monday.

A short while later, the police officer I had called showed up and was astounded at how the rookie officer had handled the situation. He filed a report and went to Derek's house to issue him a ticket for reckless driving without a license.

On Monday, friends of mine showed up at court for me; Derek showed up with Pam. I had to sit with stern-looking men in orange jumpsuits. I stared at Derek, not believing what he was doing to me. On Saturday he had begged me to go back and become a family with him. On Sunday he had charged me with assault and battery after trying to run us off the road. On Monday he had showed up to court with the married woman he was having an affair with.

Then, on Tuesday, he apologized for everything and told me he wanted to drop the charges, but in Colorado you can't drop charges. It's a law designed to protect battered women. Learning nothing was protecting me from this lunatic. Once again, he began calling my office all day long, trying to talk with me. It got so that I had to ask our secretary to screen calls for me.

The morning of the trial, my attorney sent me to a lawyer who was looking to get a start in the field and needed five hundred dollars. As my father and I walked in, Derek, nice as can be, sat with me to talk when the DA walked by. The DA asked him, "Is this the woman?" thinking I was Pam. That's when I realized that for the two months between the initial hearing and the trial, while I was caring for Ami, Derek had had been meeting privately with the DA. All of this was hard on my father, because it hadn't even been a year before that they had gone to England with us, and they had since watched what he had put me through.

In the meantime, my attorney suggested that I plead guilty to a lesser offense. At first, I refused. Everyone had been advising me to do that, but I had done nothing wrong! Finally, he convinced me, and I took the lesser plea.

When we got into the court room, the rookie policewoman was there, throwing a handball back and forth with Derek.

What happened at court that day was a blur, but after I pled guilty, I had to see a parole officer who took one look at the charges and immediately dropped them.

After that, Derek continued to call me excessively, and my attorney continued to try to convince me to file contempt citations for his harassment and also for not paying his child support. He warned me that if I didn't do something soon, I would be sorry. But I was afraid of what Derek would do if I brought him to court, so I continued to refuse. It was similar to what I had done when I had been pregnant. People couldn't understand why I wasn't fighting for myself more. They thought it was disgusting how he treated me. I had to keep things calm for the baby's sake and was afraid of miscarriage. I was determined not to lower myself to his level

CHAPTER 5

A Mother's Nightmare

One evening, after a visit with Ami, he brought her back asleep, so I let him into the house and told him to put her in her crib. When he didn't come back down the stairs, I called out his name, but he didn't answer. So I went up to check on Ami. In the past, he had threatened to take her from me. But I found her safe inside her crib. All of a sudden, from a dark corner in the room, I saw him sitting with a weird look in his eyes. "What's the matter?" he said, his voice strange and awkward. "Are you afraid I would rape you?" Afraid for my life and for Ami's, I kicked him out of the house. But that look in his eyes stayed with me. He was so strange.

By this time, my attorney's fees had reached $17,000, and every time Derek fired his cheap attorneys, he would use mine—calling him for this or that, running up my bill, and asking if we could use the same attorney as long as I paid for it. To go into trial would easily cost another three thousand dollars. So when I was asked to go into mediation, I considered it, since it would save me a lot of money. My attorney advised me to try it but told me it would never work and recommended that I never give him joint custody. That, he said, would be the sorriest day of my life.

The first day of the mediation, I pulled aside the mediator, Janice Cella, and told her that what she would see was not what he really was. She believed that he was still in love with me and thought that together we would raise a wonderful child. I asked her to write the evaluation in a way that would protect me, so that

I would be able to leave the state if he didn't stop his behavior and refused to leave me alone.

After the first day of mediation, my car broke down, and I couldn't get a hold of anyone to give me a ride. Derek offered to drive me. During the ride he said, "Wouldn't it be funny if we could tell everyone that we just had a bad fight, and that's all?" I thought that was a very strange way to look at it. But on the last day of mediation, when we both knew it was over, we hugged, and for the first time I felt that we had really said good-bye and could possibly become friends.

My attorney looked over the mediation agreement and said he could not have done a better job himself. It had been a lot of hard work negotiating. I had agreed to joint custody, but with the condition that I be the custodial parent and have sole decision-making power. My attorney said that was the same as having sole custody.

But agreeing to joint custody with me having the sole decision-making power would turn out to be my biggest mistake. Attorneys will tell you joint custody is the same as sole custody if you are the residential parent and that you can work out visitation anyway you want. But that applies only to couples who have a very amicable divorce and agree to make decisions on what is best for their children. That wasn't to be the case for me.

After that, things started to go a little more smoothly until I found out that he was not paying bills that he had been court-ordered to pay. Without any credit, he really needed to pay those bills. Because he couldn't even handle the Honda payments, I tried to pay his bills and sell the car while working full time and raising our daughter. Eventually the car was repossessed, so he got a motorcycle and rode with Ami on it. Later he got an old used car.

During this time, I would spend every minute I could with Ami. She was the cutest and happiest little girl I had ever seen. My social life became non-existent, but time with my baby was so much more important to me than going out. She was much more fun anyway. I enjoyed every minute with her and couldn't wait to get home to her every afternoon. We took the pram to the corner park every day, and my life felt content. I was relieved and felt like a ton of bricks had been lifted off my shoulders to have Derek out of my everyday life. Every morning I put her in her bassinet next to me on the vanity and sang to her. Ami would look at me as though I had a beautiful voice, when in fact I could barely carry a tune. On some quiet Friday evenings, when I knew most of my married friends were cozying up together at home and my single friends were out having fun, I would feel a bit lonely. I was proud of how I was handling things—I was paying the bills, making the house payment, taking care of a new baby, keeping up both my yard and house, and not losing my mind—but it didn't stop me from craving a little adult company sometimes.

One day, my parents called to tell me they were shipping down my childhood bed, which was also my mom's childhood bed, so that Ami could use it. It arrived at the same time Derek was returning Ami from his visit with her. When Derek saw the delivery truck, he started screaming at me, freaking out because he thought I was moving. He didn't believe me when I told him I wasn't, so he called all my friends, threatening them if they didn't tell him where I was going. One of my friends called me to tell me I should call the police. Before I could pick up the phone, a police officer appeared at my door, explaining that the man outside had told him that I was leaving town because I wouldn't go to bed with him. I had to laugh at that one! Once I explained everything to him, the police officer told me I should get a restraining order. So the next day, I did. Although it took a few weeks to get it served to him, he found many ways to avoid it and eventually he got it. Laura, a friend of mine from work, had come home with me to pick up Ami from a visitation with her father. Since the sheriff had tried numerous times to serve him and failed, Laura walked to the door with me to get Ami, and as I introduced her to Derek and he reached out to shake her hand, she handed him the restraining order. I had finally done something proactive.

◆ ◆ ◆ ◆ ◆ ◆

For the next two months, everything seemed to smooth out again. But then I received a motion in the mail from an attorney, stating that Derek was pursuing sole custody.

I had just returned from a trip to Hawaii with Ami. My sister Leslie still lived there at the time, and she had given birth to a second child. So I had decided to make it a trip for Ami and me so she could see her cousins. I had been having a recurring dream that I lived in a glass house and that he was watching my every move. If I ever let him know that I knew he was watching, he would kill me. Clearly, I would benefit from a few days out of town.

Upon my return, I received the motion. In my view, he didn't stand a chance, but I was sick over the money I knew I was going to have to spend to defend myself. I called him up, pleading with him not to go through with it. We had just finalized everything, and I didn't want to have to dole more money out for attorney fees. I didn't understand why he wouldn't let this end and allow me to start putting the little money I had toward Ami's college education. Plus, I had been told that there was a two-year statute of limitation once an agreement was signed. How could he be going back to court? In tears, I called my attorney. He told me to bring three thousand dollars with me in order to finish Derek once and for all. I sold my diamond ring and brought him the money.

During this time, Continental cut back their management department, and I was one of the many who were let go, even though a month earlier I had been told by my boss that I was one of the best supervisors in the office. In many ways, I did not fit the mold of management at Continental Airlines. They had major employee problems since their bankruptcy in 1983, and I had tried to make some major changes for flight attendants. To do so, I had gone over a few bosses' heads, straight to the vice president. Although this was definitely not the way to further one's career, I had no regrets because I had accomplished my main goals that year for the flight attendant group that helped Continental and saved the morale of the employees. I had initiated a furlough program for flight attendants so that all of them would keep their jobs and earn regular pay, and I had straightened out a huge scheduling problem that had been causing a lot of frustration for flight attendants.

On the day I was cut, my boss told me they had positions open in management in other bases, and I could go to either Honolulu or Houston. But I knew that I couldn't leave town because of the court order. I asked my boss to give me one good reason why I was getting cut. He said, "Maralee, you've had a bad year." This was certainly true, but I had never missed work, and I had done my job, so there had to be another reason. He brought up how I had gone over his head to support the reserve system for the flight attendants; that's what had sealed my fate. I then met with the vice president of inflight in Houston and applied for a position as base manager in Honolulu.

Soon afterward, I had to go back to court this time due to a new frivolous motion sent to block me from leaving the state. Although I was now taking over a two thousand-dollars-a-month pay cut, and an opportunity to further my career the judge ruled to keep me in the state; he also ordered Derek to pay for a custody evaluation, which would cost several thousand dollars. I was now forced to go back to flying, which I really didn't want to do. I had senior status, so I could pretty much fly the line of my choice and have more time with Ami, but I just did not want to fly again and take the pay cut. So I applied for a sales job with Yellow Pages advertising and got it and took a leave with Continental.

I was very happy in my new job, and Derek once again mellowed out. Three months went by with no sign of his insanity. So I asked my attorney for my three thousand dollars back. He informed me that he would give it back if nothing happened in the next few months. Though Derek was still asking Ami and me to do things with him, and I kept turning him down, there didn't seem to be any agenda behind his interest. I really enjoyed seeing the two of them together, but his previous lack of interest in her as a baby kept me on my toes when it came to Ami as a toddler. He lived like a pig and didn't keep her clean, but he loved her and was her father.

In March, I began to fly a couple of trips a month just to keep my flight status, and if I had to go overnight once or twice a month, I would give Derek the overnight with Ami. Soon Ami had a hard time sleeping and cried out in the night. By April, her cries had increased, and her mood had changed. I explained this away as her going through the terrible twos. But then my daycare provider, Ruth, began complaining about the change in Ami's behavior. She had bit another child and was becoming very aggressive. My daughter? She was so sweet; I was sure it was the other children's fault. Ruth also told me that Ami was taking her clothes and panties off, asking a little boy to touch her. Now I was concerned. She was only two, and the little boy was older; it must have been the boy's idea.

Now, the hearing was merely a week away, and my lawyer wanted to negotiate an agreement. I told him that I was concerned with going that direction again and that I didn't want to end up in the same situation the mediation had put us in. Plus, I simply couldn't afford any more legal action. Especially when the father was calling my attorney and I was getting charged for every phone call he made and conversation. I just wanted it to stop. Stan said, "Maralee, I am your attorney, representing you." This comforted me, a little. We met, and it took a long time to negotiate a new agreement. I wanted the term "sole custody" so he couldn't take me back to court any more, and I wanted my three thousand dollars he had just cost me to go toward Ami's college education. I promised Derek that I would never take our daughter away from him, and I didn't expect him to have to pay several thousands of dollars for a custody evaluation. After all, I had stayed in town and found another job instead of transferring to keep the job I had wanted. I just wanted this waste of money to stop!

At the time, I thought the only way he could take me back to court would be if I did not have sole custody of Ami. What I later found out was that it didn't matter. If one party wanted to go back to court, you would still find yourself there. Once, Derek laughed at me and said, "Maralee, my attorney told me you and I will be married until that child is eighteen," and he walked away with a smirk.

While we were negotiating, Derek manipulated my own attorney—though it wasn't that difficult, since I'm sure Stan didn't mind not having to work for the three thousand dollars. I agreed and signed the document, leaving our custody arrangement as it was. As I walked out of Stan's office, my strong intuition told me I had made a big mistake and that this would not end.

One night, I decided to go to dinner with Dan, a nice man I had met, and Derek agreed to keep Ami. At about nine, I called to see how Ami was. He told me I had to come get her, that she was sick. When I arrived, Ami was far from ill. Once again it was about control.

The next day, we left for San Francisco for my sister's wedding. The minute we were off the plane, I called Stan to stop the document. He said, "Why, Maralee? You got everything you could want."

I had a gut level feeling that was usually right. "Just stop that document. I am not comfortable."

CHAPTER 6

Disclosure of Abuse

On July 6, 1989, when Ami was two and a half, she came home from a visit with her father, and I was sitting on the couch with a friend. She started complaining, "It hurts! It hurts!" as she grabbed her crotch. At first, I thought that her jumpsuit was too tight, so I took it off for her. But she continued to complain, so I asked her if she needed to use the restroom. She said no and kept putting her hands in her panties. I told her to take her hands out of her panties. She said, "Mommy, I have an owie." She lay on the floor pulled her panties down and opened her vagina, placed her finger in the opening, and cried, "Daddy hurt me!"

In total shock, I looked at Dan, who grabbed his throat and said under his breath, "I am going to kill the sick bastard!" I calmly told him to drop it until I got Ami to bed.

I called Leslie my sister, who worked as a nurse at Children's Hospital, and asked her for advice. I told her what the daycare provider had said to me and what I had just witnessed. Leslie told me to wait until the morning, when Ami first woke up, and then to ask her what happened "down there" without mentioning her father's name. If she repeated the same story, Leslie said I should take her to a pediatrician.

The next morning when I awakened, that's exactly what I did. I asked her what happened "down there" and she repeated the same story she had given me the previous evening.

That afternoon, when I picked her up from Ruth's, she was still complaining that her "pee-pee" hurt, that it hurt to go potty, and that her daddy had hurt her. We were in Ruth's living room alone, and both of us started to cry.

I then decided to take her to her pediatrician, Stan Rosenberg, who examined Ami but didn't ask her any questions. My only concern was that she was okay down there. I did not want to believe that her father had done anything wrong. The pediatrician told me she looked okay but that he was going to inform social services. I begged him not to, but he was legally bound to do so.

Two days later, Ami came home from another visit with her father in just a nightgown with no panties underneath. She sat down next to a friend of mine, put her legs in the air, placed her finger in the opening, and repeated numerous times, "Daddy touches me here."

The next day, I called my psychologist in order to get a professional opinion on what Ami was saying and to see if he thought Ami was being abused. After I told him, he yelled, "Geez, Maralee! Of course he is doing this to her! You know the guy is crazy! I'm calling social services right now." I begged him not to, but once again, he was legally bound.

I began crying uncontrollably. It was finally sinking in. I was so scared and so sick to my stomach thinking he could do this to his own child, but I knew that I had to face this. At least with social services now involved, I thought maybe I would have someone on my side to help me and to help Ami.

Little did I know how wrong I was.

CHAPTER 7

The Awakening

The woman who appeared at my door was slovenly and aloof. My first impression was that I didn't know if someone so cold would be able to relate to a child, but still, I was glad that a professional would now be helping us. She sat on the couch with Ami and began reading with her. Ami was very outgoing and enjoyed being read to. Once I saw they were comfortable with each other, I went into the other room. When I returned, I heard her ask Ami, "Does your daddy touch you there? Does he touch you with paper when he is wiping you?" I was shocked at how untrained she seemed and how unprofessional she was behaving, especially after my sister had said not to mention her father's name. Now this woman was suggesting to her that her father was wiping her with toilet paper.

The social worker said she would start an investigation. My first instinct was to say no because I was afraid of Derek and what he would do. He had visitation that night, so I asked her what I should do when he came to pick her up. I could not give her to him. I then brought out the letter that Dr. Margolis had written two years earlier, stating that if ever my child was left in his care, she would be unsafe. I had given her Derek's collection of journals and asked her what I was dealing with. She wrote,

> These journals were written by her ex-husband during many years of their marriage. They suggest erratic thoughts, disjointed and confused cognition, and paranoid ideation and could be the writing of a very disturbed and conflicted individual. I was

> concerned that there could be some possible danger to Ms. Mclean's child if left in his care.

I told Jennifer that at the time I thought the doctor had overreacted. She read the report and told me to put a note on the door telling him that an emergency had come up and to leave the house. But I knew he would not believe that I was withholding visitation for some casual reason because I never did that. I really didn't know what to do.

Later, feeling discouraged with how Jennifer had handled her interview, I asked Ami what had happened at her father's. She lay on the floor, pulled her panties down, pointed to her vagina, and said that her daddy touched her there. I asked her what he touched her with, and she said, "His fingers."

"Does your daddy do anything else?"

She stuck out her tongue, moved it around, and then said, "My pee-pee."

I immediately called social services and told them to start the investigation. Then I put a note on the door and left the house.

◆ ◆ ◆ ◆ ◆ ◆

The next morning, I got a phone call from Derek. I tried not to show in my voice that anything was wrong, though I knew he was calling to test me. He asked me if I had read an article in the newspaper about an uncle who had abused his niece. He was trying to see where my head was at and if I was suspicious of what he was doing. I ignored his questions and said that I had to get ready for work. He brought up the subject of Ami, but I played dumb and told him that I really didn't want to hear about it. He knew something was up because I'd never withheld visitation. He called me back and said that he thought Ami was being molested by the daycare provider. All I could do was hang up the phone.

As I ran out the door with Ami, I kept going over the conversation in my head. I felt sick. I pulled into a gas station, jumped out of my small car to put gas in, and left the car door open. The car started rolling backward, and then I heard a loud crunching and screeching as my car door caught on a post and was pulled off. Ami was in the car, so I jumped in and stopped it. I had to have a service worker carry my door to the station and leave it until after work. (Ami never forgot this. Every time I would go to the gas station after this, she would say, "Mommy, watch the door.") Later, driving down the freeway without my driver's-side door, I looked pretty foolish with my hair flying straight up in the air and my whole body exposed for everyone to see.

At this point, Ami was talking frequently about what her father had been doing to her. Most of the time it was when her clothes came off, like bedtime or bath time. When friends heard what she said, I told them not to react, to just listen and change the subject. I did not want to taint anything she was saying and did not want her to quit talking. Though I was dying inside, I never said anything negative about Derek in front of Ami. When the social worker told me they were going to discontinue Derek's visitation, I became nervous and afraid. I now believed what Dr. Margolis had written two years previously about my child not being safe in his presence. I was afraid he might kill me. After all, if molesting his child wasn't outside his boundaries, why would murder be?

From then on my anxiety grew and grew, and I felt surrounded by fear. I spent night after sleepless night fearing what lay ahead. I would sleep a couple of hours, only to have a sudden electric shock shoot through my body and awake me. It must be real, I thought, or I wouldn't have this gut-level feeling. I was scared and constantly waiting and wondering what was going to happen. I could no longer read him at all; he did the opposite of what I expected. The divorce was emotionally painful and shocking for what he put me through, but now this was all so different. I was scared. Now I knew just how sick he really was. Maybe he had a split personality and he didn't believe he had done this to his daughter; maybe he could block it out, but now that his alter-ego was out, he would become sicker and sicker, and there was no turning back. Who was he? Was he a psychopath? He was scary; I was afraid he might kill me. If he could do this to his own daughter, and I barely got out of my divorce alive, what was next?i

◆ ◆ ◆ ◆ ◆ ◆

One day, the phone rang, and I heard someone crying on the other end. At first, I didn't realize who it was, but when I did, for a few seconds, I felt sorry for him.

"How could you do this to me?" he asked. They had suspended his visitation with Ami until they completed their investigation.

I told him that his daughter had said and demonstrated things that, as a mother, I had to follow up on. He asked me about the people in my life, as if one of them was the one who had molested her. I went along with the charade, knowing that Ami had identified Derek as the only one to hurt her.

The next time I went to therapy, I asked Ami's psychologist if this could all have been planted in her head, if someone could have said that it was her dad doing this to her. Her response was, "No. That's like trying to tell her you're not her mommy."

I wanted to get away for a couple of days, so I took Ami with me to New York to see my sister Judy. I would let social services know where I was and keep in contact with them. One morning during that visit, Judy gave Ami a bath. I was sick with a miserable cold, so I lay down in the other room. Suddenly, Judy came running into the room to tell me the things Ami was saying about her father. Even though she had heard the story from me numerous times, it was frightening for her to hear it from Ami's own lips. I asked her to go back in there and act like nothing happened. Later that day she said to me, "You really have changed. You show no emotion. No emotion! What the hell is wrong with you?"

To me, not talking about it in front of Ami was protecting her. I figured she was better off not knowing how wrong it was. Looking back, I should have fought aggressively from the very instant I heard those words come out of my baby's mouth. As it turned out, it wouldn't have mattered.

Later that month, one of my girlfriends came out to visit from Phoenix for a few days. One morning, out of the blue, Ami said to her, "Daddy jumps on me and rides me in my bed. He hurt my pee-pee and poopy."

◆ ◆ ◆ ◆ ◆ ◆

Ami was now seeing Derek once a week at social services, supervised. While I sat in the waiting room, he was in their visitation room, showing the social worker what a great dad he was. He had always been good with children. In thirty seconds he could take them to Wonderland. In the meantime, while I was running Ami to the mountains for her appointments with the psychologist, taking her to her social services visits with her father, juggling all of my sales appointments and trying to deal with what had happened to my little girl, Derek was spending his time planning and manipulating all the experts around us.

As part of the ongoing investigation, social services had given me a list of psychologists who worked closely with them, and from that list I picked a Dr. Brodbeck. Ami had approximately five sessions with Dr. Brodbeck. Since Ami was very advanced and articulate for a two-year-old, I hoped Dr. Brodbeck would have this out in no time. I had told her that Ami seemed to talk about it when her panties were off. She asked Ami to take her panties down. Shocked and very uncomfortable with her request, I assumed that as a therapist she knew what she was doing. It also made me sick to ask my little girl to talk about such a disgusting event in front of someone, but I did as the therapist asked. Understandably, Ami became uncomfortable and stopped talking.

On August 29, 1989, during her last session with Ami, Dr. Brodbeck called me in after twenty minutes and told me she had some good news and some bad news. The good news was that she felt I had handled this beautifully and that Ami had not been terribly affected. The bad news was that she could not substantiate the abuse.

I was shocked. After five sessions, she couldn't prove the abuse that Ami had been telling everyone about every day?

She would later report that I had coaxed Ami into saying what she had said, that although Ami had made a licking motion with her tongue when talking about what her father had done, it was just a stress-related gesture. This was after she had told me I had handled it beautifully.

Both she and Jennifer determined that Ami wasn't afraid of her father, and his denials of any sexual contact with her were credible. When they had asked Ami directly what her father had done to her, they said Ami had offered no response. On September 1st, Jennifer called to tell me that they were closing the case and that she would be recommending that Ami resume her visitations with Derek. I was irate. "Like hell you will!" I said. I knew this man was abusing Ami, and I didn't want her with him. "I'm not afraid to take this to the governor of Colorado if I have to," I exclaimed in a strong and firm voice. I no longer had any doubts about what Derek was doing to Ami. I would not stop at anything to protect my little girl.

In the meantime, Derek called to tell me he wanted to see Ami immediately. Like hell he would. Then, Jennifer called me back to tell me that Derek would have to go through Children's Hospital for visits and that I should get a second opinion from another psychologist, which was surely due to my outrage at the suggestion to resume the father's visits. He called me again, demanding visits, telling me that no one believed me. I didn't care. Ami was all that mattered, and I believed her.

The next day, I called the Aurora Police Department again and told them how upset I was that social services had closed my case. I couldn't understand why Dr. Brodbeck had not substantiated the abuse. Detective F.H. Parker referred me to another psychologist, Dr. Baker.

Dr. Baker was a warm, relatable, lovely woman. After four visits with Ami, she believed that Ami had been abused.

When she interviewed Derek, she noted that Derek referred to Ami as "the baby" or "the girl." When asked why she might have complained about his treatment of her, Derek said that he may have wiped her vagina "too roughly" after she had gone to the bathroom.

Her interview with Ruth, Ami's daycare provider, was revealing. Ruth told her that during the spring and summer of 1989, Ami's behavior had changed markedly from "happy-go-lucky" to aggressive. She occasionally bit the other children and whined a lot. When Ruth had bathed Ami, Ami had fondled her genitals and told Ruth, "Daddy hurt me." She had also put her fingers inside her, wiggled her tongue, and said, "Daddy did that." According to Ruth, when she napped or spent the occasional overnight there (when I had an overnight flight), she cried a great deal or had nightmares.

In Dr. Baker's sessions with Ami, she found Ami to be unable to distinguish between truth and lies or good touch and bad touch. She found that Ami became "observably nervous" when examining the genital areas of the anatomically correct male and female dolls. Ami had undressed all the dolls and immediately began to examine their genital areas. She had placed her index finger inside the female doll's vagina, then got nervous and asked for Dr. Baker to get her mommy.

During the second interview, Ami, once again, undressed the dolls then set the "daddy doll" some distance from where she was playing and repeatedly said that she did not like the daddy doll. Doctor Leigh wrote in her report:

> When asked…a leading question concerning her father "touching her," she just stared blankly at the examiner. She then stuck out her tongue and wiggled it back and forth. When questioned further, Ami stated that she "was afraid."

Dr. Baker explained that this fear was probably due to all the anxiety Ami was feeling about being asked about what had happened. Her normal routine, her normal environment, had all changed. She was seeing her father only once in a while for supervised visits, and she saw that her mother was very upset with what had happened. All of this couldn't help but leave her feeling vulnerable and frightened.

Dr. Baker concluded that Ami's repeated demonstrations of digital penetration, anger, and marked anxiety toward the daddy doll and her constant retelling of the same scenario were indicative of sexual abuse or exposure to sexual stimuli.

I quickly realized that I needed a lawyer, so I began my search. When I consulted with one named Barbara Stark, she encouraged me to quickly try to gain control of the situation. It was as though I were a rape victim, she said, and the courts would turn everything around and blame me. She told me that there was a great backlash going on in the country, and if the guardian ad litem—the person appointed by the court to advocate for the child—turned out to be against me, then that would carry 90 percent of the weight. If that were the case,

I could lose custody of my child. She also wanted $5,000 as a retainer and said it could cost $40,000 by the time we were done.

I couldn't believe it was as bad as she made it out to be; I walked out of her office, thinking she was exaggerating. I would later learn that she had it exactly right.

CHAPTER 8

Without Conscience: Parental Alienation Syndrome (PAS)

On October 12th, I took Ami to a supervised visit at social services and was met by a stern, abrupt woman who coldly introduced herself as Doris Truhlar. She seemed very angry and arrogant. She said, "I am the GAL (guardian ad litem) assigned to your case."

Quite surprised, I replied, "How did you get to be the GAL? Do I not have some say in this?" I guess I didn't. She wanted to see Derek and Ami together for thirty minutes, and then she would come and see me. That was fine, but little did I know that she had been on the case for two months. During that time, she had spent a great deal of time with Derek.

Later, when she came in to talk to me, I told her all the things Ami was doing and saying, but I could tell she was not listening to a word of it. She made no real comment, except that she would like me to bring Ami to her office for another visit with her father.

When I arrived at Doris's office, I was greeted with a five- page document stating that it was emotionally and irreparably damaging for Ami not to have her father in her life. "This is parental alienation!" she said. It was the first time I had heard this term, so I asked her to explain.

"I had made every effort to involve her father in her life," I said. As I read farther, I became alarmed that the whole document was so conclusive and biased toward the father. When she walked into the conference room, I asked her just how emotionally and irreparably damaging was what Derek had been doing to her.

"No one said there was any kind of abuse," she said.

I couldn't believe it. My only comment, not knowing yet what I was dealing with, was that I had bent over backward for Ami to have her father in her life. I had a great relationship with my own father, and I wanted her to have the same. Until now, this had been extremely important. But now?

Doris wanted both Derek and me to participate in a psychological evaluation. I told her I didn't think Derek would agree to one. She left the room, marched back in only moments later, and shook her finger in my face angrily. "Derek agrees," she said. "Now maybe we'll find out about you!"

Clearly, he had influenced this woman against me. Not trusting her, I went to check on Ami, to see if Doris had left her alone with her father. Sure enough, she had. Angrily I asked her secretary where Doris was and who was watching Derek and Ami. She told me they had it under control. I told the secretary that she should watch them and slammed the door behind me.

This was amazing. Doris had been manipulated, just as so many others had throughout my divorce. When Derek had convinced people at our athletic club that I was crazy, when he had falsely charged me with assault and battery, when he had the policewoman in the palm of his hand, and when he had secretly met with the DA. Now it was the social services women.

It was already five in the evening, and I was emotionally drained. I just wanted to get Ami and go home. When it was finally time to go, Doris asked me to bring Ami again on Thursday.

When I got home I told my mother, who understood Derek better than I did, everything that had gone on at social services. "My God," she said, "he is pushing them to get Ami placed in foster care." She was usually right, so I called Ted Kaplysh, a lawyer who had been recommended to me by my friend Rhonda at work. Unlike the other lawyer, he didn't ask for $5,000 up front, and he agreed to take me on as a client.

Days later, on the night of October 18, 1989, Ami was in bed with me because she was having a hard time sleeping by herself. For months, I had held everything in, not showing any emotion as my heart was ripped out every time my precious little girl told me and others what most people would describe as unimaginable. For her sake I had been trying to keep myself together, while feeling deep down as though I was dying. But that night, for the first time, I cried in front of her.

She told me, "It's all right, Mommy, you just need to sleep." "I know, honey," I said. "We're buddies."

She had never heard that word before. "Buddies?" she said. "Yes, buddies!" I said. "We will be together always." She

liked that, the word buddies.

On Thursday, I brought her for her next supervised visit with her father. We were met by Jennifer, who for seven weeks had watched this perfect father with his darling little girl while I was being labeled as a vengeful, vindictive ex-wife who could not deal with my divorce from this wonderful man. She and Doris handed me a piece of paper and said they wanted to discuss the four matters listed on it: 1. Separation Counseling. What for? I wondered. We had been divorced for over two years, and I was not the one having a hard time separating. I wasn't the one calling him every day or writing editorials to the newspaper or begging him to come back. They wanted me to sit in the same room with the person who was raping Ami and discuss our marriage? 2. Psychological Evaluation. I agreed to this. 3. Let Pam supervise Derek's visits with Ami. I didn't consider her to be a very moral, responsible adult. I was determined that she would not supervise the visits. I didn't trust her to stay there with them. But Doris said, "I met with Pam and found her to be a credible third party." I found that interesting: she had met with Pam, but not with Ruth, the daycare provider who spent a lot of time with Ami, and not with me or my friends or my family, or with Dr. Baker, the psychologist who had concluded that Ami was being abused! 4. Parental Alienation. When I heard them describe how Derek had been alienated from Ami, I knew I had to do something to stop this. I said, "I need to talk to my lawyer before we go into a meeting." But then I could not get a hold of Ted Kaplysh and left a message with his paralegal.

After a lot of pressure from Doris and Jennifer, I agreed to get started. I knew that all these people were against me, and I had been through hell for four months. But I was determined to be strong and handle it myself.

We went into a conference room where I was interrogated for over an hour. It was just like a movie. Not one question was directed toward the abuser; they were all directed at me. "Why would your daughter continue to say this if you weren't coaching her?" they asked, and immediately I'd be hit with another question, one right after another.

I said, "Because it is happening! I would never coach Ami. Maybe it is because he is doing this. Did you ever think of that?" I told them what Ami was saying for the first time right in front of Derek, who avoided eye contact with me; he just looked at the floor.

But Jennifer and Doris had made up their minds. Nothing I said sunk in with them. They did not want to hear what the daycare provider, psychologist, friends, and I had witnessed Ami saying and doing on many occasions. When the subject of Dr. Baker's evaluation came up, Doris very angrily said, "Dr. Baker says there is no abuse." (See Dr. Baker report Appendix D). I had just read the doctor's report and remembered very clearly that when she had come out of therapy with Ami, she had told me point blank that yes, Ami had been abused. Now Doris was stating that this was not true. What the hell was going on?

When Doris brought up the issue of "parental alienation" again, I told them that I had bent over backward for Derek to be in Ami's life. In fact, I had originally filed for divorce in part because he had not been involved in her life or mine, but I had a great relationship with my own father, and I wanted Ami to have the chance for the same. I told her to ask Stan Lipkin, my divorce attorney, what had gone on prior to this and how hard I had worked at mediation, and to call Janice Cella, the mediator, too. She told me that she had talked with Stan Lipkin and that he did not corroborate my assessment. How could Stan have said anything negative? We had disagreed about the three thousand dollars I had paid him and about one of the custody documents, but would he have turned on me like that? I was starting to feel crazy. Later I find out Doris was lying

Doris then suggested separation counseling. I am thinking to myself separation counseling with the man who abused me and is now abusing Ami. He has never left me alone and our divorce has been over for over two years.

The last thing we discussed was the suggestion that Pam should supervise the visits. I was appalled by this. At that moment, my attorney called back and asked Doris what the heck she thought she was doing. Had she read Dr. Baker's report or talked with the daycare provider? When she said no, he asked her how she could assign the woman who was the catalyst for the breakup of my marriage to supervise the visits. That's when I heard Doris say that the child was going into foster care. He told her, "You take that child from her mother, and I will have your ass." Her response once again was that Ami was going into foster care.

I was horrified. What grounds did they have to take my baby from me? All of a sudden, I felt my body start to tremble. I wanted to scream, but I desperately held back from doing. I knew that this was the reaction they wanted so they could say, "See, she is emotionally inept!" From somewhere I got the inner strength to hold it together. I got up and walked into another room, where I laid my head on a desk between my arms and let it all go. I sobbed as though my heart were being ripped out of me.

Doris Truhlar had planned and arranged everything beforehand, over the phone with a judge. I had been excluded from the entire process. She had the police and a foster care home lined up before I had even come in that morning with Ami.

After a few minutes, they came into the room and told me they were taking Ami away from me. One of them tapped me on the shoulder and said in a cold voice, "You can go say good-bye to your daughter now."

I pulled myself together, but I could not walk—my legs were numb. It felt as if my whole body had been removed and a shell had taken its place. A gray mist surrounded me, and voices around me sounded distant. One of them said, "Look at her! Look at her! She can't handle it. She can't say good-bye to her daughter."

I extended my arm to move them away from me and, in a low voice from somewhere inside of me, said, "Yes, I can."

I shoved them to the side, walked in to where Ami was playing, and said as calmly as I could, "Ami, Mommy has to go to work. I know we were planning on going roller skating, but I will be back soon."

She looked at me, puzzled, wondering if everything was okay. I bent down and held her as a tear streamed down my cheek.

After I hugged Ami good-bye, the police came in and escorted me out of the building.

For "The Truth about Parental Alienation", please visit MaraleeMclean.com

CHAPTER 9

Foster Care and More Trauma

I can't remember much of anything after that except getting in my car and driving directly to Dr. Baker's. I wanted to confront her with what Doris had said. I wanted to know why she was now stating there was no abuse. Then I was going to go see Stan Lipkin, my former attorney, to see why he had turned on me too.

I don't remember driving to Dr. Baker's. All I know is that I drove very fast. Once I arrived at her office, she was not in so I waited for her. When she walked in, she was shocked at how I looked. My makeup was running, and I'm sure the pain and fear I was feeling was evident in my face.

"What happened to you?" she asked.

I looked at her with tears rolling down my cheeks and said, "You know the truth!" You fight for us!" God help me! I thought. I told her they had taken Ami away from me.

"I was afraid they would do something like this," she said, "and I told them absolutely not!" She told me she had another emergency and she would be right with me.

As I waited for her, I called Ted Kaplysh, my attorney, and he said he wanted to talk to Dr. Baker. I told him that she was in her office with her door closed; she had another emergency to take care of. He told me that she was probably calling the police to have me arrested; I should get out of there right away. After everything I had been through that morning and knowing that according to Doris, Dr. Baker had said there had been no abuse, I suspected that my attorney could be right. Everything else had been completely twisted around, so why not this?

I knocked lightly on Dr. Baker's door and told her I was leaving. She came to the door and grabbed my arm as if to hold me. I pulled away from her, thinking she was trying to keep me there to have me arrested, but she gently put her arms around me as tears surfaced from her eyes. "I am so sorry," she said. "So sorry Maralee! I had an idea they would do something like this and I told them absolutely not. I have called your therapist, and he knows you are coming. Go to him now. He is waiting for you."

I drove twenty minutes to my therapist's, but while I was waiting, I called my attorney, and he told me to go back to Dr. Baker's and get the report for him. So I drove back and got the report from Dr. Baker. I don't know how I was able to drive. It was an out-of-body experience.

When I arrived at my attorney's office with Dr. Baker's report, my friend Rhonda, Ted's girlfriend and my fellow supervisor at Continental, was there. She had been with me and had listened in on Derek's phone calls when he had falsely charged me with assault and battery and when he cried and said how sorry he was and admitted that I hadn't hit him with the car. She had also witnessed his constant phone calls at work and knew that I had told our secretaries to screen my calls. She and Ted were about to travel to Indiana to see a Notre Dame football game. I looked at his big bag all packed for the weekend and suddenly felt so alone. There was to be a hearing on Monday, but he would still be away, so he wanted me to get another attorney to handle the hearing at juvenile court. He gave me the names of other attorneys in his firm, but when I called them all, not one of them was available.

I went home and called two of my best friends who came over for support. I also told Ruth, Ami's daycare provider, what had happened. Ruth called social services and asked if she could be the one to take Ami, since she had been a foster care parent in the past. But Doris said no.

Then I called my parents, and after they heard what had happened, without me knowing they decided to come down immediately to be with me. They drove nonstop from Montana and arrived at four in the morning. I have never in my life been so glad to see my parents. We said nothing as the tears streamed, just hugged one another tight and went to bed. The next day I went to see my psychologist, Matthew, because I had missed our meeting the day before. After seeing him, I drove an hour and a half to meet with an attorney who had said on the phone that he might be able to represent me at the hearing Monday morning. I was still in shock and a little incoherent, and it was difficult for me to drive. After I finally arrived at his office, he told me he already had a hearing scheduled for Monday. I asked him why he hadn't told me that before I had driven all that way!

When I arrived home, Doris Truhlar called to tell me that Ami was fine. She was in a nice home, and Doris had checked it out carefully. I asked her what the hearing was for on Monday, and in a cold, condescending tone she told me that it would be to decide if Derek or I got custody of Ami. The undertone in her voice indicated that she would support Derek. I was infuriated. This was not a custody issue—this was an abuse issue! She went on to say that I could see Ami the next day, Saturday, at a local park after Derek saw her. He was scheduled for 9:00 a.m., and I was scheduled for 9:45 a.m. That night I stayed up typing a thirteen-page letter to Doris, explaining everything that had happened, but my parents suggested that I not give it to her until my attorney saw it. (I eventually gave it to her, but it had no effect.) Meanwhile, I couldn't wait to see Ami. Every night my stomach was in knots as I looked out at all the lights of the city and wondered where my baby was. Until then, I had always known where she had been, every minute of every day.

The next day, as I drove up to the park, I saw her from a distance. She had a little jacket on that Derek had given her with "Daddy's Little Angel" written on it. It made me want to gag. So did hearing his voice. As I began to walk toward the playground area, Ami saw me and began to run across the park as fast as she could, screaming, "Mommy! Mommy!"

I ran toward her, picked her up, and pulled her close to my chest. I never wanted to put her down again. I wanted to run with her and never look back. Instead, I took her over to the swing sets while Doris escorted Derek to his car, looking quite chummy together.

When Doris came back, my visit with Ami no longer seemed real. Everything I did and said as a mother was being scrutinized.

When the visit was over, Ami was placed in the car with Doris, and she instantly turned quiet and distant. In shock, she thought, that her mommy was taking her home. I didn't know what they had told her. I felt so sick. I reached in the car to reassure her and whispered in her ear, "Remember what I said the other night, we're buddies. You and Mommy will always be together." She just turned her little head away from me and went off into a blank stare.

Later, Ami's therapist would tell me that Ami was traumatized that day. She would reenact the scene over and over. The day she was left in a park alone. Trauma, trauma and more trauma induced by the professionals.

◆ ◆ ◆ ◆ ◆ ◆

At the hearing Monday morning, I was represented by Alex Benze, an attorney Ted had found for me when I had called him to tell him I hadn't found anyone. At this hearing, it was decided to take Ami out of the foster home she was in and put her into Ruth's house. I was so thankful. At least she would be in a familiar place with someone who loved her. I grabbed Doris Truhlar and hugged her with tears rolling down my cheeks. "Thank God!" I said. "You're at least thinking of my child."

That day, Ruth and Doris removed Ami from the foster care home. Ruth would later tell me that the foster home was a filthy, disgusting place, and when they picked her up, Ami was in a trance-like state, with diarrhea caked to her leg. (By that time she had been potty-trained for quite a while.) She said she did not talk the whole way to Ruth's home, and when they arrived, she asked for her mommy. When I learned of this, I wanted to kill those idiots. What rights did they have to do this to my child?

On November 10, 1989, I received a letter from Doris Truhlar stating, "At this time Ami is exhibiting some dissociative type behavior—there are times when she seems to disassociate or almost to go into a trance-like state. This is extremely serious and concerning. It indicates to me the severe trauma that has happened to Ami. I do not know what this is. A child who was exposed to repeated bitterness, animosity and hatred of parents for each other could, in my own view, behave this way." Unbelievable she just abruptly took her from her mother a loving secure home and put her in foster care. I think this would be pretty traumatizing for a two and half year old plus the trauma of not being protected. She also said," Derek if you abused your daughter, I would very much still want you to have a relationship with her. I would want you to have counseling to assist you in having a completely normal relationship. I would want to return to unsupervised visitation absolutely as soon as possible—as soon as the professionals in the case felt that Ami was safe from re--abuse. I would not feel, even if you abused Ami that your relationship should be cut off or that you should be relegated to the position of an absentee father." How sick is this women? Doris had Dr. Baker's report, Ruth Gibbens information on the abuse, what I had told her, and other witnesses and she continued on her charade.

For six weeks, Ami was in foster care at Ruth's, and I was allowed to see her only three times a week for an hour each time. Those days and weeks seemed like an eternity. I was now in a large home by myself, surrounded by Ami's memories and wondering when they were going to give my little girl back to me. Every night, at around two in the morning, I sat straight up in my bed in a cold sweat, as if an electric shock were running through my body. Other nights I woke from a dead sleep, remembering with a shiver going down my spine the day I had dropped off Ami at Derek's, having bathed and dressed her like a little doll, only to find her naked and limp, soaked with sweat, with Derek claiming she was sick. I now was certain that that was one of the times he had sexually molested her. The smirk on his face was etched in my memory. Now that I look back on it, he was looking at me as an idiot. He seemed to be thinking, I just raped your daughter, and you don't even know it.

Later, I would see in Ruth's report that Ami was also waking every night at two in the morning, crying and crying and begging for her mommy.

◆ ◆ ◆ ◆ ◆ ◆

Ruth was under oath by the courts to stay within hearing distance of both of us during our visitations and to never leave Ami alone with either of us. She took this oath very seriously. She was also to keep a daily journal. In that journal, which was later submitted to the courts, she wrote, "One day Ami confronted her Dad. She sat on the floor with her legs spread and said, 'Daddy you're not to touch me here anymore. It's bad!' She was pointing to her vagina." He supposedly turned five shades of white and left the room. Ami had told Ruth that her daddy put his tongue in her and hurt her pee-pee.

When I would come to Ruth's to see her for an hour, Ami would say, "Mommy, I want to come home. Why won't you take me home?" I never knew how to answer this. I wound up telling her that there were some problems and that they had nothing to do with her. I loved her very much, and I wanted very much to take her home but couldn't.

When other moms came to get their kids from the daycare center, Ami would run off and leave me standing there. She was angry that I would not take her home. How could I make her understand that she wasn't the only one who didn't know what was going on?

Toward the end of the six weeks, Ami was having a very difficult time. Ruth told Doris that this poor little girl's heart was broken, that she needed her mother, and that she had cried every night, all night, for two weeks solid. Ruth was exhausted. Derek had called about visitation that day, and Ruth had told him that there would be no visitation because of what my poor Ami had been going through; she told him she was going to call Doris to suggest they change the arrangement. He insisted that he call Doris, but Ruth called and she, Doris, and Jennifer had a three-way phone call. Ruth told me later that they wanted to put Ami back in another foster care home, but she had told them that if they did that, they would kill this baby. She was missing her mother, and her heart was broken. So Doris decided to put Ami back in my home for the time being.

I can't remember much about that day. After I got the phone call telling me that Ami could come home, I drove to Ruth's house so excited and picked up my little girl, once again terrified of what they would do next. Was this for real?

We were both very excited. When we got home, she ran right to her room with a squeal.

That night, I put her to bed and sang her a lullaby that I had sung to her many, many nights, watching her angelic face as she fell asleep. Then I got up every hour on the hour, just to go look at her. She was so beautiful, so precious. I can't even express the love I felt gazing at her angelic face. How I loved my little girl. She did not deserve all this pain. I wanted so badly to protect her and for her to never have to experience any trauma. Before all this, she had been so secure and well adjusted. Everything I had worked so hard for, these outsiders, these nobodies, had quickly and callously destroyed. It made no sense. Where had these people come from? What right did they have to do this to our little family?

One of the stipulations that social services had imposed upon me was to get separation counseling, so Derek and I met with Art Jones, a therapist Doris had recommended. This, to me, felt absurd. I was to sit in the same room and discuss my marriage—which had been over for two and a half years—and minor issues like insurance, while my ex-husband's criminal abuse of our daughter was still not being addressed. On one occasion, I lost it. I had been up with Ami the night before with her crying out about what her daddy was doing to her, and yet here he was, wanting to discuss something he had spent two weeks mapping out on a computer printout. I finally said, "This is nonsense! The problem isn't these menial things you keep bringing up. The problem is what your little girl is saying about you!" (See Jone's report Appendix D).

He said, "Look, I may have put her in her car seat and pinched her down there once."

I very angrily said, "And that's why your tongue was there?" He did not know what Ami had been saying about him. She had been articulating very clearly what her daddy was doing to her. He once again just looked at the floor, and when the session ended, he hurriedly walked right past me out the door. I caught up with him and called out, "You pervert!" He kept walking until I got right up into his face. "You child molester!"

He looked at me with his steel-blue eyes and a smirk, as if to say, I know, but what are you going to do about it?

Needless to say, the therapy was counterproductive. It was cruel to make me sit with him and discuss meaningless issues. So it was terminated after a lot of wasted money. I was beginning to learn an ugly truth: this whole process was a money-making industry. All their referrals made a lot of money for lawyers, counselors, and consultants but didn't really do much for the people who actually needed their help, especially the children

CHAPTER 10

Gut Instincts in Court

My attorney and I had already scheduled a hearing to ask the court to bring Ami back to my house, and now it would be used to determine our new visitation arrangement. On the day of the hearing, when I showed up, Doris Truhlar, Jennifer, the father's attorney Steve Calder, and Pam were all in a conference room together. This was typical behavior throughout. I would be outside while they had their little private meetings, as if I were the criminal or the abuser. They wanted me to agree to some stipulations: to remove Dr. Baker as Ami's psychologist and to let Pam supervise the visits again. My attorney told me to agree with them or they would take Ami away from me again. I refused to agree. There was no reason to remove Dr. Baker. Ami had spoken with her and felt comfortable with her. Finally, after four hours of arguing, I agreed because of my attorney's strong recommendation to do so, but once again, I had a strong gut feeling that I was doing the wrong thing.

At the meeting, Doris Truhlar got up before the court and recited all her motions, which included giving Derek custody of Ami. I felt sick to my stomach. I looked down at my attorney and said, "Alex, object! Object to this hearing! I cannot go along with this." In a strong, deep voice I said, "Object now!"

He said, "Are you serious?" Of course I was serious! He immediately interrupted Doris's power play and objected. Doris reacted by throwing her hands in the air and screaming out, "I file a motion with this court to immediately remove this child out of the custody of her mother and place her in the custody of the father!"

My attorney once again spoke up. "Your Honor," he said, "there are a lot of lies flying around this courtroom. This man has sexually abused his daughter and should have supervised visits." He went on to chastise Doris and all her recommendations, considering the father had abused his child. Doris wanted to make sure Dr. Baker was removed, so she claimed the doctor was inadequate. Jennifer, her counterpart in all this, agreed. Neither one of them was a psychologist— far from it, in fact—and Dr. Baker was not there to defend herself. Dr. Baker was more than qualified and had come highly recommended from the police department's sexual abuse team. Nonetheless, the judge agreed and ordered that Dr. Baker be removed and that Derek's girlfriend would supervise his visits. In place of Dr. Baker, a doctor named

Dr. Gail Adam's would be assigned as Ami's therapist.

Doris Truhlar had been the one to recommend Gail to the court, and this should have been my first clue. She would turn out to be the most incompetent therapist, more loyal to my smooth-talking ex-husband than to Ami. But at the time, I figured it really did not matter who the psychologist was. Ami would talk again in time, and the truth would come out. I was told later by Dr. Baker that Dr. Adams was not going to give Ami any sexual-abuse therapy. Little did I know that Dr. Adams had been told to counsel Ami only on the trauma she had suffered from being taken out of her home. She was not to provide therapy for sexual abuse or even try to find out if there had been any abuse.

When Ami began her sessions with her, Dr. Adams said that Derek should be in the waiting room with me for every session. This made me uncomfortable, to be sure, but more importantly, it made Ami uncomfortable. With her father right outside the door, she wasn't about to say anything bad about him. Later Ami would ask me, "Can my dad hear what I say through the door when I am at Gail's?"

Ami began visits with her father for three hours at a time with Pam supervising. At first, the visits went well. Then one night, Ami came back from a visit and hid under the dining room table and seemed distraught. I tried to get her to come out then decided to not pay attention so she could come out when she was ready. After a few minutes, she sat on the stairs and said, "Daddy touched me again!" She had not talked about it for a couple of weeks. I thought maybe she was talking about the past—he wouldn't do this now with all these people watching for it.

"Was Pam there?" I asked her. "No!" she said.

Soon after that, her nightmares increased. She cried out, "Mommy!" in the night. "No, Daddy, no! Daddy, don't! It's bad!" One night she woke up screaming out, "No, don't get it out!" and throwing her pillow. The next night she woke up, grabbing her vagina and crying out, "Icky sticky!"

After I soothed her by saying, "Ami, your mom is here," I asked, "Why are you saying 'icky and sticky'"?

"My dad puts it in there," she replied. "What does your dad put in there?" "His peanut. It hurts!" she yelled.

I tried to comfort her, all the while feeling I might throw up, and then I tried to figure out when this had happened or the time frame. "Did he do this after he cut your hair?" I asked. "Did he do this to you when he had you last night?"

She responded, "Yes."

Her inappropriate behavior also began again, both at daycare and at home. One day we were sitting on the couch together when she started fondling herself, saying that her dad had put a blue toy in there. When I asked her what kind of toy, she shrugged her shoulders.

"Would you have a toy like it in your toy box?" I asked. She quickly ran to her toy box, pulled out her "Sing-Song" set, and showed me the microphone.

This behavior led me to believe that Pam might not be supervising her visits with her father. So I hired a private investigator to see if she was staying during the visits. Sure enough, she was leaving Ami alone with him. So now I was sure that he was molesting her again. I called social services and told them that I had evidence that Derek was not being supervised when he visited with Ami. Of course, nothing was done.

Meanwhile, Ruth, Ami's daycare provider, was having problems with Ami telling the other kids what her daddy was doing to her, along with taking her clothes off and constantly fondling herself. I didn't say anything to anyone because I was afraid they would come and take her away from me again, and I knew neither Ami nor I could handle that again. However, Ruth understandably felt compelled to call social services.

Jennifer was then taken off the case, and a new social worker by the name of Kirsten Jensen was assigned to it. She visited Ami at Ruth's house and told Ruth to bring Ami into the living room. There, Ami told Kirsten what her dad was doing to her. Kirsten listened, and then concluded that it had been too long after the fact to do anything. She could not be sure that what Ami was saying was true; her statements were too vague. It's as though they must keep the father in the child's life even if he is raping your child. Male Entitlement?

Two weeks later, Derek was given unsupervised visits

CHAPTER 11

Learning to Survive While Everyone Else Lives

At this time, I was still on leave from Continental and still selling Yellow Pages advertising. On one sales call, I met a man named Dennis Brachfeld who owned a company related to energy conservation. When I met him, I was immediately attracted to him, and it was definitely mutual. I had a beautiful blue dress on, and it had buttons all the way down the back. Ami had buttoned it for me that morning and had missed a couple. When we entered his office he said, "I see you missed a couple of buttons. Let me get these for you." Embarrassed, I told him that my little girl had helped me get dressed. I had not had a man touch me in so long, and he was so good-looking. After we met a couple of times, he asked me out to lunch.

I was very attracted to this man, so I made a deal with myself: I would not let him know what was going on in my life. I had not dated anyone for quite some time, and I just wanted to have some normalcy to my life.

When he picked me up for our first date, he revealed to me right away that he was going to be a father. Shocked, I said, "I thought you said you weren't married." He explained he had broken it off with a woman he had been seeing and that they had gotten back together for her fortieth birthday. Now she was pregnant with his child. I thought, He is sure up front with this information. Well, at least he's honest. He told me he cared for her but was not in love with her and was upset about the baby. He really opened up to me.

I had decided I wasn't going to share anything with him, even though I felt so much pain over what was happening with my little girl. Here he was revealing everything to me on our first date. He kept asking me questions but trying not to pry, and he seemed so kind and trustworthy that I finally decided to tell him. As I told him the story of how they had taken Ami away from me, I started to cry, and he held my hand and comforted me.

Not long after that, we went out again, and when we returned, he held me in his arms on the couch all night. His arms encompassed me in a way I had never felt before. When he kissed me, I melted. It was as though I had been in his arms for years.

◆◆◆◆◆◆

Meanwhile, my attorney, Ted Kaplysh, had taken a strong liking toward me. He had broken off his relationship with my friend Rhonda. I was dating Dennis, but Dennis was seeing other women. We hadn't yet made love when Ted first started courting me, and, besides, Dennis had a woman who was carrying his baby, whether he wanted the relationship or not. So, I agreed to go out with my attorney to a movie, and this was followed by subsequent dates—a game of racquet ball, kite flying, brunches, and dinners—until it was obvious that he was looking for a relationship. I was confused and felt that I might be making a big mistake, but he was attractive, fun, and even though I had fallen in love with Dennis, I did enjoy Ted's company. He bought me work-out outfits, all the way down to the socks, along with other gifts. I tried to keep my distance, but I found that all of his efforts to win me over were beginning to work.

I was still earning money strictly on commission, and with my house payments along with all of Ami's psychological expenses, lawyer bills, and the stress of having nobody addressing my ex-husband's abuse of Ami, I felt the pressure mounting. So I put the house up for sale and decided to move into a smaller place. This was a difficult decision. It was a beautiful home. It had been Ami's house since birth; it gave me a sense of security, and all my retirement money was tied up in it. But I had to do it. I prepared Ami for the move, telling her we needed a smaller home and a larger car.

The market was so depressed that my house didn't sell for months, so I decided to lease it for a year. It leased immediately, leaving me no time to find a place. So Ami and I temporarily moved in with my best friend, Kim Fowler, and her husband, Pat. They had a large beautiful home, and Ami felt right at home. Kim had known Ami since birth and had no kids of her own, so she immediately treated Ami as if she were her own little girl. It was stressful yet a fun time for both of us. Dennis and I had become much closer during this time, and he was very emotionally supportive and seemed to make my life much easier.

The day we moved out, Dennis and two of his employees helped us to move. Derek had visitation with Ami and was bringing her back when he saw I was moving out. He looked at me with a sad look in his eyes and said, "Sorry." What a twist. He had never left me alone after my divorce, caused as much pain as he possibly could, abused Ami, and now he had tears in his eyes when I moved

CHAPTER 12

Blinded Professionals

Meanwhile, Ami's behavior and nightmares had gotten worse. For a few days she would be fine, but the dreams and the masturbation never let up. She talked about it all the time. We could be driving to her ballet lesson, and she would blurt out that her daddy put a red toy in her.

She was three years old now, and what I had found out during one of our hearings was that the women working for social services were never going to help me to protect Ami. Instead, they were arguing that there had been no substantiation of the sexual abuse allegations against Derek, and in fact, what was harming Ami most was the animosity between her parents. I was being portrayed as a hysterical mother who was coercing her daughter to lie about what her father was doing to her while Derek was being portrayed as a model parent and model citizen who had cooperated fully with all suggestions for evaluation and therapy since the very beginning and against whom no accusation could be proven.

In April of 1990, Ruth had grown furious that social services were totally ignoring this child's behavior. One day, Ami had been playing in a playhouse with another little boy when Ruth noticed they were extremely quiet and went to check on them. Ami, who was wearing a dress that day, had pulled down her panties, was bending over a table in the playhouse and telling the boy to "put it here." Now, Ami wasn't just talking about it; she was exposing the other children to something they should never be exposed to. Needless to say, Ruth lost it. She called Doris and yelled, "If you do not do something about this, I am going to the radio, newspapers, and television with this!"

Doris called Ami's pediatrician, who was not experienced in child sexual abuse, and told me to take Ami there and meet her father there. I saw through it immediately. If her dad was present, then she would be less likely to say anything. According to statistics 90 percent of child-molestation cases have no physical evidence. Doris set up a hearing for three days from that day.

Ted came with me to the hearing, and I was confident in his support. I thought, Ted cares about me so much; he will fight for Ami. But at the hearing, he seemed unprepared and did not represent me well at all.

As a result, Doris gained more control over Ami's visitation, and Derek gained overnight visitation. He would now have Ami 40 percent of the time. Doris and Kirsten Jensen the social worker would make all visitation decisions. Ted let it all slide by as these women took control of Ami's visitation; he didn't even bring up the issue of Derek's abuse. I was furious, and afterward we got into a terrible fight.

◆◆◆◆◆◆

On the first night Ami was to spend with her father, I was literally ill, but I had to remember that he molested her at any time, day or night. Still, just the idea of her alone there all night made me want to die. The first night she stayed with him, Dennis came over to the Fowlers' house and held me all night as I cried and cried.

Sometimes when Ami returned from her father's, she exhibited aggressive behavior and then turned around and became withdrawn. When she didn't stay at her father's, she seemed very happy at the Fowlers' house. But once after a visit with her father, Ami came in the house and yelled out, "I hate Kimmy!" Shocked, I asked her why she would say such a thing. She had always had a sweet, loving relationship with Kim. She replied, "Daddy told me to say that." He really hated us living there for those six weeks.

One night after a visit with her dad, Ami woke up screaming out of control, kicking her legs and saying, "No! Ow! No!" She banged her head against the wall, and cried out, "No, Daddy, don't do it!" as she grabbed at her private areas. I was so angry and sick to my stomach. How could he continue this? I hoped that these were memories visiting her in her sleep, and not something that was still happening to her. I knew that I was probably in denial because the truth was too painful to accept.

On Easter Sunday, 1990, Ted, who had made up with me after our fight, asked Ami, the Fowlers, and myself to Easter brunch. Dennis was not pleased. When we went to church, he called me Scarlett O'Hara. I thought it was because I was wearing a big, pink floppy hat, but he meant that I had two men fighting over me. He said he could take a challenge; he just felt that since he was so involved with Ami's case he wasn't getting a fair shot.

I assured him that once the trial was over he would have a chance, but it was not a good idea at the time. He responded that he could keep his emotions at bay while all this was going on.

Ted bought me a beautiful Easter basket and had Kim put it by my bed for when I woke that morning. We had started playing racquetball together, and it was probably the most fun I had had in years. I loved sports and competition. I would not let him get intimate for two reasons: he was my attorney, and I had become intimate with Dennis. This helped me not to get too close to Ted.

However, as much as I liked his attention, things were starting to get a little out of hand; it seemed that he was so infatuated that he would stop at nothing until I was his wife. I decided that our dinners and our dating in general had to stop. No more dates, no more gifts. He agreed. But then on my birthday, because I told him I would not go out with him, he asked me to meet him at his office, which was in the penthouse of the building. There he had ordered in a picnic lunch with champagne, chocolates, flowers, and a bottle of perfume imported from Europe. I was impressed and flattered. His romantic behavior was hard to resist. Then, when my old clunker of a car broke down, he offered me the use of his car. I refused, not wanting to take anything from him. Although he made me laugh, and we had a good time together, I felt very on edge about this relationship and where it was going. I felt as though he had made up his mind that I was the woman he had been waiting for his whole life, and this scared me.

So in addition to feeling stressed over Ami's situation, I was also torn between the two men I was dating. Ted was the kind of man I was looking for: he was handsome, polished, funny, educated, and athletic. He loved to travel, and we had many common interests. On the other hand, Dennis was extremely handsome in a rugged way that I was even more attracted to, extremely protective of Ami and Ami's feelings, emotional and caring, and a good friend.

To make matters worse, the two men began to step up the intensity of their pursuit of me. Ted told me that he had passed by Dennis's office that day, and Dennis asked, "Have you talked to Mr. Penthouse today?" They both called me before I went to sleep, Dennis to ask me about how things were going with Ami, and Ted to ask if he could take me to Greece or Paris or "La-La Land."

In June, just before a hearing we had scheduled to straighten out Ami's custody arrangement, Dennis and I were heading out to a movie, and Ami was on an overnight with her dad. Just as we were walking out the door, the phone rang. It was Ted. I told him I was on my way out to a movie with Dennis and couldn't talk.

When we returned at about 11:00 p.m., the phone rang again, and I told Ted I was still with Dennis. At approximately two in the morning, the phone rang again, when we were sound asleep. It was Ted again. I told him I was asleep, and, yes, I was with Dennis. He hung up on me. Then he called every five to ten minutes after that until 5:30 a.m. at which time Dennis unplugged the phone and said, "Let's go to the mountains for a day and get out of here." I felt awful and guilty for being with Dennis, even though we had been in a relationship for way over a year. Dennis said he felt like he was seeing a married woman.

Strangely enough, I felt the same way. It was as if I was married and had just cheated on my husband. Instead of apologizing for calling me all night, Ted was irate about the whole thing. When I tried to call him later, he hung up on me. When I eventually talked to him, his voice trembled. "Maralee," he said, "so help me, if you are using me…"

I was disgusted. I told him I had never used anyone in my life. "I'm a grown woman," I said, "and I will choose who I want to be with. I do not owe you anything. Dennis and I have been together for a long time. I like you, Ted, but you know where we stand." Later, he apologized and said he did not know why he reacted the way he did—he had never acted like that with any other woman.

I was in a tough position with Ted. On the one hand, he had not represented me well at the last hearing and was getting way too personally involved. On the other hand, I owed him money and wanted desperately to avoid a custody trial. In divorce cases, any party could take the other party to court to reconsider the custody agreement. But this had nothing to do with custody. The only reason I had hired an attorney was to protect Ami.

CHAPTER 13

Evil, Injustice, and System Failure

At the height of this conflict, I had a hearing scheduled for June 6th. The day before, Ted had told me to come to his office at one o'clock. That day, my parents had arrived from Montana to support me, along with my brother from Phoenix. I was exhausted. I had been going through hell with Ami, who was up all night, crying out about what her dad was doing to her. I had been diagnosed with pleurisy. I was still working full-time. I hadn't slept through the night in months, to say nothing of what I was trying to do to help Ami. So when Ted called me in the afternoon, yelling at me, "What are you doing? I told you to be here at one!" I was worried. This man was angry about my relationship with Dennis, and he had my whole life—and Ami's—in his hands.

When I arrived, he was talking to Dr. Baker on the phone, telling her, "I don't care about the case."

I was incredulous. "I'm the only one who works on this case," I said. I reminded him that I had given him Parent Alienation Syndrome by Richard Gardner, which was the book I had seen Doris passing under the table at one of our meetings and now was using to base her case for Derek. I had strongly suggested he read it and had underlined the important parts for him. "This is what they are using," I had told him. "You need to educate yourself on what is going on. Gardner says, 'There is a certain amount of pedophilia in all of us and that pedophilia has been considered the norm by the vast majority of individuals in the history of the world.ii He proposes that pedophilia serves procreative purposes.iii His book is affecting this case and you have not even read it?" I was also the only one who was bothering to prepare for my hearing. For example, I had spent days putting together collages of Ami and her family so the judge would not go by what Doris Truhlar said about the relationships she had with my family. "So don't ever say that to me again," I said. "I do not need your bullshit, and I will leave."

With that, I walked out of his office.

The next day, Ted called Kim with the instructions that Dennis was not to come to the hearing. Then he called her back and told her it was okay, so long as Dennis was emotionally supportive of me. I was already there, and my parents, brother, and Dennis happened to come up on the same elevator. When they arrived on the fifth floor, my parents sort of deserted Dennis because they didn't want Ted to think he had come with them. As I talked with Alex Benze, who was working with Ted on my case as the juvenile court attorney, I could see Dennis standing off to the side, looking terribly uncomfortable. I could also see Ted's face turning red, watching my eyes as I looked at Dennis.

Soon, I saw Ted dash off for the men's room, and right behind him was Dennis. I thought, What the heck is Dennis doing? I found out later that he asked Ted if the two of them were going to have joint custody of me. Ted snapped back at him that he better find himself a good attorney.

When Ted came back, he and Alex Benze talked to Derek and found out that Derek was unwilling to agree to anything they were suggesting. My attorneys returned and told me, "This guy is just out to get you."

When the hearing commenced, Doris Truhlar asked the judge to make it a closed hearing and remove my friends and family, except Pam, she said, who should be allowed to stay. The judge agreed, so everyone on my side, except for Ruth, had to leave. (Pam and Ruth had been appointed as special respondents to the case.)

The hearing was scheduled only for one day, and it was obvious that there was no way all of the arguments could be heard in that time. So it was decided that there would be five more days of hearings in December. But at this one, Doris Truhlar had filed a motion asking that she, Kirsten Jensen, and Dr. Adams be granted the authority to determine Derek's visitation schedule. Judge John

Leopold approved this, and soon afterward, Derek had gained three more overnights per week. The courts are now allowing the abuser more time with Ami and no protection.

Meanwhile, my attorney bills were piling up, so two days after the hearing, Ted asked for the deed of trust to my house as a guarantee of payment. I was under extreme duress and began to cry. He assured me not to worry. It would probably be our house, anyway. Dennis warned me absolutely not to sign that deed—the house. But I needed representation to fight for Ami, and that was all that mattered to me. So I gave him the deed.

During this time, Ami's nightmares were severe. She woke up every night, crying out, dreaming about what her father was doing to her. It was very graphic. She would kick her legs, screaming in pain. One evening, Dennis and I were watching TV downstairs when we heard Ami crying out in her sleep. We ran upstairs to her room, and what we saw was horrible. I could not get control of her as she was thrashing her legs, grabbing at her vagina. My poor little girl! I ached for her. I gently woke her up and said, "Ami, honey, you are with your mommy. It's okay, it's okay. Your mommy is right here," and she went back to sleep. Then I ran for my room, threw myself on my bed and began to sob. Afterward, Dennis suggested that I put a voice-activated tape recorder by Ami's bed at night, so that I could document what she was going through.

I did, and we recorded poor Ami's nightmares on tape. I told Dr. Adams, Ami's psychologist, about them, but she didn't seem concerned. She was proving herself to be a terrible psychologist. She had called me once after a session and said, "I am real concerned about Ami." When I asked her why, she said, "Well, Ami doesn't say her full name." I was stunned. This three-year-old girl was screaming out in the night about what her father was doing to her and had been traumatized from being taken out of her home and placed in foster care for no reason, and her psychologist was concerned about her not saying her full name?

"Well, Gail," I said, "I don't know why. I taught her how to say her full name before she was two." What type of a therapist was she?

At that point, I still didn't know that Dr. Adams had been ordered not to discuss Ami's abuse. I expected any week that Ami would confide in her about it and that Dr. Adams would advocate for us. This was proving to be far from the case. Once when Ami was complaining to me about her father, I asked her. "Don't you ever tell Gail how you feel?"

"No," she said. "She likes my daddy."

The social worker, Kirsten Jensen, wasn't much better. I told her what was going on with Ami and got sympathetic responses, but no real action. When I became increasingly frustrated and felt like I might go crazy, she had Doris call me. I brought the tapes to Doris's office. She listened to them for a little while and then told me to make copies so she could give them to Kirsten and Gail. (As far as I know, she never gave them to Kirsten and Gail; they never mentioned hearing the tapes.) After she listened to some of the tapes, she said they were "ambiguous." If any outsiders listened to them, she said, not knowing what was going on, they would find them ambiguous too.

Just how wrong Doris was about this was illustrated when I picked up the copies of the tapes. The woman at the store handed them to me with tears in her eyes. "This is child abuse, isn't it?" she asked.

"Yes," I said. "It's interesting you would say that because the professionals in this case say that anyone from the outside not knowing of abuse would find the tapes ambiguous."

She replied, "We all listened to the tapes in here, and we all said this is child abuse."

◆◆◆◆◆◆

That summer, I had been given an ultimatum from Continental: no more leaves. I had to come back. I was having a difficult time selling anyway with the stress I was under and had gone from one of the top reps at Yellow Pages to the bottom. Not wanting to give up my sixteen-year investment with the airlines, I returned to Continental. With my seniority, I was able to take eighteen to twenty days off a month and fly "turns"— when flight attendants fly out and return the same day. Once they gave Derek several overnights a week, I scheduled myself for weekends: I would check in at 4:00 p.m. on Friday, fly to London, and be home at 4:00 p.m. Sunday. That way I would have the whole week with Ami. I enrolled her in preschool for the social aspect, but on many days I would not take her there because I was home and she was only three. However, for no apparent reason, Doris insisted that I put her in daycare, and I had to comply.

Just before one of my first trips to London, Derek came to pick up Ami, but she was still napping. I told him that I had her bag packed and that he could go into her room and get her. He went into her room, and I came in behind him to grab her bag. She was sound asleep, but when he touched her leg to wake her up, she went into a panic, scurried to the other side of the bed, and started screaming, her eyes wide as saucers. "No!" she cried, while reaching out for me. I had never seen her so frightened in front of him. He grabbed her, and she kept screaming, "No, Mommy, no! Please don't let me go with my daddy!"

So I screamed, "Give her to me!" but he wouldn't. I looked at him with a look that could kill, grabbed her from him, and tried to calm her down.

My mind was racing. I didn't want to give her back to him. My check in for the London trip, for which I was the flight service manager, was in an hour. I couldn't call that late to be replaced, and social services wouldn't let me keep Ami anyway. I would be held in contempt, and it would be used against me at the hearing. I would get in trouble with my job, and I had to have a job to be able to provide for her and pay for her legal fees so I could protect her. If I kept Ami and ran away with her, I knew what would happen, as I had thoroughly researched that possibility. Mothers who tried that were inevitably caught and put in jail, and their abused daughters lived with their fathers for years.

So after Ami calmed down, I let her go with Derek. Literally, I just wanted to die. I did not know how I would make it through that trip. When we landed in England and on the way to the hotel looking at the green endless fields all I could think about was freedom, somewhere else for Ami and me.

When I returned from that trip, Ami's hair, which had been long and beautiful, had been chopped again. It looked terrible. Chunks were missing, and her bangs were crooked. I knew he had done it to get to me, so I did not give him the satisfaction of reacting to it. I found out from Ami that his girlfriend had done it. She was rather jealous of Ami, I think, because he would not marry her and used Ami as an excuse. I don't know very many forty-year-old men who would rather be with their daughter than with their fiancée.

Later on in the month, Kim and I took Ami to Disneyland in California. We had not had a vacation for two years, and I had to beg Doris to give me the three days in a row with Ami so we could go. By that point they—the threesome of Derek, Doris, and Kirsten—had split up my time with Ami so I saw her every other day.

When we arrived in California, we stayed at Kim's mother's house. That evening, Kim's nephew and one of his friends came over, and out of the blue, Ami, who was still only three years old, asked them if they had penises. She had once asked Dennis if he had a penis, and he had replied, "Yes, all men have penises." Ami told him that all girls have holes.

We had a great time at Disneyland, and Ami saw Ariel, her all-time favorite Disney character. She danced on the dance floor with lots of people watching. It was great for us both to get away, even though it was a short trip.

When we returned home, it was time for a visitation with her dad, and she was outside with her princess hat on, playing with the girls next door. As her dad drove up the driveway, I was standing outside and caught Ami's reaction. Sometimes she would be happy to see him and sometimes extremely upset. This time, as her father honked his horn, she went into a trance-like state; she did not move or blink an eye. As the girls yelled to her that her dad was there, she just continued to stare. Finally, I walked over and said, "Ami, your dad is here." She quietly walked over and got in the car.

Another time I saw her in this trance was when I was driving to work one morning. She had spent the night with her dad, and when I passed them on the road, I spun the car around to catch up with her. When Derek pulled over, Ami was in that state. After I pulled her out of the car, she said, "Mommy, take me with you. Take me with you!" She pleaded with me to take her. By her despair, something must have happened. The pain I felt as a mother was unbearable.

On another occasion, on a Sunday afternoon, I drove up in front of his house to pick her up and found her sitting on the lawn in that same state, as if her mind had left her body.

In the meantime, I was still taking her to therapy for ninety dollars an hour, just to play with the incompetent therapist. I couldn't believe Gail was hearing nothing about the abuse, when during this period I was up all night with her as she cried out about her dad. She was constantly touching herself and telling me her dad was sticking a toy in her. Each time, I had to sit in Gail's waiting room, two feet away from the pervert who was molesting Ami. I wanted to kill him but prevented myself from showing any emotion because of the professionals, who found him absolutely charming.

During one of those awful hours, I looked at him in the waiting room, and I couldn't imagine ever having been married to him. He wore the same watch I had given him. In fact, every article of clothing he was wearing I had picked out for him many years earlier. His hairline was receding. All I saw was this inhumane pervert sitting across from me. Chills run up and down my spine. The next time I glanced up at him, he was looking at me. We were the only two people in the office waiting area. I said, "Why? Why did you have to abuse her? She is a beautiful, perfect child in there. Why do you have to ruin her just because you had a horrible childhood? Give her a chance!"

He got up, not looking me in the face, and said, "I didn't!"

I said, "She knows you did it, and I know you did it, and that is all that matters."

He left and locked himself in another room. When he came out he said, "Are you finished?"

"Yeah, I'm finished!"

CHAPTER 14

A Mother's Dream

The next month, I actually had a few days in a row with Ami, so I took her to Honolulu to see her cousins. I wanted to make it into a mini-vacation for the two of us, so we did not stay with my sister. I got a place for us on the beach. I took the voice-activated tape recorder with us because during the past three months, she had been having terrible nightmares.

We flew at night, and Ami fell asleep during the flight. She woke up on the plane screaming out, "Don't, Dad!" and almost kicked the pregnant woman sitting next to us. I felt very uncomfortable that other people heard what she was saying. I didn't want everyone around us to know that my little girl was being abused by her father. It was difficult keeping her quiet, and I had to wake her to remind her that she was with her mother. The pregnant woman looked shocked, but I decided not to say anything.

When we arrived in Honolulu, Ami was very excited upon checking into our hotel. They gave her a lei made out of candy. It was late, and we were both very tired, so we quickly fell asleep in the king-sized bed. When my leg accidentally touched hers, she began to cry out, "No Dad, don't! Owe! Owe!" I had the voice-activated tape recorder on, and she continued to cry out in such a painful, heartbreaking way with her eyebrows scrunched. It took a long time before I could calm her down. This was absolutely heartbreaking. I was so angry now at these professionals for not listening.

After I got Ami back to sleep, I went into the bathroom with the tape player. With my voice full of fire said, "If you so-called professionals don't do something about what Ami is going through and you let this sick despicable man get by with what he is doing to her... She is thrashing her legs and moaning, as you can hear on this tape, obviously in pain." The anger in my voice could have pierced Satan. I could not say another thing; I was too upset.

The next day, Ami never knew she had been up all night crying, and things went on as usual. She was always a pure joy to be with. I had more fun with her on that vacation than I ever had with anyone. She never got cranky like most kids; she could play on the beach all day long. When we returned to the hotel, she would want to go swimming some more. I used to be a swimming instructor, so I taught her how to swim before the age of two, and now that she was three she was pretty good, a little fish who loved the water. When we went out to dinner, she ordered shrimp, and I order a grilled-cheese sandwich—the opposite of what most parents and children would order—and the waiter laughed. Ami had a magnetic quality about her, and people were always commenting on her. When we went to a luau, she found the lead singer, who impersonated Elvis, to be very handsome. She stared at him as she slowly moved closer to the edge of the stage. Then he looked down at her and asked her to come up on stage. There were at least five hundred people there, and Ami did not even hesitate as she sang and danced with the Hawaiian dancers— not shy at all. When she got down, everyone clapped and yelled, "All right, Ami!" What a kid!

CHAPTER 15

Stop at Nothing

Back home, her nightmares continued. One night my parents came to see us, and Ami cried all night, just as she had on many previous nights. My dad couldn't take it; he went downstairs to sleep. It really broke him up to actually see and hear Ami's suffering. The next day, when they were leaving, their flight was delayed so we decided to have lunch at the airport. Out of the blue, Ami asked me, "Do you love your daddy?"

I replied, "Of course I love my daddy."

She then said, "But your daddy doesn't touch you?"

"No, Ami," I said, "my dad doesn't touch me!" My dad turned white, and I could tell he was going to throw up.

For the next couple of months, Ami's behavior intensified, and I grew more and more impatient with her therapist. During one visit, Dr. Adams had Derek and me sit in a session together to discuss Ami's table manners and how Derek could better discipline her. Although Ami was a very well behaved three-year-old, her table manners were about what could have been expected of a child her age. I couldn't believe we were even talking about these things. We had bigger issues at hand here! It was exasperating to deal with people like her. Here I was, trying to obey the law and do what was right, but I was dealing with some pretty inadequate professionals who had been forced upon me by the court system. I was so exhausted, both physically and mentally, but I was determined to find someone who would help us.

I went to see Ted. I gave him the tapes, explained what was going on with Ami, and how exhausted I was. I told him I wanted Dr. Adams removed. She couldn't possibly be a good therapist if Ami's condition was getting worse, and she saw nothing. What was Ami doing in therapy with her?

I then visited the Kempe Center, a National Center for Abuse in Denver, and met with a well-known child advocate, President of the Kempe Center, Dr. Richard Krugman. One of the captains at Continental, my friend Duke, came with me because he knew one of the psychiatrists at Kempe. I gave Dr. Krugman the tapes and the reports, and he said he would help me. I was told not to worry; my case would not fall through the cracks. He called me before he left on a trip to Europe and told me that he and my attorney and detective Perry did not feel that Ami was safe. However, weeks later, he got in touch with one of his counterparts, who passed along to me that Dr. Krugman was currently too busy. When social services found out I was looking into this, Kirsten called to remind me that she knew a lot of people at the Kempe Center. All of a sudden, my phone calls to the center weren't returned.

I still didn't know what was going on, and my attorney wasn't doing his job, so I wrote letters to Barbara Bush, just reaching out for help any way I could. Her response was to advise me to get in touch with social services at the federal level. When I did, they gave me to a supervisor, who in turn talked to Kirsten's supervisor—another dead end.

I called a nurse from Children's Hospital who worked with their Child's Advocacy and Protection Team and left a message. Then I called Kirsten. I tried to describe to her how hard of a time I was having with Ami, how she was waking up at least four times a night and masturbating constantly—she was always putting her hands in her panties. Kirsten's response was that Dr. Adams had seen no signs of abuse. I angrily asked Kirsten if she knew what kind of therapy Ami was doing. She said, "Ami and Gail have a good rapport."

I said, "If you do not believe me and do not want to talk to friends of mine who are doctors, lawyers, and professionals who have witnessed this, then I will pay you to send one of your social workers you trust to just stay with us a couple of nights and see what my child is going through." She refused.

Kirsten replied, "Maybe she is picking up on your vibes because it is close to the hearing."

To say the least, I lost it. "You mean to tell me while I am in the other room cooking dinner, Ami masturbates because I'm thinking of the hearing? And she wakes up in the middle of the night, screaming and moaning, grabbing at her vagina, yelling 'Daddy, don't!' because I am asleep in the other room thinking about the hearing? Oh, Kirsten, that's good. That is very good."

The phone clicked, and I saw that I had a call waiting—Carol, the nurse from Children's Hospital. I was extremely upset, so she set up an appointment for Ami to be seen in six weeks. That was the soonest they could get her in.

The next day, I called Carol from San Francisco, and she truly seemed to be concerned. I was still reaching for someone to help. I called my attorney and told him once again that I wanted him to file a motion to remove Gail as Ami's therapist. He said he wouldn't do it and began yelling at me. "No one believes you, Maralee. No one." Even he didn't believe me.

I didn't need this. If he didn't want to fight and do something about this case, then fine. "Do you want to withdraw?" I asked him. Before he could answer, I said, "Better yet, you are fired. You are off the case."

I felt so alone.

As it turned out, I had to keep him on. He had the deed to my house. But I told him that I couldn't date him anymore—after the trial, maybe we could date again—but he couldn't handle it. Between this day and the final hearing, Ted withdrew from my case four or five times. He was still emotionally involved with me, and he alternated between wanting to help me and pulling away.

My poor parents, I called them daily with pain piercing in my voice, hoping they could take some of it away. It was as if I got so full of pain that I couldn't bear even a half-inch more; I was full to my neck. In order to relieve some of that ache, I would try to lay it on them so I could take more in. But they couldn't handle it. They couldn't bear to hear my pain and to know that the granddaughter they cherished was suffering. My mom at this time began writing letters to senators, congress, and the governor. She was an incredible writer, and this was her way of helping. So my main support at this time came from my friends and from Dennis, who had always been able to calm me and help me think more clearly again.

How much longer could I let this go on? No wonder women were forced to go into the "underground" or run with their children. But that was no answer for me. The underground would be a horrible life for both of us. I would have to cut all ties with my family as if we were dead, live off other people because I would constantly be on the run, and probably get caught and go to prison. I would have to change schools all the time and be looking over my shoulder. This would be subjecting Ami to more trauma on top of the trauma she was already going through. Her father would look for me to the ends of the earth. The F.B.I. would be on our heels.

I felt that there was a hole in my stomach, and it was getting larger—so large that it threatened to eat me up inside. When Ami went back to sleep, after her nightmares about her dad, I lay awake with my insides aching, and the hole grew larger and then swirled so fast that I couldn't breathe. My heart pounded, and I experienced severe chest pains as if I were having a heart attack. I told myself not to breathe or move, because if I did, I would probably die. I lay very still until the pain subsided. How much longer could my body and mind take this intense stress? I was so sick of fighting a whole system alone. How stupid to think it would all turn around, that the evidence was so obvious, and that the system would eventually do the right thing. What if my body didn't make it through this intense pain. Derek now had increased his visitation with her. On the evening of November 7th, after she had spent the weekend with him, I picked her up from his house. When she got into the car, she said, "My dad touched me again." I said, "While you were at this visit?" "Yes!"

"I'm sorry, honey. I'm doing everything I can to stop this.

I don't know what else to do."

"Well, could you hit his hands for me?" I told her I am doing everything I can!

She said, "Sometimes he is good, and sometimes he is bad."

When we got home, it was bedtime, and I turned on the voice-activated tape player by her bed before she went to sleep. She did not know what the voice activated tape recorder was. Before she went to sleep, she started demonstrating what her father did to her. She put her legs in a V shape in the air and began bouncing on the bed, moving her body up and down. She said her daddy made her move like that and that he puts candy inside of her and licked it out. He put salt and pepper there too and told her it was food and that it would make her grow. "That won't make me grow, will it, Mommy?"

"Does he hurt you, Ami?"

"Sometimes," she said. She told me he would whisper in her ear, "Ami, am I hurting you?" and she would yell, "Yes, Dad!"

I felt like I was going to throw up. After I got her to sleep, I called my best friends Kimmy and Pat and played the tape for them. Pat was so upset he said, "That's it. This has gone on long enough." And he called the police.

The next day, I got up very early with severe chest pains. I had decided to go over everyone's head and bypass the court orders to get help for Ami. I would go to Dr. Krugman at the Kempe Center, to the Children's Hospital's Child's Advocacy and Protection Team, to the police—someone was going to help us. I called my neighbor, a police officer with daughters Ami's age, and told him that I had this tape of Ami stating facts about her father touching her. I was also having severe chest pains and was scared I could be having a heart attack.

He came over immediately. First, he told me that my chest pains were probably caused by stress. "It's not a heart attack," he said. "Just try to breathe." Then he listened to the tape and was sickened by it. He called Detective Dave Perry, who specialized in sexual abuse, in on the case. (At the same time, the police that Pat called had filed a report.)

Detective Perry showed up later, still in the early morning. He was a nice-looking man, with sandy-blond hair and a gentle voice. He said he needed to review all previous reports from this case before he would interview Ami. He told me to get all the reports from my attorney's office. He would be back in the evening to pick them up.

When Detective Perry showed up again at six p.m., I showed him the reports. He said he wanted to try to interview Ami or just to talk to her. At the time, Ami had taken a late nap and was still asleep. He was worried she would be too sleepy to talk clearly once we woke her up, but we decided to give it a try. He told me I could stay in the room but that I should not talk to her or respond to anything she said.

Once Ami woke up, she quickly warmed to Detective Perry. He had a boyish way about him. Before he talked with her, he told me that I could not encourage or help Ami answer any questions. She had to answer them on her own.

He reviewed good and bad touches with her. He asked her, “If anyone punched you in the nose, would that be a good touch or bad touch?” Ami said that would be a bad touch. Then she identified a hug as a good touch. “Mommy touched me here,” Ami said, pointing to her knee; she said that was a good touch. Then she pointed to her genital area. “Daddy touched me here,” she said. “That’s a bad touch.” She offered this without any provocation from Detective Perry.

When he asked what kind of touch it would be if a doctor were to check her “pee-pee” to see if she was okay, Ami said it would be a good touch only if it was done to help her to feel well. When he asked if changing a baby’s diaper would be a good touch or bad touch, she said it was good, because it would make the baby clean.

Finally, he asked, “Has anyone ever touched you in a way that hurt you or made you feel uncomfortable?” She nodded her head and said yes. He asked her where, and she pointed to her vagina. He asked who touched her there and she said, “Daddy did.”

“Does anyone else?” he asked. “No.”

Detective Perry then pulled out a diagram of a white preschool-age female and a white adult male and asked Ami to name the body parts. To my surprise, she called the penis a “peanut.” The night before, she had said her father put a peanut inside her, and at the time, I hadn’t understood.

Then he gave her a red pen and asked her to mark on the drawing of the girl where she had been touched. Ami colored the genital area and the buttocks.

Detective Perry then pointed to the drawing of the white adult male and asked her what it was a picture of. “A daddy,” she said. He then asked if there was anything on the diagram she had been touched with, and Ami pointed to the penis. He asked her to mark what she had been touched with, and she colored the penis on the drawing. He asked Ami what that was, and she said, "A peanut."

When he asked what color her daddy's "peanut" was, she said that it was red and hard. He asked where she was touched with it, and she said, "My pee-pee and bottom," and pointed to her vaginal area and buttocks.

"When did this happen?" he asked. "At Daddy's house, downstairs."

"When did it happen?"

"Lasterday," she said. Detective Perry tried to establish what she meant by "lasterday," but Ami wasn't specific.

"Did anyone tell you to tell me this?" "No."

"Did your daddy say anything to you about telling anyone?" "No."

"Has anyone else ever touched you in those places?" "No."

Detective Perry then asked her why she hadn't told Dr. Adams about this.

Ami responded, "Don't want to. I forgot to." "Why did you tell me?"

"Because I like you."

◆ ◆ ◆ ◆ ◆ ◆

Afterward, I asked my neighbors to watch Ami for a little while so I could talk with Detective Perry alone. She had told him things in fifteen minutes that she had never told me. He told me that the next day he would be filing criminal charges with the Arapahoe County District Attorney's office. He said it would be an uphill battle with social services, but he would go around them through the Kempe Center. I told him I had already tried to get Ami in for an evaluation there, but I couldn't do it.

He said the process would be grueling. "It wouldn't matter what you have on tape or what you have said to me," he said. "The only thing that matters is what your little girl has told me, and nothing can change that. She was very spontaneous."

He gave me a number for victim's compensation and the names of some people who would help. He promised to file the report in the morning. He also warned that we were in an uphill battle against social services.

I told him that I couldn't possibly give Ami to her father for his visitation now.

He said, "Do what you need to do. Just keep in touch with me, and I will stand before the judge and testify that I approved you to go."

The next day, Ami was to have an appointment with Gail, and he told me to take her as planned. As always, her dad was in the waiting room while Ami had her session with Gail. I tried not to show any emotions, but my disgust for him was overwhelming. I could no longer sit in the waiting room with him, so I went into an adjoining room and shut the door, wondering if Ami would tell Gail now after everything that had happened. During this specific session with Gail, Ami ran out of the session at least four times and hugged her dad. Gail asked him, "When is the last time you saw Ami?"

He said, "Just yesterday."

Gail was surprised at how much Ami was hugging her dad, but it seemed clear to me that she was letting her dad know she was not telling Gail and feeling a lot of anxiety about keeping her secret. I'm sure this never crossed Dr. Adams's mind.

When the session was over, Gail walked into the waiting area and said the session went very well. I looked at her. Had she not picked up on anything? At the beginning of the session, in front of Ami, I had said, "Maybe your dad and I will go for a walk," just trying to get him out of the waiting room so Ami might be more apt to talk, but her father had refused. As we were leaving, he notified me that he would be taking Ami to LA for a week for Thanksgiving. He was not even scheduled to have her for Thanksgiving, but I guess his three ladies didn't know an investigation was going on.

I told Gail I needed to talk to her in private. I went into her office, sat down, and told her I couldn't believe she hadn't seen anything in Ami during her hour with her. I told her that Ami had revealed so much the night before, but I couldn't tell her about the detective yet—she would surely tell social services about it. She could tell I was upset and said the only thing that Ami had done while playing with the dolls was to put salt and pepper down there. I exclaimed, "Gail! That's what she told me about last night!" She completely ignored me and asked me about her bill. I got up, grabbed Ami, and walked out. I was not going to pay this sick so-called therapist another dime.

At about three p.m., I started getting ready to go to the mountains with Kimmy and Pat. I told Ami we were going for a short vacation. Before I left, I called Detective Perry. He said he had not had a chance to file the report, but he had talked with social services and was going to investigate further. I sighed and turned silent. After his interview with Ami, he had told me that nothing could ever change his mind, and now I was feeling him hesitate. He said, "Don't worry, Maralee. I believe you, and most of all I believe your daughter." I told him where we were going in Vail and left a phone number where we could be reached.

We drove up to the mountains in silence. I had told Kim that I didn't want anything said in front of Ami, that we would talk when I got up there. Besides, I was very nervous. Once we got up to the mountains, a lot of the Fowlers' friends were there with their kids, who Ami already knew, so she had a good time.

That night, she woke up screaming, as she had so many nights before, and everyone in the condo could hear her. They didn't know what was going on.

The next day, everyone went cross-country skiing, so Ami and I had the condo to ourselves. We went for a walk on the golf course and rolled down the hills in the snow, threw snowballs at each other, and I chased her all over the course, which was her favorite thing for us to do. When we stopped and sat down, to my surprise her first comment was, "Mom, have you stopped it?"

"Yes, Ami," I said. "I think I have."

"Maybe my dad and I can be friends." I was silent.

"Are you going to marry Dennis?"

"I don't know. But I will get married someday."

"And he will be my daddy and love me? And he won't touch me?"

"No! Ami, he won't touch you."

It was so sad to hear my poor little girl talk like this. But looking back, my mistake was letting her think that I had finally protected her. I hadn't. She wanted me to get married, I think, because she wanted a new daddy. That way she wouldn't have to go to her dad's ever again.

CHAPTER 16

Defying Logic

Detective Perry called me while we were in the mountains and talked me into bringing Ami down off the mountain for a session with him and Gail together. He was having a hard time with the people at social services and needed more support. If he could get Gail, he needed me to help him out by bringing Ami down. I agreed, but I was concerned they would try to take Ami away from me again. He assured me no such thing would happen.

In retrospect, I should have agreed only if it was with a different therapist, but you could say I was not thinking clearly. When we arrived at home that day, November 15th, Detective Perry came over, but Ami did not want to go with him to Dr. Adams's office. She hid under the table and acted very apprehensive. I was a little apprehensive myself. I trusted Perry, and he told me not to worry, but still, it was hard to give my little girl to him. But I decided that I needed to put my trust in someone who could help us turn this whole mess around. So I reassured Ami that it was okay to go with Perry and that he would bring her right back to me. When Ami saw by my face and by the way I was acting that everything was okay, she went with Perry.

When he returned with Ami, Detective Perry told me that things had gone well. Ami had talked in front of Gail. He reassured me that it had been a good idea.

I would later learn that at this session, Ami had told Dr. Adams that her daddy touched her on her pee-pee. When asked what her father used to touch her, she said it was blue. Ami then said her father needed help. And when Dr.

Adams asked what kind of help, Ami said "Blue." When Dr. Adams asked why Ami thought her daddy needed help, she said "Because my mommy said so."

The next day, I received a phone call from Kirsten Jensen, wanting to know if Ami wanted to see her dad. I asked Ami, and she said no. Kirsten insisted on talking to Ami, so Ami got on the phone and adamantly said to Kirsten, "No, I don't want to see my dad." Ami was so defiant and still no one listened to my child's wants or needs.

I knew something was going to happen—I could sense Derek pulling strings in the background—so I called Kim, and she came over for support. Next thing we know, Kirsten came to our house in person and tried to convince Ami in person to visit with her dad. "Don't you want to see your dad?" she said. "He's at the park."

Ami responded, "You can tell him I can't come!" "He has a present for you," Kirsten said.

Kim and I couldn't believe what we were hearing.

Earlier that day, I had called Gail and said, "Can't you guys give her some time to deal with this before seeing her dad? This has nothing to do with me. These are her feelings. She has finally opened up and is terrified of seeing him. Give her some time. She wet her panties this morning. She feels guilty for telling you, Gail."

"She could feel guilty for two reasons." "What are those?"

"She could be lying."

"My God," I said, "she doesn't even know what a lie is!" Ami ended up being coerced to go to the park that day.

◆ ◆ ◆ ◆ ◆ ◆

When Ami returned from her visit with Derek, she told me that her father said he had only touched her with paper.

The next day, I brought Ami to Children's Hospital where she was examined by Dr. Susan Reichert, who was with the Child Advocacy and Protection Team. Dr. Reichart asked me if I wanted to come in the examining room. I told her no—I didn't want anyone to accuse me of influencing the results— and waited outside. When Dr. Reichert was examining her genital area, Ami told her that her daddy hurt her there and on her stomach and buttocks too. When Dr. Reichert asked what her daddy had touched her with, Ami said, "Paper," in a robotic manner. (Her dad had a visit with her the day before, so it seemed obvious to me that he had trained her in what to say.) In her report, Dr. Reichert noted that Ami had seemed very anxious when she responded, as though she had it in her mind that was what she would say no matter what the question was. But then Ami made a spontaneous comment: "I can't go back home to my dad." When Dr. Reichert asked why, she said, "I don't like to go to my dad's."

"Why?" Dr. Reichert asked.

"He touches me," Ami said, pointing to her vagina. "What does he touch you with?"

"A bottle."

"What color is the bottle?"

"Pink."

"What's in the bottle?"

"Milk."

After the examination, Dr. Reichert told me that she had not seen any physical evidence of the abuse but that she was very concerned for Ami.

◆ ◆ ◆ ◆ ◆ ◆

For the next three weeks, the so-called professionals worked on Ami, supervising her visits with her father and telling her how great he was. Slowly, they eased her back into her father's arms. At first, she did not want to be alone with him, but they continued to reassure her that he was wonderful and safe, and of course her dad did too. Ami became convinced that everything would be okay and said that she wanted to stay overnight at her dad's again. I was shocked, but this was right after a supervised visit with Kirsten, and they had all convinced Ami how wonderful her father was. After Kirsten left, Ami said, "My daddy won't touch me anymore. He won't!" I felt sick. A few nights earlier, she had been screaming and holding onto my legs at the thought of being with her father, and now all of a sudden she wanted to go back? What was going on? They were convincing this poor little girl that it was okay to spend the night with a rapist. If it was a neighbor and not her father, you can bet the pervert would be in jail. But since it was her daddy, that relationship must be maintained at any cost. This was a sick system.

At first, Ami seemed to be fine, but then her nightmares started up again. It was almost as if I could tell by her sleep patterns when she was safe and when she wasn't. During this time period she told me her dad says he won't touch me anymore, but he still does.

In the meantime, Detective Perry was continuing his investigation. I didn't know any of this at the time, but Derek had contacted him, denying any abuse. Derek provided him with a report from Dr. Brodbeck, who claimed that I had been pressuring Ami to talk about the abuse; a report from Gail, who stated that Ami had never told her anything about any abuse; and a letter to Judge Leopold from Kirsten Jensen, which documented the court hearing from February when it was decided that my sexual abuse claims weren't substantiated, that the animosity between us was harming Ami, and that Derek had been fully cooperative in all evaluations and therapy sessions.

He was also contacted by Kim, who told him that she had witnessed Ami's behavior firsthand and could verify that she had been abused. She had personally witnessed Ami saying that her daddy put a toy inside her, Ami masturbating when she didn't think anyone was watching her, Ami crying out, "I don't like my daddy, I don't like my daddy!" and Ami having nightmares, during which she screamed, "Don't, Dad, it's bad!" All these events had happened at her house or while she was with me. She also told Detective Perry that Derek was a philanderer who had tried to have an affair with her, who had had affairs with women she knew, and who had unusual sexual behaviors. He had once asked one of her friends to have a threesome and told her that he wanted to experiment with bondage.

Detective Perry also contacted Gail to ask her for her assessment of the session they had had on November 15th. Dr. Adams told him that while Ami had in fact admitted her father had touched her, she suspected that I had coerced her into saying so.

◆ ◆ ◆ ◆ ◆ ◆

The hearings that had begun in June were scheduled to continue December 17th and 18th. On December 3rd, I received a motion from Doris Truhlar, stating that Detective Perry said that there was no abuse and that if there was, it was not her father that was doing it to her. Now I was at my wit's end. How could Detective Perry have said that? He knew that Ami said it was her father, and he had believed her. Was Doris changing all this around?

This was the help that I had desperately counted on, and now it was backfiring on me. I began to cry uncontrollably and went over to Kim's. She had also talked with Perry and thought, as I had, that he was going to protect Ami. Kim and I immediately headed for my attorney's office. Ted had also just read the motion. He told us to go the police department, ask Perry if he said any of this, have him write out on the document where Doris had lied, and initial everything that was false.

We drove to the police department and met with Detective Perry. He had not said the things Doris had filed in her motion. Quite the contrary, he said. My case was still open, pending a decision by the Kempe Center to review it. However, he didn't feel that a criminal prosecution would result from his investigation. We had him write down what he said and rebuke most everything Doris was claiming.

Even the social worker, Kirsten, was "very frustrated" with Doris's motion. She wrote me a letter, apologizing to me for what Doris had done and stated that Ami had been talking to Dr. Adams about her dad touching her. However, she went on to say that she had been supervising Ami's visits with her father for the past two weeks, and they were going well. "They should continue," she said, "because it made things more relaxing for Ami." She wrote in a letter to me:

> If the next two therapy sessions with Dr. Adams support my current feeling that nothing is going on between Ami and Derek now or in the last eighteen months or so, then I planned to arrange an unsupervised daytime visit on either Saturday or Sunday. I would pick Ami up from Derek's after the visit

> to bring her home—so that I could see how she is and what she says—if, after that, I feel Ami is safe with Derek, then I recommend visits return to the old schedule.

Clearly, I didn't want this to happen. So for the next few days, I called the Kempe Center repeatedly, trying to get a hold of Dr. Krugman. Finally, on December 7th, I spoke to him. He agreed to review my case and said he would call Detective Perry once he returned from a morning meeting. I called Detective Perry and told him that Dr. Krugman would be in contact with him after 11:00 a.m. I felt that if I had the Kempe Center behind me, Detective Perry would have the professional backup he needed to indict Derek for sexual abuse.

Dr. Krugman never called.

Later that day, after calling the Kempe Center and being told Dr. Krugman would call him back, Detective Perry suspended his investigation.

> Based on the information that I have received on this case from all parties involved, it is still unclear whether or not Ami Walker had been sexually assaulted by her father. Based on my interview with Ami Walker, there is a suspicion that some type of sexual contact had occurred; however, it is unclear when this contact occurred. Ami is receiving therapy from Dr. Adams, and it appears that protection issues are being met. This case will be filed as Inactive until such time as additional information becomes available. The case would then be reopened if the Kempe Center and Dr. Krugman decided to review the case.

This was surely not what he had said the day he interviewed Ami, when he claimed that he believed her and that nothing could change his mind. Perry had told me this would be an uphill battle against social services. Had he succumbed to not protecting Ami after what he had witnessed and told me nothing could change his mind?

CHAPTER 17

In Whose Best Interest?

As the December hearings approached, Ted told me to take a week off work, so we could prepare. So I took a week off work, and we did no preparation whatsoever. One day, when I walked in, he was wrapping all his Christmas presents on the floor for his family. He told me that he had thought of a new approach to our case. We would minimize the sexual abuse and go with the argument that I was an excellent mother and a stable force in Ami's life and that I had virtually raised her by myself.

I was irate. The whole reason I was going to court was that Ami has been abused by her father and was still being abused by her father. What did custody have to do with this?

"Maralee," he said, "no one believes Ami has been abused. You go in there trying to prove abuse, and you are going to lose your child." What about the daycare provider, Dr. Baler's report, Dr. Reichart's report?

Another day when he said we would work on the hearing, he told me he had some errands to run, and we could talk in the car. So I got into his car, and he took me to a very expensive men's store and proceeded to buy several shirts. It was like getting slapped in the face—first the Christmas presents, now the expensive shirts—as if he was saying, look what I can buy. I was incredibly frustrated. All I wanted was for Ami to be safe, and my lawyer wasn't doing anything about it.

◆ ◆ ◆ ◆ ◆ ◆

The hearings were held on December 17th and 18th, and then continued on February 5th and 6th. On the first day of hearings, Ted tried his new approach, assuming he could ask Judge Leopold to see him in chambers before the trial got started and ask him to alleviate the sexual abuse issue and focus on custody. The judge said, "Mr. Kaplysh, I will talk with you provided social services and their attorney, Doris Truhlar, and opposing counsel are all there."

They all went into the judge's chambers together. When they came out, Ted looked shaken. Behind him, Doris stormed out angrily with the others. I asked, "What's going on?"

He said, "These people don't want your blood, Maralee. They want your meat."

Kirsten's face was tight. There was a lot of whispering going on. Then we were all asked to leave the courtroom. As I left the room, thoroughly confused, I watched "the clique"— social services, Derek's attorney, and Doris—all gather together again, looking very upset. I was sitting by myself, still confused. So I got up to ask Doris what was going on. She said, "You mean you don't know?"

"No," I said. "What?"

"Ted is withdrawing from your case," she said.

My heart hit the floor. We had waited over six months for this hearing. What was Ted doing? Why would he do such a thing now?

When we returned to the courtroom, I asked Ted what the hell was going on, but he didn't reply. The judge suggested we take the morning off, go have lunch together and decide whether Ted stayed on or off the case.

All the way back to Ted's office, he wouldn't talk to me. He seemed completely freaked out. I guess he assumed the judge would just alleviate the sexual abuse issue, and now that the judge had refused, he had no backup strategy.

In his office, he still didn't talk to me. I followed him around, trying to get answers, but he still wouldn't talk. When we were getting ready to go back, I reminded him that the reason we had taken this break was so that we could talk. He still didn't level with me; instead, he told me to take my own car back to court. I insisted on us going back in his car, because we still hadn't discussed what was going on. I was bound and determined to get answers. This man had Ami's life in his hands.

While we were driving back, I kept trying. I said, "How can you do this? Ted, why are you doing this?"

"You are a security risk to me," he said, raising his voice. "And I am not losing my twenty-year practice over you."

I didn't know what he meant, but I assumed it had something to do with our personal relationship. Doris and her gang must have said something to indicate they knew that he and I had gone out. I said, "If you ever really cared about me, don't leave me now. I would never do anything to jeopardize you. I need you now."

His answer was that he was withdrawing from my case. I couldn't figure out why, except that he was scared to death because he wasn't prepared.

Back in court, Judge Leopold asked me if I still wanted Ted to represent me, and if I did, the hearing needed to proceed without further delay. Still an optimist, still believing that after he got over his panic Ted would do the right thing, still believing that once the truth was heard, the judge would then protect Ami, I said yes.

So the judge officially ruled against Ted's approach, and the hearing continued. The first witness was Jennifer, the social worker who had come to my door and asked Ami leading questions. Ruth had told me that when Ami was in foster care at her house, Jennifer had put Ami in the bath tub and had asked her questions that had made Ami very upset. I was sickened by this and very angry. I was so careful to protect Ami and can't imagine a stranger putting her in the tub to be questioned like that; it was creepy. As Jennifer and other witnesses testified, I wrote notes to Ted, giving him things to ask each witness in cross-examination. Ted did nothing. He seemed to have lost it. His plan to change the focus of the hearing had been shot down, and he didn't have the slightest bit of a back-up plan. Listening to the social worker's testimony, I was sickened and in disbelief to hear her say that the father, Ami's abuser, should get custody of my daughter. I kept writing notes to Ted. Finally, the judge said, "Don't worry, Ms. Mclean. You will get your chance."

I never did get that chance.

Detective Perry was in the courtroom, waiting to testify that day. Later, referring to the way Jennifer, Doris, and the rest of the people on Derek's side behaved, he told me that he had never seen anything quite like it. It seemed like a game that they were determined to win, not a case in which a child's life and safety was at stake.

"If you lose your daughter," he said, "I hope I never have to look you in the eye and feel what a great injustice has been done."

When the court was adjourned, everyone filtered out, until I was sitting in the empty courtroom alone with Ted. I had never felt so depleted and alone in my life. I turned to Ted and asked him for a ride home.

"No," he said. "I told you at lunch today to take your own car. I have something to do." With that, he left.

No words could convey how I felt at that moment. I had spent the day listening to lies about me and hearing how I should lose custody of Ami, sitting next to a comatose attorney who let me get eaten alive. In my entire life I had never been through something so horrible.

When I got off the elevator, it was dark out. I called my dad and told him what had happened. Then I called Kim—Ami was at her house—and had her come get me.

When Kim picked me up, I was so upset and drained that when I got to her house I asked her to keep Ami occupied while I went home to be alone. I felt as if a truck had run over me one way and then backed up to finish the job. Kim kept Ami preoccupied while I tried to pull it together. I was so utterly depleted all I wanted was for someone to put him away. I wanted the sickness surrounding me to just end.

◆ ◆ ◆ ◆ ◆ ◆

The next day, I came in ready to fight. The first thing I did was hand Ted a list of things I wanted him to do. I wanted him to bring in Detective Perry, not just to ask him what Ami said, but to also show what Ami had drawn on the diagrams he had shown her. I wanted him to put it on the A-frame display stand in the courtroom, so the judge could get an idea of what was really going on. How Ami had marked with a red pen on the drawing Detective Perry had of a female the genital area and the buttocks to where she had been touched by her dad. She stated, "He touched her with his peanut which is red, and hard and hurt." Then I gave him a list of witnesses I wanted brought in.

Ted refused. He said that I was going to lose custody of my child.

"Screw you Ted!" I said. "If I'm going to lose custody of my child, then I am going to go down fighting, so you had better get in there and fight!"

As the GAL and social worker were testifying, I kept writing things down for Ted to say and coaching him on how to represent me. Then Art Jones was brought in to testify. It had been way over a year since he had seen Derek and me in his separation counseling that Doris Truhlar had set up. At one point when Doris was questioning him, she referred to a beautiful and poetic book that Derek had written about his daughter, which was in the courtroom as Exhibit 6. I told Ted to ask for Exhibit 6. He asked me why, and I told him again to ask for that book. He did, and as Doris continued to question Art Jones, I found some passages in the book where Derek had written romantic phrases about Ami. For example, in one part he had described himself sipping sherry, waiting for the moments that he and Ami would be together again. "We are as one," he wrote. In another part of the book he wrote, "Your mother and I hugged tonight. You relinquished her spot, your body laid on top of mine. Our lips met, your eyes wide open." I put yellow tabs in these places in the book, and I said to Ted, "Now, ask Mr. Jones if he would write this about his two-year- old daughter."

When Ted asked this, everyone became quiet. Mr. Jones said, "No, but Derek tends to over-indulge himself with his daughter, and we worked on that."

Dr. Jones had not seen either of us for over a year, and he had never seen Ami, but he still stated that he did not believe Derek to be a child abuser. He also stated that through his testing, I did not prove to be a liar. At that, Judge Leopold raised his eyebrows.

The next witness was Dr. Brodbeck, the first psychologist to see Ami—the one who had told Ami to take off her panties and talk. She was the one who had told me that I had handled the situation beautifully, that Ami had not been traumatized in any way. Later, I found that she had reported that I had ripped off Ami's panties and told her to show the doctor what daddy had done to her—an outright lie that to this day makes me sick. I had been so protective (far too protective, in retrospect) of Ami—not wanting to make her uncomfortable, making sure people listened to her when she brought it up but then changing the subject quickly afterward. In fact, a friend of mine, when he had heard what Ami said about her father, had encouraged me to tell Ami straight out what her father was doing and how wrong it was. But I had wanted to protect Ami. I hadn't known what to do or what was the best way to handle such a situation. I had such a hard time coping with what was happening to Ami and I did not want her to be afraid to continue to talk. Looking back, I believe that is why she continued to talk.

I got my chance in court to rebut Dr. Brodbeck. I told them how she had told me that I had handled things beautifully. During my testimony, I wasn't allowed to talk about anything pertaining to sexual abuse, nor was I asked anything about it. I was also warned that I should drop the issue altogether.

It was then Dr. Baker's turn to testify. She described how Ami had placed the anatomically correct Daddy doll a distance away from her and said she didn't like him. Based on Ami's comments and behavior, Dr. Baker had concluded that Ami had been subjected to sexual stimuli. (See Appendix D.) While my attorney didn't bring out the abuse as he should have, still her testimony seemed effective and relevant.

Next came Dr. Adams, who admitted that at one point it seemed that Ami's behavior was indicative of a child being abused, and that at times, she had believed that Ami had been abused. But she also said that it was very important for Ami to have her father in her life, and it was her opinion that Derek would be the better parent for Ami. It was so important for the father to be in her life, but nothing about the safety of my child. Fathers rights superseded the protection of Ami as if Male Entitilement is paramount.

Another witness was Ruth, Ami's daycare provider. She described what Ami had said and done under her care, incidents that I have already related. It was enough to make a person gag and certainly enough to convince anyone that my little girl was being abused by her daddy.

Kim Fowler also testified to the same kinds of behavior—to what Ami had been saying about her father and to her nightmares as well.

In Detective Perry's testimony, he did not put the anatomical drawing Ami had circled on the A-frame, and Ted didn't ask too many questions or bring out important information. Ted had never even subpoenaed Perry. Perry had been angry about Ted's attitude toward him, and he hadn't intended to show up for the trial. I had tracked him down while he was in some kind of training, and he told me he wasn't coming because of the way my attorney had approached him. I begged him to come to the trial; I told him I really needed him. He had agreed to come. When he showed up, I overheard Ted discussing with him whether or not he should go on the witness stand. I was shocked by this. Here was a detective who had evidence pertinent to our case. How could the evidence of abuse that he had spontaneously received from Ami hurt the case? I insisted to Ted that Perry be put on the stand. I demanded it. Among other things, Doris was banking on being able to cite me for contempt of court for the time I took Ami to Vail. She didn't know that Perry had covered for me, and I never told her he had. So she and Steve Calder, Derek's attorney, had assumed they would get me for contempt; however, Perry's testimony saved me there. I was upset that Ted did not ask Perry more questions, but then again, I wasn't the attorney. At the time, I really didn't understand just how terribly Ted was representing me. Now that I look back, I would have done a much better job representing myself.

Judge Leopold then asked Doris Truhlar to take the witness stand to defend her lies and biases toward Derek. She had already written a statement to the court before I had even testified, which was unprofessional and unethical. Judge Leopold told her to take the witness stand. When she took the stand, she sat back in her chair and tried to be cute with her answers and with the judge. The whole thing was an embarrassment. She and the rest of her gang had been acting very unprofessionally, not only before the trial, but also during it. At one point I had overheard Doris say of me, "She used to model, can you believe that?"

And Kirsten said, "I didn't know that!" And they all had laughed. These were supposedly professional women, who looked and acted so unprofessionally.

As it turns out, she had written her custody recommendations days before I had even testified at the last custody hearing. In fact, her recommendations had been written two months previous. The judge found this alarming; he chastised her in front of the whole courtroom then took her into his chambers.

Unbeknownst to them, I had a friend in the courtroom taking notes, a reporter from the Rocky Mountain News.

A few months before the trial, I had read an article in that newspaper with the title "Runaway Moms" describing cases in which mothers were losing custody when they accused their husbands or ex-husbands of sexually abusing their children. I immediately called and asked to speak to Linda Castrone, the reporter who had written the piece. I met in person with her and her editor, and she asked if she could sit in on my trial. So she was there that day and afterward told me that she found Doris's behavior pretty pathetic, as was that of other professionals in the case.

For the next two days I was on the witness stand. I had the collages I had put together of Ami with her extended family entered into evidence. Doris was saying how his girlfriend and her 80-year-old grandmother would be wonderful as an extended family. I had an attorney doing a lousy job and my ex had two attorneys for the most part: Steve Calder—a tough little Texan with a short man's complex—and good ole Doris, who was totally mesmerized by Derek, and as far as I could tell, had never thought about Ami from day one. They did not want to bring up the abuse, so mostly they brought up visitations or other topics that would keep the focus on me, hoping I would mess up. However, I was very poised and stuck to the truth, even though they never gave me the opportunity to talk about the abuse. I did an excellent job on the stand; I could not have presented myself any better. But nobody—not even my own attorney—wanted to bring up the abuse.

During the trial, friends of mine had slipped in and observed. They said I did a beautiful job but that I just wasn't going to be able to prove the abuse. But I felt certain that we could have proved it if anyone, including the judge, would have wanted to hear the tapes and asked me to describe what I had been through with my little girl. (See Ted Kaplysh Closing Argument to the Court, Appendix D.)

At the end of the hearings in February, I was exhausted, but I thought the judge had heard enough to be concerned that abuse was going on. I hoped that he would see fit to protect Ami. I was pretty confident I would keep custody. I had been Ami's sole caretaker since birth. I was not the one in question; Derek was the one molesting his daughter. The judge, after hearing all the witnesses, would have to look at the abuse issue and make the right decision.

CHAPTER 18

Fathers' Rights

On February 27, 1991, I received notice that a conference call was to be taken at my attorney's office. The reporter who followed the hearing asked if she could be present, and I told her it would be okay. My heart was racing as the phone rang. Judge Leopold began by stating that Doris Truhlar had misrepresented the court and that none of her recommendations would be taken into account. She had been too biased. Throughout the case, he would later write that Doris had demonstrated a dominance over both representatives of the Department of social services, giving the appearance of successfully influencing their attitudes and opinions with respect to me and in favor of Derek; was instrumental in facilitating the removal of Dr. Baker and securing the appointment of Dr. Adams; and in general attempted to orchestrate the entire proceedings, including those in the courtroom. "Her open and notorious fraternization with Mr. Walker along with that of social services and his counsel both in and out of the courthouse have further substantiated the contention that she, the Department of Social Services, and Dr. Adams have not had the objectivity necessary to give valid recommendations to the court."

I grabbed Ted's arm, and he grabbed mine. We both grew confident. If the judge wasn't taking her recommendations into account, then all the other people she brought in and the testimonies she had controlled would go by the wayside.

Then Judge Leopold continued reading his order. He ignored the testimonies of Detective Perry and Dr. Baker and discounted Kim Fowler's and Ruth Gibben's because they were considered friends. He ordered that we maintain our now 50 percent visitation arrangement but was awarding custody to Mr. Walker because Mr. Walker was more able to nurture the relationship with the mother and the child than the mother was able to nurture the relationship with the father and the child.

"It is clear that Ami is a fortunate child, in that she has two parents who love her very much and are devoted to her. Social worker Jennifer testified it would be in the best interest of Ami for her father to be awarded custody. Dr. Adams testified that Ami's father was better able to encourage the sharing of love and affection and encourage the relationship with the mother. The mother testified that, if she were awarded custody of Ami, she would not do anything different than she had done previously. The guardian ad litem believes the father should be awarded sole custody."

Dr. Jones states in the separation counseling that he found me to be quite credible with respect to her story about the initial complaints by Ami and her initial disbelief about the abuse. Dr. Back recounted the events as he remembered them, and his account matched mine exactly. My call to him was his concern about Ami's welfare and he would have to rule out the theory about the abuse was to get back at Derek.

On June 5, 1990, December 17, 18, 19 1990, and February 5 and 6, 1991, this matter came before the court. Judge Leopold's order read, "The conduct of the guardian ad litem was subject of an in chambers meeting of counsel. (a) On Feb. 5, 1991 the GAL testified under oath that she had not formed an opinion for recommendation to the court and would not until all evidence had been presented. The GAL made a recommendation before Ms. Mclean's testimony favoring the father. (b) The court's file contains several pleadings filed by the GAL which, when read in the context of her actions favor the father well before this trial. The GAL's testimony creates an impression of bias to question the integrity of the adjudicative process. (c) Accordingly the court strikes the GAL's written recommendation and gives it no weight and all are disregarded by the court. Ms. Mclean spent more than two years in unceasing beliefs to validate her beliefs."

The judge ordered I put this issue behind me, but her statements lack conviction and credibility. This court order is after all the reports of abuse, Detective Perry's report, officer daycare provider, pre-school teacher, Dr. Lee's report stating abuse, as well as many other witnesses. (See Judge Leopolds Order, Guardian's misrepresentation, check paid to Dr. Richard Gardner. See Appendix D). Judge Leopold never acknowledged any of this testimony and dismissed all claims of abuse. He stated he was not taking the GAL's recommendations into account however he took all her recommendations. (See Judge Leopolds Order, Appendix D.) I sunk to the floor. I thought I was going to scream, so I ran out of his office into the hallway. There, I lost it. I felt far away from everyone. Here the reporter had written about cases where the mother loses custody to the father by trying to protect the child, but I had never dreamed this would happen to me.

In the hallway, I began to kick the elevator door as hard as I could. I screamed out, "She is my baby! How can they take my baby away from me?" A man came out of his office and asked if I was all right. Other people came out of their offices, and I could only scream, "My baby, my baby!" The pain overwhelmed me. I didn't want to hear what anyone was saying to me. All I could do was scream. I melted against the elevator door and sunk to the floor.

My attorney's paralegal, who was a mother, came out to hold me. "How could they?" I asked her. "How could they? I'm a good mother. I have done nothing wrong. Oh, God help me! Help me!"

After a while, I pulled myself together and went back in to see Ted. He was talking with Linda, the reporter, seeming more concerned with how he looked than with what had just happened. I was trembling with anger. I could feel myself losing control. Through all the torment these people had put me through, I had never acted hysterically. I had long found it amusing that when a man yelled or raised his voice, he was considered forceful; but when a woman did so, she was quickly labeled hysterical. Did they want to see hysteria? I would show them what hysteria looked like! I picked up a pen and threw it as hard as I could at a window. Ted yelled at me to get control of myself and pushed me out of his office.

After I left the office, once again traumatized I felt a separation from my body. I used the paralegal's phone to call my mom. I told her, with my voice cracking, that I had lost custody of Ami. Then I called Dennis, who lived close to the office; he told me he was on his way. After that I called Ruth and Kim. They both said they would be there as soon as they could. I went out into the lobby, feeling as if I might die on the spot.

When Ruth arrived, she looked angry. She hugged me first then said she was going up to talk to Ted. I followed her up the elevator to the penthouse, and as she went in to say a few words to Ted, Dennis showed up and just held me tight, which is all I wanted. Ted then walked out of his office and saw Dennis holding me. Immediately Dennis told Ted he wanted to talk to him. Then Kim showed up, and we all went out into the hallway to discuss what had just happened. That's when the reporter came out of Ted's office, and everyone told her how involved Ted was with me and how he had screwed up my case.

In the meantime, Dennis headed into Ted's office. He had told Ted he wanted to talk in private, so the paralegal wouldn't hear. Ted said it was fine to talk right there and then. So Dennis proceeded to tell Ted he was too emotionally involved with me to handle the case and that he should have withdrawn from the case a long time ago.

Ted said, "I am not emotionally involved!"

Dennis said, "Remember, I was there when you called all night long. I'm the one who unplugged the telephone at six in the morning. You bought her gifts."

Ted said, "This is extortion!"

Dennis then suggested that he release the deed of trust that I had signed on my house, so I could appeal what had just happened.

I had been so confident that the judge's decision would be in my favor that I had planned on going straight to work from Ted's office. So I called my base manager, who knew what I had been going through, and told him what had just happened. He told me it wouldn't be a problem; he'd have me pulled off my next trip, and he gave me an emergency drop. My friends then drove me home and gave me some sleeping pills, which totally knocked me out. I do not remember much else from that day.

The next day, by a weird coincidence, I ran into Detective Perry at Target, with his two sons. I looked him straight in the eyes with tears welling up and told him in a choked voice that I had lost Ami.

He could not bear to look at me. Keeping his head down, he barely managed to say, "I'm sorry."

Why couldn't he have done more? I thought to myself. He knew the truth and so had Dr. Krugman at the Kempe Center. I felt that so many people had let Ami and me down.

Where was justice?

CHAPTER 19

When Power and Control are Given to the Abuser

The next time I saw Ami, her father had cut off her hair again—a short, blunt cut this time, with a thick cluster of uneven bangs—all for my benefit, to let me know he had control now and could do whatever he wanted. When I drove up to his house I noticed it right away, but I didn't react so as not to give the psychopath any satisfaction. He handed me a visitation schedule specifying when I could see Ami. When I took Ami home, I acted as if nothing had changed. She knew nothing about what had gone on in court, although Derek had made it very clear to me that the courts had just handed me to him on a silver platter—exactly what he had always wanted. Abusing Ami had actually worked in his favor. He had now gained back the one thing he had lost when I had divorced him: control.

In the days that followed, he called me constantly. I took to screening my calls again and not answering my phone during waking hours. So he decided to call me very early so that, half asleep, I would accidentally pick up the phone. One morning he did this and told me I was supposed to take Ami to Dr. Adams that day, and then he asked if I had the money to pay her. It wasn't a question of money, I told him. I didn't approve of Gail. But, I said, I would take Ami. To that point, he had taken Ami to all her therapy sessions. He wanted to make sure that Ami didn't ever say anything to her again.

I said, "Let me talk to Ami."

When Ami came to the phone, she cried, "Mommy, I want you! Mommy, I want you!"

She had never acted like this on the phone. Maybe, I thought, this was why Derek was so nervous about her appointment with Gail. Ami was really upset. For her to wake up so early and be this upset, something must have happened. "I will come and get you right now," I said. Then her father grabbed the phone away from her and hung up. I immediately left home and went to pick her up.

◆◆◆◆◆◆

After we came home from Ami's session at Gail's, it was about 11:00 a.m. Ami looked exhausted; she wanted to take a nap. This was a little girl who always had a lot of energy, but lately, when she returned from her father's, she was sleeping for long periods of time. That day, she lay down and slept from 11:00 a.m. until 6:00 p.m. When she woke up, her panties were on the floor, and she was in bed touching herself. When I asked her why her panties were on the floor, she said, "I wanted to touch myself!"

We discussed it no further. But a little later, I went over everything in my head—why she had been crying that morning, why she had slept all day, and why she had been touching herself when she woke up. I asked her if she remembered when I had talked to her that morning, when she was crying. She said she did. "Why were you crying?" I asked her.

She said, "Because before you were on the phone, my daddy was touching me!"

I felt sick. Ami was now four years old. How much more of this would we have to endure?

This whole experience had changed my outlook on life. Whenever I was in a grocery store where there were little kids with their dad, I would wonder what kind of fathers they were. Or I would see moms who were mean to their children, or possibly drug addicts or alcoholics, and I would feel bitter, knowing that those moms were allowed to keep their children. Whereas a mom like me, who was told many times over what a great mom I was—the best mother people had ever seen—was not. Here I was, just trying to protect my child from the worst crime imaginable, and I had lost custody. When would society, judges, lawyers, and courts be educated enough to deal with this so that an abused child would be protected? When would we get to the point where the protective parent wouldn't be punished by this inadequate system?

Later that week, I still had not given up. I was resolved to try to get help for Ami no matter how hard it would be. I met with a woman from NOW who was familiar with the underground. She gave me pertinent information and advised me to what it would be like if I chose to run away with Ami. She confirmed what I already knew: that most women in my situation got caught sooner or later or went to prison. The government spent enormous sums of money through the FBI hunting you down, ironically protecting the perpetrator. Then the child wound up with the perpetrator for life, and the mother, in jail, was helpless to provide her daughter with any assistance. She said if I chose to run, there were places I could go to get a new identification, but I would never be able to contact family or friends again. The thought of running from home to home for food and clothing, of changing schools for Ami and not having any stability for me or my child, did not seem to be the answer. I later went out and bought a red wig and started contemplating how I would get Ami a passport. I thought of going to Australia, but the extradition laws had changed, and Derek knew how I loved Australia so that would be the first place outside the US that he'd look for us. Surely there had to be another way. Why should Ami and I have to give up our lives and run because no one would believe or protect her?

I began looking for a new attorney to represent us, a woman this time. I was done with male attorneys. I met with several, all of whom were shocked at the outcome of my case and even more astonished at how my lawyer had acted. I had Dennis come with me to these meetings. Before, I had dealt with everything by myself, but I had been so shaken up by losing custody that I wanted to make sure that I heard everything people told me and that they heard me as well. I didn't trust anyone anymore. And after the decisions I had made with Ted, I didn't trust my own poor judgment either. I needed Dennis's support, feedback, and judgment. And it was great to have him with me. He was very low-key and a good judge of people's characters.

One lawyer we talked to referred us to an attorney named Steve Zaplier to handle a malpractice case against Ted. She was livid. She felt that I had been poorly represented and that Ted had mishandled the case. A lawyer should never become involved with his client, she said, as he had done with me. She immediately called Zaplier and made an appointment for us. When we arrived at Steve's office, he was a ball of fire, filled with outrage at what had happened. He immediately began making phone calls. He wanted to file a civil suit against the father so that he would have to go through a jury trial, but since I no longer had custody, I could not file such an action. Steve found an attorney to represent me who would end up pursuing the case against Ted for a long time until I had too little money and too little interest to retain him any longer. Getting back at Ted was the least of my worries. I had to concentrate on helping Ami.

Then I was referred to Mary Jane Cox, who had a very good reputation with Arapahoe County. Dennis and I met with her, and we both found her to be the best lawyer we had met thus far. I explained to Mary Jane that I no longer had any money left; I was looking for someone to take on my case pro bono. She said she would first have to talk to her partner, Randy Mustain Wood, and that they would get back with us. When she and Randy got back to us, they said they couldn't take us on pro bono, but they offered us a payment plan: $1000 up front and $500 monthly. Dennis and I talked it over, and we agreed to it. We were both impressed by Mary Jane and Randy and felt that they would represent me well.

Mary Jane set up a meeting with her partner Randy, Steve Zaplier, and the newly assigned guardian ad litem, Paula Tomko. Dennis came with me again. At the meeting, I felt like I was back on trial, explaining again to everyone what had happened and explaining why I wanted to regain custody of Ami and protect her at the same time. Paula Tomko, whose opinion would now carry a lot of weight in my case just as Doris Truhlar's had, was not very impressive: she was very young and seemed not to be able to grasp what was going on. But, I thought, anything was an improvement from Doris.

On Miss Tomko's first—and only—visit to our house, my parents were there with me. Paula made comments in front of Ami about the abuse that I found to be very unprofessional. I never discussed the abuse with Ami unless she brought it up, and now—in front of my parents, and in a very awkward way— she was speaking in a frank manner, using adult language. I said, "Excuse me," and immediately removed Ami from the situation. I asked my parents to take Ami for a walk so I could talk alone to Ms. Tomko alone. I didn't want to expose Ami any further to that language.

At first, Paula seemed eager to help, but as time went on, I tried contacting her several times, and she did not return my phone calls. For five months, in fact, she did absolutely nothing and saw Ami only for those fifteen minutes at our house. Ami was still complaining that her pee-pee hurt and still crying out in the night that her daddy was touching her. One evening, before she went to sleep, Ami told me that her dad touched her with his fingers and then he put white stuff in this hole and in her "pee-pee."

I said, "White stuff? What are you talking about? Where does it come from?"

She said, "From his peanut in his hands!"

The next morning, I called Paula Tomko and continued to call her until she finally returned my call. I told her what Ami had said and that something had to be done. She told me to make sure that Ami told Dr. Adams what she had told me; meanwhile, Paula would call Gail and tell her what she told me to do.

I told Paula that in the past, when I had been told to tell Dr. Adams what Ami was saying, social services wound up using it against me. In court they had turned it around, saying that I had coached and instructed Ami to say these things about her father. And Gail had done the same thing and had betrayed Ami as well. Once Ami had come home from a session with Gail absolutely elated. "Mommy," she said, "Gail believes me, and she is going to tell Kirsten Jensen, and she is not going to tell my dad!" I had never seen her so excited and relieved. But then Gail had immediately called Derek to report what Ami had just told her.

Nonetheless, for two weeks I encouraged Ami to tell Gail what she had told me. I said, "You must tell Gail, honey. I can't help you, but Gail can."

At this point, Derek and I were taking turns bringing Ami to therapy. When her next session came up, on Wednesday, it was my visitation day. However, Derek insisted that he be there in the waiting room. On the Tuesday evening before Ami's appointment, I talked to my parents; they wanted us to come to Billings to see them. Since I could fly for free, and it was only an hour-long flight, I decided to take Ami for a couple of days. Ami was elated—how she loved her grandma and grandpa! Since her father was insisting he take Ami in to Gail's session, I left him a message, asking if he could possibly drop Ami off at the airport after her session so we could make a flight for her to see her grandparents. When he returned the call, Ami answered the phone and asked, "Can you, Daddy, so I can go see Grandma and Grandpa?" He told her it would be no problem; he'd be happy to. She exclaimed, "Oh good, Daddy! So after I talk to Gail you will take me so I can go to see my grandma and grandpa!"

Since Ami had answered the phone late, my answering machine accidentally taped the whole conversation. When I listened to it later, I heard him pause after she said that. In effect, she had just warned her father that she was going to talk to Gail. In the past, she had always said that she was going to see Gail. He picked up on it immediately.

When he arrived to pick her up, she was all ready to go with a darling sailor outfit and a hat. But he told me in front of her that he wouldn't be able to take her to the airport after all. "Why not?" I said. Just minutes earlier he had said he could. This was a man who rarely worked, so I knew that couldn't be the problem. "You told her you would," I said, "and look at her—she is all ready to go."

Ami got very upset and started to cry. "Look at her," he said. "Now look what you've done." He told me to just go ahead and take her to Montana and skip her appointment with Gail.

I wasn't fooled; I knew he didn't want Ami to go to Gail's because he was afraid she would tell her therapist what her father had done to her. I knew that by now Paula Tomko had probably told Gail what was going on and that this would be an important appointment. But he knew that since I was standing there with wet hair and no makeup, I was obviously not ready to take Ami to her appointment. He also knew I didn't care for Ami's therapist in the first place and that I couldn't possibly make it both to the appointment and to the airport. He also knew that I would never disappoint Ami by not making it to the airport on time, so I would choose going to the airport over going to the appointment.

In general, I tried to talk to him just as little as possible and tried never to show my anger, because that's what he wanted. Any reaction from me tended to thrill him. But this time I just looked at him and said, "Screw you!"

"Oh, that's good, Maralee," he said. "In front of Ami." "Screw you!" I said again as he walked away.

There was no way Ami was going to miss this appointment. So I quickly made a plan. I had everything packed, so I would just go to Gail's with wet hair and get ready there while Ami was in therapy. I looked at my little girl and said, "Don't worry, honey, we are going."

When we arrived at Gail's, much to my surprise, there sat Gail with Derek, the mastermind manipulator. He was sure I had left for the airport. Both were very surprised that we had shown up at another one of their private meetings. Gail looked at me with such disdain you would have thought I had just committed a serious crime.

"What's going on?" I asked Derek. "What are you doing here?" Even though I knew exactly what he was doing there.

Once she got her wits together, Gail insisted that Ami get into therapy, and Derek insisted that he stay. I told him there was no reason for him to stay. This was my day with Ami, and as soon as the appointment was over, we weregoing to Montana. Gail agreed that he go ahead and leave, but he still insisted on staying. Then he told Ami that he would be waiting in the waiting room. However, what he didn't know was that earlier that week, Ami had asked me, "Can my dad hear me through the wall? He tells me he can." I had told Ami that even when her dad was in the waiting room, he couldn't hear what she told Gail. The door was closed, I told her, so she shouldn't be afraid to tell her anything. After fifteen to twenty minutes in the waiting room, looking pretty foolish for staying after Gail had suggested he leave, Derek finally left.

Ami came out early; Gail had cut the session short. The first thing she did was ask me for the money I owed her, which she was doing on a regular basis.

However, after Ami had told her in the fall about what her father had done, and Gail had believed her father instead, I had decided that I was not going to pay someone so incompetent. I just could not justify doing so. Instead, I wanted to file a lawsuit against her for not protecting my little girl.

I ignored the subject of money and said point blank, "Let's go in your office. Well, did she talk?"

She answered that we would talk about it later.

"No!" I said. We were going to talk about it now. "Did she talk?"

Her reply was yes, she had talked, and Ami was quite proud of herself. She said this in a very sarcastic tone.

"What do you mean by that?" I said. My blood was boiling.

She was turning this around on me.

She was visibly angry. She said that Ami had said that she told me what her father had done because she was getting to go home to see her grandma and grandpa.

"We had not even decided to go to Montana until last night," I said. "The reason she told you is because Paula Tomko told me to encourage her to tell you, due to what she has been saying recently."

Then Gail threatened me with calling social services and said she would now have to reopen the case and call Kirsten Jensen, the social worker. The mention of social services made my skin crawl, but the way she said it even scared me more. Then she went on to say what a shame it was.

"What a shame it is," I said. "What her father is doing to her!"

She asked, "Why did you not encourage her to tell me before now?"

"Because if you remember right," I said, "when I was told by Kirsten to get her to tell you, you used it against me in court, saying 'Ami told us her dad was touching her, but she told us her mom told her to tell us that!' Remember?"

She then called Ami into her office and said in a calm voice, "We are all friends. You can talk to me."

Ami hung her head, looked up at Gail with the saddest eyes, and said, "Gail, my daddy hurts me!" It was as if she was screaming Gail, help me! She went on to say that he put his fingers in her and that she never slept at her dad's. She had only slept there once.

Gail looked at me and said, "What does she mean by that?"

I said, "She means she can't sleep at her dad's."

Ami then said, "I never close my eyes!"

I told Ami to tell Gail about what she told me about the white stuff, and she described to Gail what her dad was doing. Gail asked her if it was a cream, but Ami did not know what a cream was. She said it came from his peanut in his hands. "He makes me so mad at his house," she said. "I don't like it"—she paused—"to stay with my dad. Maybe someday when I grow up."

Gail seemed very angry. I could see that her view of herself as a professional—her ego, in other words—was obviously more important than admitting she had made a horrible mistake.

"I'm confused," she said.

I once again could not imagine hearing what my child had just said and how she could be the least bit confused. But this woman with a PhD was confused. After a year of therapy, she hardly knew Ami. Whenever I asked Ami what she did with Dr. Adams, she said, "We play." She never bothered to speak to her, to listen to her, to find out who she was close to, or what she liked or disliked. Was she now going to protect her?

No, she was going to cover her butt.

With all that Ami had told her in the past, with all I had been through, her reaction—"I'm confused"—just blew me away. She was still not going to help Ami. I guess it should not have surprised me, but I never dreamed that someone in the position to help children, not destroy them, could turn their back on the very helpless beings they were paid to protect. I was beginning to feel that those who did not help my child were themselves guilty of abuse.

We left Dr. Adams's office, drove to the airport, and flew to Billings to see her grandparents as if nothing had happened that day. When we arrived, Ami ran as fast as she could off the jet way and into her grandpa's arms, screaming, "Grandpa! Grandma!" with her face lit up and her eyes dancing. Oh how she adored her grandparents, and how they adored her.

We had a great visit and I pretended for everyone's sake we were okay.

CHAPTER 20

Mounting Evidence

After we came back from our visit with my parents, she was with Derek for the next couple of days. When she returned, she had a new problem: she had a thick, clear sticky discharge from her vagina and was complaining of pain there. I called Mary Jane Cox, my new attorney, and asked what I should do about this discharge problem. It was pretty severe and her vagina was very red. Mary Jane insisted I take her to the doctor, especially since in the past we had sent Derek letters telling him that Ami needed medical attention, and he had ignored them. Since I had lost custody, Derek was now in control over which doctor she went to or whether she even went to one. I told Mary Jane that if I took her to a doctor they would use it against me, but she explained that I couldn't ignore this problem; for health reasons I had to take her. Since her father had shifted all of her previous medical records from her pediatricians to Kaiser, I proceeded to take her there.

When the doctor came into the examining room, I saw that he was Joe Marion, a football player I had dated in college. We were both surprised to see each other after so many years. But being a professional, he quickly got right to the point. He had no idea why we were there and asked what was going on. I told him that Ami had some sticky discharge and had been complaining of pain in her vaginal area. Then Ami said, "My dad touches me there!"

The doctor was quite surprised. He said, "Does your dad touch you there a lot?"

"Yes," Ami said.

The doctor held up five fingers and asked if it had been more than five times. Ami said that it had and went on to tell him the same thing she had said at Gail's a few days earlier—that she couldn't sleep at her dad's.

Dr. Marion continued to examine her and took samples of the discharge for any STDs; the cultures came back negative. He said that her vaginal opening was large for a four-year-old and that he would be notifying social services and the DA of Arapahoe County. He said Ami needed to see a specialist. When I asked him if I should see someone at Kaiser, he said "That would be like taking your Ferrari to a Volkswagen dealership."

In his report, Dr. Marion noted "Some crusting on the superior aspects of both labia majors" and called Ami's vaginal opening, "somewhat larger than expected," and said that her "vaginal vault…appears erythematous" (abnormally red, from irritation or infection). He concluded this was a case of "possible sexual abuse." (See Kaiser Report, Appendix D.)

Social services never responded to Dr. Marion's phone calls.

Her father was to have a visitation day the next day. At this point I was worried, not as much about his physical abuse of her but about the mental abuse he would chastise her with for telling the doctor. I talked to my attorneys, and while they couldn't officially suggest that I refuse Derek visitation, I could tell that they thought I should. So once again, I took Ami to my friends' condo in Vail to stay there until I heard from my attorneys about what I should do.

◆ ◆ ◆ ◆ ◆ ◆

When returning from Vail, I began to drive toward our home. Before leaving, I had asked Ruth to go by my house and see if the police were there. If they were, she was to come back and honk her car horn at me. When she came back, she honked and told me there were two police cars in front of my house. I could not go home. So I got off the main road and stopped at a payphone so I could find out what was going on. Randy, one of my attorneys, suggested that I come to his office with Ami until he knew we were safe. We stayed there all day, both of us exhausted as we slept on my attorney's floor in her office. All I wanted was to get

Ami into her bed safely and to let her sleep. By 5:30 p.m., I was finally told we could go home, and we would not be bothered. But I was worried they would give her to her father or place her in foster care.

The next day my attorneys called me to tell me they had made some progress. It was agreed by all parties involved that Ami would be seen by the Kempe Center and that Derek would no longer be able to sit in the waiting room while Ami was at therapy with Gail. But in return, I would have to return her to her father on Father's Day. How ironic. I wasn't worried about her being abused, what with so many people scrutinizing Derek's behavior at the moment. But again, I was worried about what he would do to her for telling on him.

I begged Gail to protect her. I said that Ami had been wetting the bed, something she hadn't done since she was a baby. But Dr. Adams insisted that Ami needed to be with her father. Then I begged the new guardian ad litem, Paula Tomko, to protect her. Paula's response was that they had confronted Derek, and he had agreed not to discuss the subject with Ami. Yeah, right! A perverted child molester wasn't going to say a word! We could all rest easy now! He was going to stop. What a travesty! Once a perpetrator always a perpetrator.

Meanwhile, behind the scenes, they all conspired to abort our meeting with the Kempe Center.

Needless to say, Derek spent Father's Day with Ami, and since he still had legal custody, he made up the days he had lost when I had taken Ami to Vail. Ami had a very difficult time during this stretch. He would not let her talk to me, and he was keeping her out of school too. She was being punished I was sure of it. On Wednesday, he finally put her in school, and I went to see her. She looked unkempt. Her blue eyes had lost their sparkle, and she had deep, dark circles under her eyes. When she saw me, she looked frightened. "Mommy," she said, "you can't take me out of school." What was he doing to her?

The teacher said, "All Ami has wanted to do all day is sleep on her mat."

I then responded to Ami, "I know, honey."

She then asked me if we could go lie down. Her teacher told me she had been asking to lie down ever since she had got there that morning. I told her,

"Sure, honey, we can go lie down." And in a matter of seconds she was fast asleep on her little mattress.

When she woke, once again very frightened, she said, "Mommy, you'd better go." She was worried that her dad would be there soon and this wasn't my day with her. Her father had warned the school not to let me take her from there, and Ami was worried for me. I assured her not to worry. They say your eyes are the windows to your soul; what I saw in my little girl's eyes was pain and fear.

The next time I had her in my house, she told me that her father was mad at her. When I asked her why, she said, "Because I told Gail, and he says he doesn't touch me, but he does! I told him he does!" Here was a four-year-old standing up to her father. I was so surprised and so impressed with her.

Maybe, I thought, she would make it through this nightmare after all.

There was a hearing scheduled for October of that year, 1991. I had filed a motion for a custody evaluation and for the Kempe National Center to review and ask for the removal of Dr. Adams as Ami's therapist. And Derek had started playing his games again. As soon as I gave him my work schedule for August, which showed that I was working only on weekends, he scheduled his stays with Ami through the weekends. In his defense, he stated that he had the control to do as he chose.

That week I had to work late on Wednesday, so I asked Kim to pick up Ami from school. But when she went to pick her up, she was told that Ami's father had given specific orders not to allow Kim to pick her up. So the teacher had to stay late with Ami and could not get a hold of Derek. Ami was extremely upset she could not go with Kim, who she loved very much.

After working a very long, hard day, I called Kim to see how they were doing only to find out what had happened. Kim was very upset about it. It was only an hour after I usually picked her up, but the school charged by the minute, and I also did not want to put them out. By that time, I had taken on a renter by the name of Connie to help me pay my mortgage. When I called my home number, Connie picked up and told me Ami was home. Her teacher had brought her there, and Connie was now reading her a story in bed.

When I arrived home, I opened the door and heard her little footsteps running down the hallway and her voice crying out my name. I was so glad she was home safe and not with her father.

Since my house was large, it was nice having a roommate around. Connie was concerned that my phone lines may have been tapped—she heard clicks on the phone when she was talking. She was also concerned about the sliding glass doors. Someone had tried to break in and had used a crowbar or some other tool to pry them apart. The framework that stabilized the door had been removed along with the nuts and bolts. I called the police and had them check my doors, and I called the phone company to have the phone lines checked. I was now becoming a little paranoid. Every day I was dealing with something whether it was creditors, malpractice suits against my old attorney, or my psychopathic ex-husband. I was so very tired.

Then, my lawyer called me to tell me that Derek's lawyer and social services had blocked the October hearing. It wasn't going to happen.

◆ ◆ ◆ ◆ ◆ ◆

About a month earlier, I had met a nice man at my athletic club who looked a lot like Dennis. I kept staring at him, thinking it was Dennis looking for me. The man, whose name was John, saw me staring at him and came up to me. After talking for a while, he asked me out. We began dating and seeing each other regularly, though I still carried a torch for Dennis. Dennis, however, had decided to be close to his former girlfriend who had given birth to his son. I had been too exhausted to fight for that relationship; I was having a difficult enough time just getting through each day. My life was consumed by all that I had going on. I went in and out of focus, and I didn't have much available to give someone else. When I was with John, I tried not to share any of my pain but instead tried to enjoy life again—at least a little.

Since John was financially well off, he took me to the finest restaurants in town. It had been so long since anyone had made me feel pampered and special. One day he picked up Ami and me to go for a drive in his Jaguar. It was a beautiful day, and we went to Washington park and fed the ducks and had a great time together. I could tell that Ami really liked him. As he returned us and was getting ready to leave, she said, "You can stay longer with my mom. It's all right. Please stay!"

To say the least, I was embarrassed. He said, "Let's let your mom make the decision."

He came in for a while, and when he left, I kissed him at the door. Ami said, "Oh! You two are lovers. John, will you marry my mom?"

I didn't know what had gotten into her! We all shared a laugh over it. But in the morning, I told Ami that I was embarrassed when she had asked John if he would marry me. "I will get married someday," I said. "But I have not known John that long, and before someone can marry someone else, they need to know them longer."

"Then marry Dennis," she said. She told me she wanted a new dad and sister before her birthday, which was just a few months away. I laughed and told her that it would be impossible to fulfill her wishes before her birthday.

"Then I wouldn't have to go to my dad's house anymore," she said, "and I could always live here."

That's when I realized what was going on. She thought she had to go to her dad's because I was not married and did not have a dad for her at my house. No wonder she was eager for me to get married!

What Ami was expressing was her dire need for a clean, stable home environment. Her father ran her ragged all the time. He was constantly dragging her along to his adult activities and leaving her at daycare at the club until as late as 9:30 p.m., after she had been in pre-school all day. He usually fed her dinner after that, which was very late for her. When she came back from a visit, she was usually exhausted, dirty, and in need of nurturing. The minute she returned from her father's she ran up to her bedroom, took off the clothes her father had put her in, and put on one of her nice dresses.

She was living in two opposing worlds. One was a fun, nurturing environment, and the other was a nightmare. How was she really coping with this? What was it doing to her? Was I doing enough to make her strong? Was I doing my best to help her to feel loved enough and not feel responsible for what he was doing to her? Were we both strong enough to survive this?

Every time she told me what he was doing to her, I felt as if I myself were being raped. I ached every day and every night for Ami. I hoped and prayed that the next day it would all end somehow and she would be protected. Some of my friends had told me to look at our situation as if Ami had a handicap: she would survive it, they said. But this handicap had not been caused by a birth defect. It had been inflicted upon her by her father and by society. This was something that I as her mother should have been able to control and stop. For a system to allow the perpetrator, her father, continued access to the child he was abusing was exactly the opposite of what should be happening. Was there no such thing as justice?

◆ ◆ ◆ ◆ ◆ ◆

Meanwhile, although there was so much strife in our lives, Ami and I couldn't have been any closer. She was so much fun to be with, a pure joy. At the time, she was the only delight I got out of life and had become the center of my existence. We visited New York together and saw the Rockettes, we skied together in the Rockies, we baked cookies and watched The Little Mermaid at least one hundred times, we went to Washington Park and fed the ducks, and most of all, we talked a lot. I wasn't sure it was healthy to be so thoroughly devoted to a child. For one thing, years were passing by, and I hadn't managed to maintain a good relationship with any man. John had quickly left the picture, and it was obviously very hard for a man to date a woman in my situation. A typical man couldn't even fathom the idea of abusing a child and had a hard time coping with the pain involved and with feeling so helpless to stop it. I did not want to bring a man into my life that I could not emotionally give myself to. And if he started to care for me, I could not be there. My only focus was on protecting my little girl.

CHAPTER 21

Analyzing the Enemy

One night, I found Ami touching herself before she went to sleep. She said, "My dad isn't touching me anymore. He tells me to touch myself, and he watches." Could she be saying what I think she's saying?

It made me think of Jeffrey Dahmer who had murdered thirteen young boys. He had probably started out by raping these young boys, and then began killing them. Or Ted Bundy. They say he started by looking at porno magazines, then he raped women, then he killed them. Sometimes, just for the thrill of it, he would kill two in the same night. These kinds of sociopaths or psychopaths tended to start with a small crime and work their way up to the big ones. What would Derek do next? What could be worse than molesting and raping your four-year-old daughter and asking her to masturbate for your own sexual entertainment?

The night before Ami told me this, I had remembered something a Vermont attorney named Allan Rosenfeld had said to me, back in February, when I had called him so distraught after losing custody of Ami. I asked Mr. Rosenfeld if he thought Derek was still doing it to her, and he replied, "I know he is still doing it! These people are sick and do not stop. And if you persist, they will try to take all of your visitation rights away and say you are obsessive. The best thing you can do is give Ami your best the fifty percent of the time you have her and keep her as stable as you can. And for the next couple of years, bide your time and save every dime so you can hire the best attorney you can get, because you will need the best." My response to him was, "How can I bide my time and let Ami be subjected to this?"

"If you fight it," he said, "you will lose her altogether."

After Ami told me about Derek's latest sick behavior, my mind kept going over and over what Mr. Rosenfeld had said to me. My God! Was this where we were heading? Was this where Derek's attorney was heading? To try to take her away from me completely? After the latest doctor's report, verifying his abuse of her, after Ami's statement to Dr. Adams, and after he had been ordered to allow Ami to be seen by the Kempe Center (an order that Derek had since fought with all his might), that would be the only route they could take to cover up all of their crimes. Oh! Would this ever end? Would Ami ever be protected? Would we ever have the chance to lead normal lives?

The next morning, I called my lawyer Mary Jane Cox and told her what I had discussed with the attorney from Vermont months earlier. I expressed my concerns to her. After I got off the phone with her, I called Allan Rosenfeld again, but instead I reached Garnette Harrison, another attorney diligently working to try to change the system and the laws regarding child sexual abuse cases. Garnette sent me a package with information of case after case similar to mine and how misrepresentation of these cases could crucify the mother. I immediately faxed this information to my attorneys—once again educating my own attorneys to prepare for the great injustice, corruption, denial, and abuse within the system.

After another sleepless night, I called Mary Jane first thing in the morning. What did she think? Was she seeing what I was seeing? From my conversation with her, I sensed that she was just starting to realize just how controlled this case was by professionals who had made big mistakes and were now trying to cover their asses.

I studied the most recent motions of Derek's attorney Steve Calder, and yes! This was where they were heading. They had filed a contempt citation on me for taking Ami to the doctor when she had a severe discharge and was complaining of pain in her vagina. According to the new custody agreement, she was not to be seen by a doctor without a court order. This was now six months after Doctor Marion had said that Ami needed to be seen by a sexual abuse expert, ASAP. By now, the discharge had worsened. The "professionals"—Gail, Paula Tomko, and the social workers—had finally agreed that Ami should go to the Kempe Center, but after my attorneys had set up times for her to go on two different occasions, they had recanted. They were obviously afraid of what the Kempe Center would find out. (See MaryJane Cox motion for Kempe Center, Appendix D.)

One Wednesday morning in September 1991, Ami woke up complaining of another discharge. "Mommy, look! I've got it again!" I called my attorney who told me to take her to the doctor. Again, I was afraid to do so. I felt certain it would be used against me and against Ami, but my attorney said that since it was for health reasons, I must do it. On an earlier occasion, I had spoken to Detective Perry, and he had told me the same thing—that I should take Ami to Humana Hospital Emergency Room. They were well trained and would know what to do. Even after I told him of my catch-22 situation, he had urged me to take her.

I knew what would happen if I took her. It was getting close to my new custody hearing, and they would use this against me. But Ami's discharge was horrible. I worried that if I didn't take her, this would render her sterile, and she wouldn't be able to have children when she got older.

The discharge had a foul smell and was thick, yellow, and crusty; it even ran onto the outside of her vagina. My poor baby was constantly pulling at her crotch and was terribly uncomfortable. I couldn't allow my little girl to suffer just because I was afraid of the consequences. I had to do something, but I was terrified of losing visitation, both for my sake and Ami's. I decided to wait until the next time she had it, and I vowed to myself that no matter how afraid I was, I would take her immediately.

That Thursday she was with her dad, and on Friday she was with me. She did not complain all day until six that evening. My friend Liz and her daughter Jessica had asked us to go get ice cream with them. On the way home, Ami was riding in the back seat, playing with Jessica, when out of the blue she exclaimed, "Mom, I have it again."

I quickly responded, "Okay, honey, we will talk about it when we get home."

Liz, who knew the situation and had witnessed this all too many times, said, "Take her."

I got out of the car at my house, sick to my stomach. I had an overwhelming feeling that this would cause big problems for us, but I had to go with what was best for Ami.

Well, she was right. It was an unbelievable amount of the same kind of discharge, clear and sticky with small, yellow globs. It smelled awful. I calmly told Ami that we were going to see a doctor.

When we arrived at Humana Hospital on September 20, 1991, the nurse in the emergency room approached and asked me to describe what was wrong. I gave elusive answers and very little information, except that Ami had a discharge problem. Because I would not answer a lot of the nurse's questions and did not want anyone to later claim that I was putting words in Ami's mouth or manufacturing accusations against the father, I let them talk directly to Ami. I had seen too often already how Derek's team of liars twisted my words and actions and used them against me. I was giving so little information that the nurse finally exclaimed, "You are her mother, aren't you?"

The hospital staff handled everything beautifully. Everyone was careful not to traumatize Ami, which eased some of my fears. When the nurse approached Ami, she told her she was there to help her, asked her what was the matter, and spoke to her kindly. Ami told her that her daddy touched her there and it hurt.

Dr. Drew Greer then came in and started asking me questions about what I thought was going on. I told him I wasn't saying anything and that he should ask Ami. I didn't want Gail, social services, and Derek's lawyer to claim that I influenced the doctors in any way. I just wanted to stay in the background, so they could not twist anything that happened.

Doctor Greer began by telling Ami he was not going to hurt her and that he just wanted to make her feel better. He spoke to her for a while. It was quite some time before he actually examined her. She told the doctor that her dad put his fingers in her. As he examined her, I was on the other side of the room, but I caught the astonished look on his face and on the nurses' faces when they saw the thick discharge. In his report he would describe it as "a crusty yellowish discharge in the perivulvular region. She is erythematous and tender to touch over both vulvas. There is approximately a one millimeter vertical laceration on the posterior forchette." He also tested Ami for gonorrhea and Chlamydia—something surely no four-year-old should ever have to go through.

After he examined Ami, Dr. Greer recommended an examination at Children's Hospital and called in the police. They arrived shortly and began talking to Ami. Ami took a liking to one of the officers in particular whose name was Tim King. He seemed to have a way with kids. (See Humana Hospital Report, Appendix D.)

Officer King asked her if she knew the difference between telling a lie and telling the truth. For example, he said, if Ami said she was ten years old, would that be a lie or would that be the truth? "It would be a lie," Ami said. When Officer King then asked Ami to tell him what she had told the nurse when she came in. Ami smiled at him and tried to hide behind me. I reassured Ami that it was okay to talk to him. Officer King then asked Ami if someone had touched her.

"My daddy did!" Ami said.

When he asked, "Where did he touch you at?" Ami pointed to her vagina. "What do you call that?"

"Pee-pee," Ami said.

Officer King then held out his notebook, swept his hand across it gently, and asked Ami if her father had touched her in that manner. Ami said, "He put his fingers in!"

"How many times did he put his fingers in?"

Ami held up her hand with all of her fingers spread.

"Did it hurt when his fingers were in?"

"Yeah," Ami said.

Another officer in the room, Sergeant Crooks, asked Ami where it had taken place, and Ami said it had taken place in her father's car.

"Where was your daddy sitting, and where were you sitting?"

"He was in the big seat, and I was in the little seat." She told them that her dad had touched her in the car on Thursday after he had picked her up from the house, and she was still in her ballet outfit. She said, "He would pull down my panties, I would pull them up, and he would pull them down, and I would pull them up…"

"Did you have your underwear on?"

"No." (See Officer Tim Kings report, Appendix D.)

She was so brave to talk about it like that. Everyone at the hospital was very attentive to Ami, and we were there quite some time. The hospital receptionist had a little girl Ami's age, so she made it a point to play and talk with Ami. She was like a magnet. Everyone liked her. She was such a doll.

Afterward, when I spoke to the doctor alone, he told me that her discharge was not normal for a four-and-a-half year- old girl. "You would see this kind of a discharge in a sexually active adult woman," he said. He also told me that she had a laceration on the inside, which was a sign that there had been penetration. I could not tell you the words that came to my mind at this time. I thought to myself, with tears springing to my eyes. He wanted Ami to be examined by a sexual abuse expert immediately. The evidence was consistent with sexual assault cases.

When I came back out, Ami did not seem traumatized in any way. I acted as normal as possible for her sake, all the while I was aching inside. My poor little girl.

Even while I was happy that everyone had handled Ami's care so professionally, I dreaded what was to come. At this point, I was so sick of having to handle everything on my own and having to be so strong. I just wanted someone to hold me for a minute and tell me it was going to be all right. It was now very late, but before I left the hospital I paged Dennis, and we talked. He seemed to think that maybe now everyone—social services, the police, the psychologist—would decide to do the right thing and protect Ami now that there was physical evidence of the abuse.

Officer King then told me he was going to notify social services, and naturally, I became alarmed. I warned him that they were the very reason we had been through all this and that they had messed up this case from the start. I did not trust them. He told me he had to contact them for legal purposes. He then handed me the phone to talk to the social worker on duty.

As I grabbed the phone, my heart was racing. After I explained what had happened, the social worker said that under no circumstances was my child to be released to her father and that she would set up a hearing for Monday. Officer

King then told me he would have a police car at my house on Saturday morning when her dad arrived to pick her up. Under no circumstances was I to release Ami to her father.

When Ami and I walked out of the hospital, she asked me if she was going to see her dad the next day. I said no, and when she asked why, I didn't know what to tell her. I didn't want to tell her she was being protected. I had told her that before and had been wrong. Far too many times had I thought that she would be protected from her perverted father,only to see her given back to him again and again. So I said, "Because the policeman does not want you to right now."

When we got home, I was wiped out. It was late at night by that point, but Ami was happy and had a ton of energy—probably because she felt relieved. It took a while, but I finally got her to sleep.

When I awakened the next morning, my anxiety began to build. Her father was to arrive soon. Suddenly, a policewoman showed up at my door. As I opened the door I thought, Déjà vu, here we go again. Usually her father arrived early. He must have seen the police car out front, called the police, and turned around to pick up Pam, his old standby, to give him some credibility.

By this time, friends of mine had arrived at my house to give me support. I had Ami go upstairs. I had taken her there and put on some cartoons so she would not be subjected to any of this. In the meantime, Derek got the papers showing that he had custody and that I had a hysterical personality disorder. Little did he know I had doctors' reports and police reports to back up what I was doing.

The female police officer spent a great deal of time out in front of my house listening to Derek, talking to the officer in the car, and talking to me. As it turned out, she didn't have the information from social services or from her own department. The other officer who was there was the one who was supposed to be handling the situation. It was mass confusion once again, even though it should have been so simple. The policewoman came to my door and said that she had been told I had a hysterical personality by the father, and maybe my child should go into a foster home if we couldn't work out our differences. I calmly pulled her aside and said, "That little girl up there is suffering tremendously due to the incompetence of people like you. If you had read the reports from last night, you would not be in my home questioning me. Instead, you would have done your job, which was to keep him away from our home and not to cause a scene."

I shut the door and immediately went up to check on Ami. I found her nervous and stressed, her eyes glazed over. She looked at me as if to say, "Is it all over?"

After two hours of his manipulation, the scene finally came to a close, and Ami was left with me. Why had there even been an argument? Why had I been told that under no circumstance was I to release her, only to have to go through all that drama?

On Monday morning, Mary Jane wanted to meet with me first thing. When I came into her office, she told me she was continually hitting a stone wall. She had never seen anything like it. She told me that my ex was a very powerful and controlling man. When I had told her how manipulative Derek was, she had no idea how controlling and had not believed me. Now she was seeing it for herself. She wanted to find out from the hospital if Doctor Greer had wanted Ami to see a sexual abuse expert right away. She had me call Dr. Greer, and when I reached his nurse, I asked her if Dr. Greer wanted Ami to see a sexual abuse expert right away.

"Yes!" she said. "Social services should be taking care of it."

I told her, "Well, social services aren't moving on it," and my attorney got upset.

"Geez, Maralee! Don't say that! That's what got you into trouble in the first place."

"It's the truth," I said.

She was learning very quickly what I was dealing with and that I was right. That weekend would be the only time that social services would issue protective orders for Ami.

Mary Jane then got Dr. Greer on one phone line and social services on the other. The newly assigned worker from social services, a woman who had never seen Ami, said that Ami was traumatized but that Dr. Greer did not think Ami should see a sexual abuse expert. Then Mary Jane brought Dr. Greer himself in on the conversation, and he told the social worker directly that this child needed to be seen by a sexual-abuse expert right away. Apparently, social services were once again trying to save face. It was good my attorney was catching on and had a three-way call going on.

Mary Jane then told me that social services and Dr. Adams wanted to see Ami that very day. I told my attorney that I didn't trust them; I wouldn't take her. She insisted that I do it, but I argued that I couldn't do that to Ami. What if they tried to take her away from me again? Ami couldn't take that, and neither could I.

Eventually, I was given no choice. I had to comply with what social services wanted me to do, or they could hold me in contempt and take away my visitation.

When Ami and I arrived, Gail wanted to see Ami alone. While I sat in the waiting room with the new social worker, she started up some small talk with me, asking me what airline I flew for. When I told her I worked for Continental, she said—in a condescending tone—that she never flew Continental. She only flew United. She went on to say that she knew Jennifer—the first social worker on our case—the one who had screwed up royally from the beginning. So what she was trying to tell me was that they all knew each other, and they were all watching each other's backs.

Gail then came out to summon the social worker, and they were in Gail's office together for over an hour, which seemed like an eternity to me. In the meantime, my mind was wandering, and my anxiety was building. What if they were sneaking her out the back of Gail's office through the sliding glass doors?

Finally, they came out, and the social worker told me that Ami did tell them her Dad was touching her. She also said that he was touching Rustle, the dog, who was living at Derek's at this point. Because she said that Derek was touching the dog, too, they didn't believe her.

I was stunned once again. Since she had been two years old, this child had explained in explicit detail about what her father had been doing to her. To be honest, I wouldn't doubt that he was molesting the dog as well. They told me that they would resume visits with her father as soon as possible.

On Thursday evening at 6:00 p.m., the GAL, Paula Tomko, called to tell me to resume the father's visits at 7:00p.m. That gave me no time to explain to Ami why she had to go back to her father. I told Paula that if she thought Ami should see her father, she should be the one to tell her. "You come to my house," I said, "and tell her yourself." Paula said she would call me back, but she never did.

Earlier that day, I had told Ami she may have to go back to her Dad's, trying to prepare her just in case, even though I had expected that the new medical evidence would finally protect her. She responded by saying, "It's okay, Mom, because when my Dad touches me, Rustle barks"—she began barking like a dog, imitating Rustle—"and says, 'Ami, pull up your panties, Pull up your panties!'"

I was amazed by my little girl. In spite of all the pressure on her, she persisted in telling the truth and expressing her feelings. Earlier, we had gone to the children's museum where they had a fake lion that talked to the kids. It said, "Pick up an egg, open it up, and make a wish. Close the egg and throw it into the lion's mouth." As Ami followed instructions she said, "I wish my Dad would stop touching me!"

◆◆◆◆◆◆

So that evening, while Ami was playing in her playroom downstairs with her friend Jessica, her father—the child molester—showed up to pick her up. Jessica's mom, Liz, was upstairs with me. Derek kept ringing the doorbell over and over as Ami cried out, "I don't want to go with my dad!" I didn't answer, so he went around to the back and tried to open the sliding-glass door. I sent Liz downstairs to be with the girls while he banged on the windows. I heard Liz tell him to just go away. She told me later that Ami was clinging to Jessica and saying, "I don't want to go!"

◆◆◆◆◆◆

The next time Ami was with Derek, I called to talk to her, and Derek hung up on me.

Soon afterward, on September 23, 1991, I received more bad news from the Aurora Police Department. Detective Parker, who had received the police report from Tim King and the report from Humana Hospital, had decided not to file criminal charges against Derek, because in his view I lacked credibility. This amazed me. Detective Parker had never met me. How did he know how credible I was? And what did my credibility have to do with it anyway? It was about Ami and the evidence they had found of her sexual abuse.

Later that week, my attorneys told me not to withhold visitation. They had an idea. They called me into their office on a Wednesday morning to sign a document that stated that Ami needed to be seen by a sexual abuse expert at Children's Hospital and asked for an immediate hearing. However, I told them this was risky. Physical evidence was rare in these cases, and I didn't want to lose any more of my visitation with Ami. "Maralee," they said, "you are the one who has told us about the possibility of them pushing you into supervised visits. To ask for the evaluation this way, the judge could order the GAL to comply. If you don't, they could claim you're not looking out for your daughter's health."

"Wow!" I said. "You expect me to sign a document that may cause me to lose Ami and get supervised visits? I can't make that decision right now."

"You have to decide," they said. "We have a courier waiting right now to get this over to the judge ASAP. You must make up your mind."

"I can't!" I said.

"You're giving Derek too much power," Mary Jane said, shaking her head.

At the same time, they gave me another document to sign that would guarantee I wouldn't file a lawsuit against them if I lost my visitation rights. I realized how scared they were.

I called my mom, only she couldn't understand what was going on. Someone had to help me in this catch-22 situation. It had been ten days since Ami was at the hospital; a physical exam probably wouldn't turn up anything by now. However, if I didn't sign it that may be exactly what the other side was looking for. Finally, after much duress, I signed the document then immediately panicked about it. Had I done the right thing? My attorneys seemed anxious to get this off and were pressuring me, but legally they couldn't make the decision for me. However, their mannerisms convinced me to go ahead with it.

Within a couple of days, we went to court. To our surprise, the newly assigned social worker from social services was there along with her supervisor. Everyone was wondering why they were there. What was their stake in this petition? Nobody had filed a DNA (Dependency and Neglect Action), which puts protective orders on the child and automatically involves social services. We concluded that they were just there to see what was going to happen.

Before and during the hearing, I kept questioning Mary Jane with what questions she had prepared. She finally smiled and realized why I was so afraid: my previous attorney had never prepared for my hearings. She reassured me that she was not like Ted Kaplysh and asked if I wanted to see the questions she had prepared.

As we expected, the judge ordered a Children's Hospital evaluation immediately.

It wound up being held up for weeks because Derek wanted to be the one to take Ami. I had just spent $8,000 for this small hearing and for having my attorney escort Ami and me to the hospital for a morning. Derek insisted he have her for up to a half-hour just before the scheduled appointment, and he won that concession. It was obvious he wanted to work on Ami before she was examined.

When Mary Jane first came to my house, so we could go get Ami together, I showed her our lovely home and Ami's pretty little room. I told her we would have to probably come back to my house to change her because Derek would probably have her dressed inappropriately. I told Mary Jane to be sure to get a look at his disgusting apartment, where he didn't even have a table for her to eat on. However, when we got there, he was too quick. He had Ami out the door before Mary Jane even got there. But I was right about Ami's clothing. Mary Jane agreed we should go home, change her, and fix her hair before going to the hospital.

Finally, we arrived at Children's Hospital, a month after the doctor at Humana had recommended we go there immediately. I was sure that Ami's laceration had healed by this time. A physician's assistant named Donna Nelligan examined Ami and interviewed her alone. Mary Jane and I waited in the waiting area.

In the report Dr. Nelligan later filed, she provided specific details about her interview with Ami. When she asked Ami to tell her about some nice things that happened at her two homes—her mother's and her father's—Ami said, "Well, at Mommy's house, we get up and make breakfast, and we have fun doing that, and I think that's nice." When Dr. Nelligan asked about her father's, Ami said, "I don't know… Daddy doesn't do anything nice."

Dr. Nelligan then asked Ami to tell her about some of the "not so nice" things that happened at either her mother's or her father's house. She said she tried not to be bad at her father's house. "He touches me down there," she added, "and I don't think that's so nice." When asked what she meant by "down there," Ami pointed to her vaginal area and said, "That's my pee-pee." When asked what he touched her with, Ami pointed to her fingers. She said it happened in her bedroom at her daddy's house. He pulled down her clothes, she said, "And he shouldn't do that." It hurt her, she said, and she tells him to "stop it, Daddy."

Dr. Nelligan then asked her whether or not she really lived in two houses or if she made that up. "No," Ami said seriously. "I really live in two houses." Then, she asked if Ami really had a dog named Rustle or if she had made that up. "No, I really do have a dog named Hustle," she said. Finally, she asked whether or not her father touching her had really happened or if she had made that up. "No," she said, "it really happened."

Dr. Nelligan asked Ami to pretend she could spend as much time as she wanted at her mommy's and daddy's houses. What would she do?

"Well," Ami said, "I would like to spend a little time with my daddy, but I think I would like to spend more time with my mommy." When asked why she felt this way, she said, "Well, I like my daddy, but I do lots of things with Mommy, and she talks to me a lot."

During her physical examination of Ami, Dr. Nelligan repeatedly asked her how this or that body part felt to her. When she got to her genital area, she said, "When my daddy touches me there, it hurts."

Upon close examination of this area, Dr. Nelligan found a "tear-drop shaped hymenal opening, and an eight-millimeter horizontal diameter with gentle anterior traction on the labia," along with "an abraded noted from 3 to

5 o'clock" and a "generous vaginal opening." She reported that after reading Dr. Reichert's examination notes from a year earlier, "It is worrisome that this child's genital examination has undergone marked changes in one year." Because of these changes, she recommended a follow-up examination in three to five weeks' time, and it would helpful, she wrote, if Ami could be brought in when there was discharge present. (See Children's Hospital Report, Appendix D.)

Meanwhile, my attorneys had scheduled a hearing to petition the court for protective orders for Ami, so that she would never be left alone with her father again. We now had Dr. Nelligan's report in addition to Dr. Greer's and Dr. Marion's, and most importantly, Diane Baird from the Kempe Center was trying to schedule an interactional assessment with everyone involved: Derek, social services, Dr. Adams, and so on. Things were finally coming together!

CHAPTER 22

New Attorneys, More Hearings, and Continued Use of PAS

A motion for a new hearing on our custody agreement had been denied, but for this hearing, many motions were before the court: we had moved for a new child therapist for Ami, for an evaluation of our case by a mental-health professional to judge whether the custody agreement was working (we had in mind a psychiatrist named Susan Van Scoyk), and a motion for the Kempe Center to evaluate all involved to review the allegations of sexual abuse. Derek had also filed motions to hold me in contempt for not paying Gail, for interfering with his visitation (when the police told me I could leave), and to further limit Ami's visitation time with me. In response, we had filed a motion to limit Derek's visitation time but more importantly to have a full visitation evaluation done.

On the day of the hearing, Officer Tim King and a teacher from Ami's school were set to testify on what they had heard from Ami regarding her abuse, and the three doctors from three different hospitals—Dr. Marion, Dr. Greer, and Dr. Nelligan—were also scheduled to testify on their physical findings on the sexual abuse. There would be a barrage of evidence verifying Derek's sexual abuse of Ami.

The morning before the hearing, my attorney Mary Jane called me to ask me to come to her office. She was very excited about a therapist/social worker she had met at a seminar she had attended in the mountains over the weekend. Little did I know that the seminar leader was Richard Gardner, author of Parental Alienation

Syndrome, which Derek's representatives were using as their bible. Gardner saw parent-child sexual abuse as an often benign activity and was reputed to say that sexually abused children sometimes enjoyed the experience. Therapists not very well trained in the area of sexual abuse were latching onto his ideas, which had never been recognized or verified by the American Psychological Association. The woman my attorney had met was Leona Kopetski, who, though I didn't know it at the time, was a disciple of Gardner's. (She would later contribute a chapter to the book, "The International Handbook of Parental Alienation Syndrome.") I did not have time to check her out. I had to trust my attorney's instincts. She was going to have Leona Kopetski testify and have her do the evaluation.

When we arrived at the courtroom, I was very nervous, and I kept asking Mary Jane if she was going to ask this or that question. Finally, she smiled, understanding why I was so nervous. She showed me her notes and told me not to worry. Unlike my previous attorney, she said she was prepared. I tried to relax. I had two good attorneys from Arapahoe County with good reputations. I had to trust them.

When they put Leona Kopetski on the stand, they told me that she was going say a lot of things I did not want to hear, but that I shouldn't show any emotion. I should just go along with it. As Ms. Kopetski answered questions, everything seemed to happen quickly. I kept asking Randy, "What about Ami? Everyone keeps forgetting about her! We are not a family. Why does she keep referring to us like we're a family and saying, 'family evaluation?'" I was confused. I had left him when Ami was six months old. I was also wondering why the policeman and the doctors weren't testifying. Leona Kopetski was taking all the court time, testifying on how we needed a family evaluation, while I knew that doctors were standing by to testify over the phone, along with the policeman and Ami's teacher. What was going on?

To my dismay, those witnesses never testified, and the judge ordered a family evaluation to take place. All of the sudden, the Kempe Center, which had lined up a date for Ami's physical evaluation, was out of the picture. Instead, my attorneys asked if Leona and her partner Claire Purcell could do the evaluation. I was extremely uncomfortable with what had just happened, but both my attorneys seemed elated and asked me if I would agree to Leona. I went along with it, thinking they must have known something I didn't. They were two highly respected attorneys— nothing like Ted Kaplysh—surely they knew what they were doing, or they wouldn't have been so happy about this decision.

But after the hearing, I sat in my car for almost two hours with Liz, who had come to court with me. I felt sick. I didn't understand why Ami wasn't being protected from her father and why the evidence against him never seemed to come out. "My attorneys were elated," I told her, "but I was sick that no one critical to my case had testified." We were back at square one with Ami in the hands of her molester, and no one was doing what was right by Ami! I looked at my friend and began to cry. "My God," I said. "What just happened? Nothing! Absolutely nothing! No testimony by police or preschool and no doctor reports!"

When I arrived home, my other friends had shown up at the house to see how the hearing had gone. Ami was at Derek's house. We were sitting around the table talking when Ami called. She talked to everyone there, including Jessica. The next day she told Jessica, who was a little older than she, that right after she got off the phone talking to her, her dad had touched her. I found this out from Jessica about a week later. So after we had been in court all day on this issue, he went home and molested her? How sick!

That same evening of the hearing, the phone rang. It was Diane Baird from the Kempe Center, asking if the court had confirmed the date they had set for their evaluation of Ami. I told her no, they had set it with someone named Leona Kopetski instead. "Leona Kopetski!" she screamed, and my heart sank. "Oh my God, Maralee. I hate to tell you this, but Leona Kopetski? She's known for never finding abuse and always siding with the male."

Now I was even sicker. I trusted Diane Baird. This woman knew the system and the people working in it. I immediately brought this up to my attorneys, and Diane Baird called them too. Mary Jane was extremely upset with me that Diane called her. As she saw it, we were building a solid case. She had urged the Kempe Center to become intimately involved and things looked like they were heading our way. She had given Kopetski a long list of professionals to contact as well as some important documents, including Derek's diaries—with all its revealingly inappropriate language—with explicit instructions to be sure to return them to me. Mary Jane seemed to feel confident that she would see my side of things.

After my first session with Leona, I could tell that this was not the direction it would be heading. She would not listen to a word I had to say. All she wanted to know about was my marriage, which had nothing to do with Ami being abused by her father. When I tried to tell her of my concerns for Ami's safety, both emotionally and physically, she once again ignored what I had to say.

I left her office, not letting her know that I was extremely upset, but as soon as I got into my car, I started crying. I don't know how I drove or where I was going, but I just kept driving. Eventually I realized I had driven to the Survivors United Network (SUN), which was a part of the Kempe Center. It had been founded by former Miss America Marilyn Van Derbur Atler (a survivor of thirteen years of incest) and

D.D. Harvey, a minister I had met a year earlier when I had desperately needed some advice. D.D. was the first person who had really listened intently to my pain, and since then, we had become very close. When I walked into the building and saw D.D., I really broke down. I rarely allowed myself to cry in front of others—usually I did so at night when I was alone. I always felt that I had to show I was strong and that the people working against me were not going to break my spirit. D.D. knew immediately that I was extremely upset. He grabbed my hand and led me to his office. I told him that my own attorneys had set me up with this woman who would not listen to anything I said. It was a re-enactment of exactly what I had gone through three-and-a-half years earlier with social services. I was back to square one. "I'm calling my attorneys right now," I said.

"No," he said. "Cool down first."

D.D. always had the ability to calm me down and knew the right things to say. After he and I talked, I went home and called my attorneys. I got Randy, and I lit into him. What the heck was going on? He reassured me that it was going well and told me to give it some time.

Why did my little girl still have to go to her father's house with no protection and with physical evidence that proved that he was abusing her?

Meanwhile, Ami's discharge was still severe and very uncomfortable for her. Children's Hospital believed the discharge to be abnormal and had suggested Ami be taken to University Hospital to see a sexual abuse expert there. They believed she had an object or foreign body lodged higher up in her vagina. At University they would give her a general anesthesia and insert a colposcope, which was a kind of microscope that enlarges objects about thirty-five times their size, into her vagina to determine if there were any abnormalities.

Ami's first appointment at University Hospital was scheduled with an expert in abuse. Her father showed up with two presents for Ami: she could have one before she went in and one when she came out. In other words, he was bribing her.

I pulled myself away and watched intently to see what other people saw and how he acted with Ami. I made myself forget what he had done and tried to observe him as an outsider. What I saw was remarkable: he seemed to be a wonderful father. He took control of Ami right away and kept her in his la-la land. No wonder nobody else could see right through him. If I had not witnessed Ami's cries, if I hadn't seen her clutching at her vaginal and anal areas all night long while crying out, "No! Daddy, don't. It's bad!" and if I hadn't seen the documentation that her father put "white stuff" in her that came from "his peanut," I too would think he was a wonderful father. He was darn good at mimicking one.

The staff at the hospital called me to go back with Ami, but Derek insisted that since he had custody, he would be the one going back with her. They ended up taking her into a room alone, while he called out to Ami outside the door to make her aware he was within hearing distance. I knew exactly what he was doing and told him to step away from the door.

When Ami came out, the doctor asked to see me. But again, Derek insisted that since he had custody, he would be making the decisions. The doctor asked him several questions about Ami as a baby, which of course he could not answer. I played along with him because I wanted to get the papers signed for the surgery so I was very submissive and let him take control of everything. I even spoke to him, although I really wanted to gag. He brought her a present. He said, "Watch this, Maralee," as he placed his hand on her head and moved her down towards the ground in a squat keeping his hand on her head. He then told her, "Okay, Ami, you can now come up," as he kept his hand on her head. "See she is my puppet and she will do whatever I want."

The next week, for her second appointment, I took Ami back to the hospital for her to see the anesthesiologist and to have her blood drawn. It was difficult for her; she was petrified of the needle and of her blood being drawn. It was so hard putting her through this. In the past she was not afraid of needles but now absolutely terrified. But she got through it, and her surgery was scheduled with Dr. White. This would be the surgery using the colposcope, and it would likely determine the source of Ami's discharge. It would probably provide indisputable physical evidence that she was being sexually abused.

The next day I called the hospital about a question, only to find that Derek had cancelled the surgery and had written a threatening letter to Dr. White. My attorneys called and told me he just wanted a second opinion, but the result was that the surgery was cancelled. Apparently, he had threatened the University Hospital doctor with a lawsuit, and she had refused to do the surgery and then was so angry that she refused to reschedule it. So now, I had to schedule it at Kaiser. My attorneys were dumbfounded. If I had not been on the ball, we would never have known until after the fact. Dr. Marion, who was the first doctor to see Ami, said she needed to be seen by a sexual abuse expert not from Kaiser; he himself was a Kaiser doctor. Dr. Greer from Humana Hospital had said the same thing; and the doctors and nurses at Children's Hospital had as well. Now the doctor was cancelling after the papers had been signed, and we had to take Ami to Kaiser where the father had decided.

Derek then scheduled an appointment through Kaiser with an OB/GYN who had never done one of these surgeries and only dealt with adults. Ami, poor thing, was rescheduled for a blood test. While at work, I called from the airport to talk to Ami, and she told me that the doctor at Kaiser had given her dad a tube to take a swab of her discharge. I stood at one of our ticket counters, in view of passengers, trying to remain calm. I told her that her dad was not to touch her there for any reason. I hung up, shaking, and immediately picked up the phone to call the doctor who had authorized this. Unbelievable! What kind of an idiot would authorize this man to take samples of her discharge with the knowledge of the Children's Hospital report?

I called the emergency number at Kaiser because my flight was getting ready to leave. I got another doctor on the phone who knew Montgomery, so I asked him to give Montgomery a message. "You tell Dr. Montgomery," I said, "that if she has authorized Mr. Walker, who is sexually abusing his little girl, to take swabs of her discharge, she had better think twice, and she will have a lot of answering to do. She is giving him a way out! 'Of course my fingers have been in her vagina,' he could say, 'I was told to take swabs by the doctor!'"

I call Mary Jane the next day, and she called Dr. Montgomery, who denied authorizing Derek to take a sample of the discharge. She said that Derek was only to take the samples from her panties. I knew this to be a lie because on a previous occasion, when Ami had gone to this same doctor for a cold, she had her discharge, and this doctor had told me you couldn't get a sample from her panties. Everything was being done behind my back and behind my attorneys' backs as well. They were always shocked to hear about the information I was finding out either by coincidence or luck or just by perseverance.

CHAPTER 23

Incredible Strength

By this time, it was close to Christmas. I wanted to make it a wonderful day for Ami, because I had a fearful sense of foreboding that it might be our last Christmas together. I called everyone in my family, asking them if they could all come to my house for Christimas day—for Ami's sake. I admit I put a lot of pressure on them, and it worked. Everyone except my sister Judy could make it.

Ami and I decorated the house together, inside and out. We put little white lights around the pine trees outside and around the front of the house as well. Ami and I had justseen a movie in which Chevy Chase put Christmas lights on his house and stapled his arm to the roof, so at one point, as I was on the ladder with a staple gun, I started yelling to Ami that I had just stapled my arm to the roof! She laughed and said, "I can't handle this. I'm going inside!"

Inside, we had a wonderful time decorating the house. I garlanded the staircase with maroon ribbons and lights and the fireplace mantle with more of the garland and lights. We had a beautiful tree that took up most of the living room. Ami took out all the ornaments, found the ones she remembered from when she was a baby, and put each one in a special place on the tree. We played Christmas music the whole time and danced together while baking fudge and icing Christmas cookies. It was tradition in my family to make beautiful plates of Christmas sweets and deliver them to all the special people in our lives. So I broke Ami in on the tradition, and we delivered our plates to friends, wishing them all a Merry Christmas.

When my family arrived, they were impressed with all that we had done, considering what was going on in our lives, but I told them that I wanted this Christmas to be one that Ami would always remember. She loved it. She ran all over the house playing with her cousins. She got a kick out of watching home movies from when I was a little girl, and we all laughed and laughed. She and her cousins actually got to see Santa's sleigh in the sky—an airplane with a sleigh and Santa trailing behind it. The kids ran for the window screaming, "It's Santa, it's Santa!" They squealed like crazy and ran through the house.

Unlike me, Ami had a great singing voice, and she decided to sing a song for the whole family. She and her cousin Kristin had been entertaining us with dances they had made up all day. "Wait," I said, "let me get the movie camera." Ami's face was beaming. She wore an emerald-green velvet dress, and her face was lit up with her baby blue eyes and freckles on her nose. My old Ami was back. As clear as a bell she belted out the song, "I'll be home for Christmas. You can count on me." Her voice was so clear and beautiful that the whole family started to cry. She had obviously been practicing the song for years, and it came from her heart.

After all the excitement of the day, the kids got in sleeping bags under the adorned tree, their faces pink from the cozy fire at the other end of the room, and Uncle Alvie told them bedtime stories. My house was full of family in every room. With the nightmare we had lived through and the nightmare to come, no one could take away this special day that Ami and I had shared with family.

The next morning, the kids were up early and opened gifts, but as time went by, I could see Ami's facial expressions changing. She was very sad that she had to leave with her dad. She never once complained, but her face showed it all. I took her up to change her back into her Christmas dress, wishing that she was going to someone else's house for Christmas, because her father's house was so depressing and gloomy, wishing she could be around someone else's family and not alone with him. When she had to leave, she went over to her grandpa, sat on his lap and hugged and kissed him. Then she went around the room to the rest of her family members, sadly hugging and kissing them good-bye.

Later that day, after her father had picked her up, I called her about 6:00 p.m., and she was already asleep in bed. The next day, when I asked her about

Christmas with her dad, she said they hadn't gone anywhere to visit, and he only had a couple of small gifts for her. I didn't care about gifts, but I did care that she had such a gloomy time at her father's that she didn't even want to talk about it.

◆ ◆ ◆ ◆ ◆ ◆

The Rockettes were still doing their Christmas show in New York, and since Ami loved dancing, I really wanted her to see the show. I decide to take Ami to see my sister Judy in New York. While we were there, I debated whether to call her paternal grandfather who had not seen her since her birth and was very ill. I figured he wasn't the one abusing Ami, and she should be able to see her grandfather, so I called him. But he refused to see her. He told me that Derek had asked him not to.

Still, we had a wonderful time in New York. We got all dressed up and dined at the River Café, a five-star restaurant where my sister was the manager. Ami thought we were on a real boat and kept looking in the river for Ariel. She was a pure delight to be with. We went to Rockefeller Center because she wanted to ice skate in her beautiful black velvet dress with white lace sculpting hem.

When we returned home, I found that her father had been diligently working on Ms. Kopetski and the doctors. There was a message for me from Leona to meet with me the next morning. I wondered why.

The next morning,Derek called to tell me that the session was also with him. Then I was extremely upset. Why would she need to see the two of us together all of a sudden? Why did I have to sit in the same room with the person who was raping my child?

I gave Ami a bath and sent her off to pre-school. When I arrived at Kopetski's office, I was aggravated—to say the least. Leona took one look at me and said, "You seem a little distressed." Well, yes, I was!

"First of all," I told her, "I knew nothing of this meeting until last night, and now I find out this morning it is joint. I'm concerned with how long you both have planned this meeting and"—I turned to Derek—"just how long have you known about it, Derek? A couple of weeks?" When Derek didn't answer me, I said, "I see you have your briefcase with all your printouts and typed questions you want to ask." I turned back to Ms. Kopetski. "You see, this is all too familiar. I have been through all this before. So how long have you known?" Derek still said nothing, and finally Leona told me she had left me a message about two days earlier. "I was in New York with Ami," I said. "I'm sure Mr. Walker immediately called you and informed you of that."

Kopetski then began her interrogation. Why had I gone to New York? I told her I had taken Ami to see the Rockettes and my sister. We had not had a vacation for two years. Very angrily, she asked, "Why did you call Derek's father? Don't you think that was cruel to Derek?"

"No," I said, "I wasn't thinking of Derek, only of Ami. And I was trying to be nice. He's her grandfather."

"You did not talk to the media or anyone while you were in New York?"

"No! I did not!" "Are you sure?"

"Yes, I am sure." Here we go again, I thought. It's me being interrogated while the rapist sits there smugly with the professionals on his side.

She then questioned me on whether or not I had been to the Kempe Center that week. I had not, but what business was it of hers if I had? The Kempe Center was a National Center for abuse, with trained professionals in sexual abuse working there.

I was getting irritated at her line of questioning, so at that moment I handed her an issue of Lear magazine, which had a twenty-page, in-depth article on incest. I was hoping to open her eyes to her ignorance, maybe provide her with a little more education on top of her master's degree in social work. I had learned to have little respect for people with an MSW. I kept running into those who had never been married, had no children, had no common sense, and had marginal intellects, and yet they had all been "trained." Trained for what, may I ask?

"Have you read this?" I asked her. "I suggest you read it. It will enlighten you to my case."

Her response was "I read plenty. Where did you get this?" I told her it was from a friend, and she asked, "What friend?"

Now she was pushing it. I said, "From a friend you don't know!"

Then I then turned to her and in front of Derek I said, "Ms. Kopetski, why don't you explain to me why my little girl wakes up in the middle of the night many, many times screaming, 'No! No! Daddy, don't. Owie! It's bad!' and grabbing her vagina and rear end, or why she says her daddy puts white stuff in her that comes from the peanut in his hands? Why don't you explain why she screams and cries when she has to go with him and sometimes when she goes she is in a trance- like state?"

"Are you saying she has a split personality?" she asked. "No," I said, "I am not a doctor. I can't determine that. But there are definitely two very different children. Sometimes she is okay, and sometimes she is not. I've seen a real change in her in the last year."

Derek started to say something, but Kopetski stopped him and said, "No, don't even try." He then brought out the vial a doctor had given him, so he could take swabs of her discharge. Of course, this was for show; he knew this would anger me. I kept my cool and told him I didn't think it was the time or place to discuss that. He kept it out, insisting on showing me how to use it. Now I became angry. This pig was abusing his own little four-year-old girl, and Dr. Montgomery and Dr. Campbell had authorized him to take swabs of the discharge that he himself had caused. I calmly pulled myself back together. I knew what he was doing.

I said, "You will not be taking any samples of her discharge. What Kaiser doctor would authorize such a thing?"

He then said, "Well, we have an appointment today."

I told Derek and Leona what Doctor Marion had said: that taking Ami to Kaiser would be like taking a Ferrari into a Volkswagen dealership. She needed a specialist in sexual abuse. Kopetski then jumped in and said that Kaiser doctors were good doctors.

"I am not saying they aren't good doctors," I said. "However, I have my concerns about Derek's private doctor, Dr. Montgomery." She was another woman he had manipulated—in this case into letting him take swabs of her discharge. "I will not be taking her!" I said.

Kopetski shrieked, "Derek, you go ahead and go to the appointment!" And to me she said, "There will be no colposcopy."

From that point on, I was told there were to be no other exams of Ami unless they were court-ordered. I had just spent $8,000 getting a court order for Ami to be seen by a specialist. I figured I had better go check out this doctor because as soon as Ami was back in her father's control, he would schedule her exam through her.

Following our meeting with Kopetski, I went immediately to meet with Dr. Campbell and asked if I may speak alone to her. I asked her why she would authorize Derek to take swabs of Ami's discharge, knowing that the discharge had been caused by his molestation of her. She assured me that she did not and would not have done that. When I asked her who had authorized it, she said possibly Dr. Montgomery. She was being evasive and not helpful at all.

When Derek came into the room, he was surprised that I was there. In front of them both, I brought up the question of who had given him the authority to take samples from Ami. Dr. Campbell repeated that she did not approve of this. He became very upset and told her he would do it anyway. "I know what you are doing," I said. "You want a medical excuse for why you've touched Ami."

When it came to making arrangements for Ami's surgery, Derek tried to schedule it three months down the road. I suppose so he could make sure she had healed first. During the conversation, I found out quite by coincidence that he had scheduled an earlier appointment with Dr. Campbell, so they had already planned everything out. I now felt completely marginalized from the process. She said that she would not be performing the same surgery as Dr. White, the specialist, was going to. She was going to use a different scope and would not be looking for sexual abuse. She was told by the social worker that there had been no court order to look for sexual abuse. I was shocked by this; there had not been a social worker legally assigned to our case in almost two years. "What social worker?" I asked.

Dr. Campbell and Derek tried to change the subject, but I didn't let it go. I repeated, "What social worker are you talking about?"

Derek's face turned ghost white. Judging from their body language, both he and the doctor had become very uptight. I insisted that she tell me who had called her. At first, she said she couldn't recall, so I said, "Wouldn't it be in your file?" She stumbled through her file and pulled out the name Leona Kopetski. My hair stood up on my neck. "She is not a social worker on this case," I said. "She is doing an evaluation. She had no right to call you and tell you any such thing. This is totally out of line!"

It was Friday at 4:00 p.m. They had scheduled the surgery for Monday morning at 6:00 a.m. I was frantic to stop this surgery. Why put Ami through a surgery with a non-expert and without even using a colposcope?

I ran to the phone to call my attorneys, but they were no help. They were more lost than I was, even more so because I had been the one finding out all the information lately. If I hadn't been calling and checking on things, everything would have happened without anyone being the wiser.

I hung up and called Dr. White at University Hospital to explain what kind of surgery was going to take place. Dr. White wasn't in, so I spoke with another doctor familiar with our case. She told me that I had to stop the surgery. I told her that would be impossible. Derek had custody of Ami for the three days before the surgery and for the day of the surgery.

There was nothing I could do about this. After worrying about this all weekend, I met Ami at the hospital, and,for her sake, I was calm. I did not want her to go through any more stress than she had already been subjected to. When they finally carted her down for her surgery in a little red wagon with her head covered and a gown on, she hugged and kissed me, holding onto me tightly. Then the nurse said, "Give your dad a kiss,"and she turned her head away and wouldn't let him kiss her.

Ruth had come with me, and we waited together for Ami to come out. I was dying I was so worried about her. When she finally came out of the anesthesia and we could see her, she started crying out, "Mommy! Mommy!"

I ran to her bedside, but her father shoved me away. I went around him to get close to her and was able to hold her. My heart was aching. My poor, perfect angel. What she had to go through because of this evil, hateful sociopath.

Her father and Kopetski had determined his days with Ami before and after the surgery, but Ami was pleading to go home with me. I turned to him and said, "Please let her go home with me. She needs her mommy." Ami chimed in, begging for me to carry her out.

Dr. Campbell then came in and said that the surgery had gone fine. Ami did have a little white discharge in small amounts, she said, but nothing else. Then she handed Derek a cream to put on Ami. I looked at her with disdain, and she then told him to have her put it on herself. I was once again in disbelief. As she handed him the tube, I grew so furious thatI was beginning to hate all of society.

I picked up Ami and left the room with her. As I carried her out, Derek motioned for the nurse to follow us, in case I ran home with Ami when I didn't have visitation. Ruth was waiting just outside the recovery room with a stuffed animal for Ami. When we came close to the front door, Derek grabbed Ami out of my arms, and she became very frightened. I looked at him and said, "Don't take her out like this.

Go and get your car and drive it up front. I'll hold her." He handed Ami back to me and told the nurse to keep an eye on us. I looked up at the nurse and said, "He is a very, very sick man!"

When Derek returned, I asked Ami if she wanted to take her stuffed animal back with her or if she wanted me to take it home with me. Most gifts that went home to her dad's house were destroyed or lost. I think he was afraid I had hidden a taping device in each one. Ami replied, "Take it home with you, Mommy."

At that, her dad started freaking out like a madman. "That's it!" he screamed. "That's it! I heard that!" and he ripped Ami out of my arms. I looked over at Ruth, dumbfounded. It had been so long since I had been forced to witness one of his out-of-the-blue outbursts. I didn't move. I was too shocked at his craziness. Finally, I moved quickly out to the car, wanting to say good-bye to Ami, but when I pulled on her car door to give her a kiss, I found that he had locked her in. He then shoved me up against the car and brushed me to the side.

I had hardly talked to this man in two years except when subjected to by Ms. Kopetski. But I wasn't going to take being shoved aside for the second time that day. I reached out suddenly, grabbed the lapels of his coat, and shoved him up against the car. "You are so sick!" I screamed. And at that moment, I felt as though I could have lifted him up off the ground. I literally wanted to kill him. I saw him look over his shoulder and thought suddenly that it could have all been a setup—he had the police waiting for me to lose it—so I immediately let go. But nobody was there. If I hadn't thought that, I probably wouldn't have stopped. I might have tried to kill him.

Later that day, when I called to talk to Ami, she quietly whispered on the phone. "I have something to tell you when I come home tomorrow. I can't tell you now."

"Okay, honey!" I said. She was supposed to stay home and rest, but he had taken her to the movie Hook for literally the twentieth time.

The next day, when she was with me, she said, "Mom, remember when I said I had something to tell you?"

"Yeah," I said, dreading what she might tell me.

"Well, I was so glad when you hit my dad. I was mad at him all day.!"

At that moment, I realized that she had never seen me fight with her dad in any way, no yelling even. She didn't know what all the papers meant or what it meant when I met with my attorneys. Nothing of what I had been doing had any meaning to her. The only time she had seen me fight for her was on that day.

◆ ◆ ◆ ◆ ◆ ◆

The few days after the surgery, Kopetski called me at home to tell me to come to her office on Saturday so she could go over the results of the evaluation that she and her partner Dr. Claire Purcell had written up. Dr. Claire Purcell had met with Ami and me for a half hour, during which time Ami colored, and Dr. Purcell asked one question after another about my marriage. I didn't think it was appropriate for Ami to hear most of my answers to her questions, so I wound up having to spell out most of our conversation as we talked.

I politely asked Ms. Kopetski if she could schedule this during the week because I could not be there on the weekend. I was working then, and I couldn't afford to take the time off. However, I had every day during the week free. But she insisted I be there; they had no other time available. So I went and wound up losing $700 in pay. Because once again, they had all the cards, and I didn't want them to claim that I wasn't cooperating.

I then called my friend Duke, one of the captains at Continental. He had followed my case for over a year, ever since he had first come with me to Kempe and we met Dr. Richard Krugman there. Duke said he would be happy to come with me and be of some support.

When that Saturday came—March 22, 1992—a blizzard had hit Denver, and the roads were icy. As Duke and I approached Kopetski's office, I was very anxious. I knew that Derek had already wrapped these two ignorant women around his finger.

Duke looked a lot like John Wayne, a very large and somewhat confident-looking man. When Kopetski and Dr. Purcell saw him, they quickly and loudly objected. "Oh, no!" they said. "He cannot come to this meeting." They were quite surprised that I had brought someone with me.

I said, "Why not?"

Her response was, "He just can't!"

Duke then said, "I know all about this case."

Kopetski then said that there were things about Ami and Derek that would be said that he could not hear.

"Who are you?"

"I am Duke," he said. "I am closely related to this case," he said.

They refused to let Duke in with me. However, on another occasion they had a private session with Derek and his supposed past fiancée, Pam, the woman who would do anything to cover for him. Pam and Derek weren't evenseeing each other at this time and had not for a year. Now he was bringing her to Leona to make him look stable.

I then told Leona that I was going to call my attorneys, but I couldn't get a hold of either one. So I decided I would go in and listen to what they had to say. But the first time they said something I didn't want to hear, I would walk out. I thought to myself, "Here we go again, more punishment from these heartless, inept, incompetent, overpowered, degenerate women."

As I entered their office and sat down, Ms. Kopetski said, "We do not believe there is any abuse. However, you did go through something horrible in your divorce." Yes nodding, and thinking to myself domestic violence, emotional abuse, stalking and physical abuse.

With that statement, I quickly got up, walked toward the door, and called down for Duke to come up. They ran for the door, waving their arms, screaming out, "No, No! You can't do this!"

As we stood in the doorway, I said, "Do you realize that I have been divorced for almost five years? The divorce has nothing to do with child abuse. You two ladies don't know me at all. You know nothing about me or who I am. I had full custody of Ami before the abuse. And furthermore, do you think I would give four years of my life, fighting with my body and soul, if this was not really happening? For what? You two have just touched the surface. You have no idea what you're dealing with. Why don't you explain to me why my child was waking up in the night for over two years, screaming out, 'No, daddy, don't!' while violently grabbing at her vaginal area. Explain why you never contacted the daycare provider or the police to hear about what they had witnessed and learned or why you completely ignored doctor reports and police reports! Why does she have abrasions in her vagina and a laceration with an eight- millimeter opening and discharge described by a physician to be that of an adult female who is sexually active? Explain this!"

Silence.

"Do you hear my voice? I just want to make sure that it goes down on record that I am not hysterical. Okay ladies? Oh, and one more thing: This will all be out within a year. I promise you both that you will have to answer to Ami and me for what you have done."

As I walked out with Duke, I walked tall and confident.

The minute we got into the car, I crumbled.

CHAPTER 24

An Abuser's Tactic: Illegal Ex parte Hearing

On Sunday morning, before I went to work, I called to talk to Ami, but her father hung up on me. Usually, I would not play his games, but this time I called back and said, "It is court-ordered to let me talk to her. I demand to speak to my little girl!"

He said, "I'll see you in court on Monday," and hung up.

Everything this man had said he was going to do, he had done. Was it possible he had scheduled a hearing for the next day without me knowing about it? He had worked and manipulated the courts so far, so why not now?

I had to leave for work. I was scheduled on a flight to Spokane, Washington, but now I was extremely upset and cried the whole way to the airport to check in for my flight. When I got there, I called Mary Jane Cox at home and related what Derek had just told me. She reassured me not to worry. There was no way to get a hearing that quickly. I told her that if Derek said there was a hearing, there probably was a hearing. Even my mom, who I got on the phone, told Mary Jane that Derek always meant what he said. I called my mom from the airport and she called Mary Jane and said if Derek said he has a hearing Monday he has a hearing.

I went on my trip to Spokane, and when I got there, I called my attorney's office and got the paralegal, Lynn. She told me, "There's an emergency hearing on the phone onyour case right now to take your daughter away."

I needed to talk to Mary Jane, but she was home sick, so I tried to get a hold of Randy. I thought I might throw up, and my heart was racing. I told the paralegal that whatever she did, she should not take that phone call. I told her I was not in the state. "You tell Randy not to take that phone call." She told me that Judge Deanna Hickman was on the other end, holding. I said, "I don't give a damn. This is my child! I demand he is not to take that phone call!"

She said, "I have to go, Maralee."

I had to go, so I ran for my flight, but the whole time I was on the plane, I felt sick. My heart was pounding, and panic set in. My God, how could they do this? What in the hell was going on? I flew out of Spokane, holding back the tears, but I knew I couldn't hold back much longer. I ran for the bathroom and locked myself in, and as the engines of the airplane began to roar, so did I, moaning deeply as if someone very dear to me had just died.

Once we landed in Denver, I did not want to make the phone call to my attorney until I was at home. I wanted someone with me when I made that call. I called my friends Kim and Liz over, and then I called Randy at home.

"What happened?" I asked.

"Maralee," he said, "you lost your child."

CHAPTER 25

Flipping the Tables

Incredibly, Kopetski and Purcell had rushed over their seventy-page report to the judge with a full docket, forcing an emergency ex parte hearing without notifying my lawyers or the guardian ad litem. They claimed that Ami was in imminent danger of being taken by her mother and fleeing the state. (This would have been difficult for me to do, obviously, since I myself was out of the state at the time.) The judge, believing them, had immediately signed the order. If I was even considering running with her, I would have run when she was two.

The order by judge Deanna Hickman from the Kopetski report states:

> A. It is inconceivable that (the child) could have had the perverse experiences and physical injury by her father that her mother describes and still behave toward him and with him as she does. (The mother's personality characteristics are consistent with descriptions given by Wakefield and Underwager about parents who make false accusations of sexual abuse during custody disputes. They are also consistent with paren- tal alienation syndrome, as defined by Gardner and as developed from experience by this team. (Id, p.69). It is very important that the mother be held financially responsible for all the costs of procedures related to litigation (the mother should pay child support).

The court issued this emergency order after considering their testimony and the report behind my back. The court finds their evaluation, and investigation, to be very thorough, accurate, credible, and professionally well done, in review of the history and evidence. Where were all the police reports, three hospital reports, and at least twenty other professionals and witnesses my attorneys had given them to review?

Kopetske and Purcell quoted in the report their renowned mentors, Underwager and Wakefield, whom have written two books on child sexual abuse, which are false. Underwager has been quoted as saying that "sex with children is a responsible choice for the individual." The supreme court held that "Underwager's analysis and conclusions are not accepted by the scientific community, making it appropriate for a trial judge to preclude him from testifying."

Paidika Brief The Journal of the Pedophilia quotes from Underwager and Wakefield, "Pedophiles can make the assertion that the pursuit of intimacy and love is what they choose. With boldness they can say, 'I believe this is in fact part of God's will. Pedophiles need to become more positive and make the claim that pedophilia is an acceptable expression of God's will for love and unity among human beings.'"

As you can see, the child's rights and what sexual abuse does to the child is never mentioned, and people like Kopetski and Purcell are destroying children, not thinking for a moment of what child sexual abuse does to a child. The court order also quoted Kopetski's report about the mother's personality. ("The mother's") personality characteristics are consistent with descriptions given by Wakefield and Underwager about parents who make false accusations of sexual abuse during custody disputes. They are also consistent with parent alienation syndrome, as defined by Gardner and as developed from experience of the team (Id. P.69). In the report, a child who had been abused by her father would not volunteer spontaneously that she has fun with and loves her father. It is inconceivable that (the child) could have had the perverse experiences and physical injury by her father that the mother describes and still behave toward him and with him as the child does.

Kopetski and Purcell did not mention any of the doctor reports, daycare provider reports, police reports, foster care reports, family and friends, or any of the therapist reports who believed my child was being abused. Obviously, the custody evaluators are not very educated in child abuse or the accommodation theory when the child is forced to live with the abuser. (See witness list Appendix D).

Most child sexual abuse is incestuous. Perpetrators are overwhelmingly male, and victims are overwhelmingly female. Fathers are the largest group of offenders, and paternal incest is "potentially most detrimental." At the same time, fathers are the group least likely to be held accountable. Numerically, biological fathers are the most prevalent. The mother who raises the charge of incest finds herself in a catch-22. The allegation suggests that she did not adequately tend to her child's safety. To do nothing now that she has the knowledge is to ignore the child's efforts to obtain help. She must keep the child from private, unsupervised time with the father or fail as a protector. If she denies the perpetrator all opportunity to molest the child and determinedly seeks to build a legal case, she is seen as sacrificing the child to endless interrogations, examinations, and emotional trauma for the sake of attacking the perpetrator. If she fails to sustain the accusation, he is likely to get custody of the child. In other words, "There seems to be no safe way to raise the possibility of sexual abuse."iv

I was speechless and began sobbing.

"Why, Randy? How can they do this? What grounds do they have? Why did you take the phone call?"

"I had to!"

"You have known Kopetski for a long time," I said. "She is known for siding with the male and never finding abuse. If you have known her for so long, why didn't you know that part of her? Give me some answers!"

"Maralee," Randy said, "you come first thing in the morning, and we will let you know what we will do to attack Kopetski's report, and we'll go from there."

The next morning, I arrived at my attorney's office with another good friend, Janice. She went with me to listen to what my attorneys said because I felt that I might not be coherent enough to hear everything clearly. My lawyers told me that they were just sick about what had happened and that they planned to attack Kopetski's report. Mary Jane just said that Leona had dropped the ball. That was a lot of help. I had just lost my child to a pedophile who happened to be her father, and she was telling me that Leona had "dropped the ball." That's it? It seemed I was surrounded by clueless people.

After discussing what they had to do and explaining that Randy had had no choice but to take the phone call, they told me that Leona's report had a lot of holes in it, and it could be torn apart.

I spent the rest of the day going through the report and correcting the un truths. It was so hard to stomach. The first thirty pages, which were about our marriage, were pretty accurate. The next twenty or so pages were about Derek, describing him as a man who could practically walk on water—he could have invented the polio vaccine for all they knew. Their conclusion was that Derek could better meet Ami's needs than I could. I guess if you sexually abused your child, that made you a better parent, and the child should be taken away from her mommy and her grandparents and all her relatives and friends. As I read through this report, I crossed out, underlined, and filled in a great deal of information that Kopetski and Purcell had conveniently left out of their report—numerous reports, police reports, doctors' reports with physical evidence, teacher's reports and dozens of witnesses. Once again, the issue of abuse had been ignored, and I was the villain for trying to protect my child.

From 9:00 a.m. to 6:00 p.m., I poured over this report. I read every page, every word. My conclusion? I had been stripped of my child for no apparent reason. I had no illness or deficiency that would harm my child. All I had done was to believe my child whereas they had chosen to believe her father. There was no mention of the Children's Hospital report or police reports; there was just a brief mention that Ami had stated to Dr. Claire Purcell after her father had dropped her off that she did not like her Dad because he touched her. Dr. Purcell, not wanting to hear this, stated, "But Ami, you seemed to like your dad so much when he was here last time." Her response, according to the report, was "I pretended for that one day." She had also been asked to finish some "stems"—for instance, "I wish my dad…" Ami's response was "…would stop touching me!" Ami also was quoted as saying her mommy said a lot of people were trying to help her.

The therapist responded by asking, "Who are they?"

"I don't know."

They also stated that I had taken Ami to "dozens" of exams. It was later proven in court that I had taken her only twice in three years when she had severe discharge. The other exams had been court ordered. So where else had they gotten that information from but Derek Walker, who they quote throughout their report. When Kopetski was later asked in court where she had gotten the information that there had been "dozens" of evaluations, she pointed to Derek and said, "Mister Walker."

The next day, my mom flew into Denver to be with me. I told her I was very worried about Ami. I didn't know what these people were telling her about me or what kind of shock she would be in when I next saw her. In the report they mentioned that even after just two days with her father, she would ask them when she could see her mother. She could not wait to be with me again.

I took my mother to my attorney's office so she could see the report for herself. At 11:00 a.m., there was to be a phone conference regarding my visitation. Mary Jane took the phone call. There was no arguing or questioning the judge's decision. It was purely to set up my visitation. This had already been set in stone, as if I were a criminal. I remained silent as I was given what you could call a mother's death sentence. The judge, Deanna Hickmann, said that I could see Ami one hour a week, supervised, and that I was to pay eighty dollars an hour to a social worker named Bob Hovenden to supervise the visits. This was a judge who could not possibly have read a seventy-page report on a Monday morning with a full docket, and now she was telling me I could see Ami one hour a week, supervised.

I asked Mary Jane, "Aren't you going to ask for an emergency hearing to deal with the Kopetski report?" I felt sick and frustrated. After all the work that Dennis and I had done to find a good attorney, this one was being about as helpful as Ted had been.

Mary Jane told me she would handle it. She set up a meeting with Diane Baird of the Kempe Center, but when Mary Jane asked Kopetski and Purcell permission to send their report to the Kempe Center, they refused to do so, saying that the consent must be signed by Derek on behalf of himself and Ami. Furthermore, they refused to attend any such meeting and refused to respond to the Kempe's Center's invitation for them to attend along with all the professionals involved in this case. (See letter from Kempe Center and a threatening letter if Kempe proceeded Appendix D).

◆◆◆◆◆◆

A month later, Mary Jane told me that my case had taken a toll on her. She was having problems at home. Just like Ted, she was going to have to withdraw from my case. Mary Jane, not the type of woman to have tears in her eyes, now did, and she handed me a huge box of very organized files.

I felt devastation so unbearable that it is hard for me to write about it even now.

Randy and Mary Jane told me they had set me up with a different attorney who handled my type of case. I begged them to stay on, but they refused.

So I went to meet the attorney they had chosen for me. He was indeed familiar with these kinds of cases, and he also knew the people who I had been dealing with. He said that they were a clique. I could have searched all of Denver, and I wouldn't have found a worse group of people to deal with. He described how they acted even before I had told him what had happened in my case. He would have been an excellent lawyer, but he would not take my case pro bono and was very expensive. I decided I would have to represent myself. When I gave him the facts of my case and the motions that were filed by dates in a chronological order from memory, he said, "I have never known anyone to be able to do that unless they were an attorney on the case." He was very impressed. I wanted to hire him, but he also said another $40,000.

CHAPTER 26

A Mother and Child's Love Survives

My first supervised visit with Ami, now four and a half years old, was absolutely heart wrenching. My mom went with me, and she waited in the car. I was so sick I didn't think I would make it. I once again pulled myself together. It was held in the very same building that housed the office of my former attorney Ted Kaplysh. I walked into the building and saw the same elevator door I had kicked over and over when I lost custody a year earlier, only on the penthouse level.

When I came in, Ami did not seem overjoyed to see me although she hugged and hugged me. I wondered what they had done to my baby. She had asked me to bring her kitty—I guess she had been crying for her kitty quite often. When she saw Sarah, her kitty, she hugged her over and over, saying, "I am your mommy, and I love you. I will never leave you." I felt as though she was transferring her feelings onto her kitty and trying to suppress her feelings for me, as if she was not allowed to cry over her mommy.

I got on the floor beside her and I said, "I am your mommy, and I love you. I did not leave you." Oh God, what could I say? I wasn't allowed to talk about the case, and I didn't know what they were brainwashing her with. Oh Ami, be strong, honey. Hang on to our love. You know the truth.

I looked into her eyes and saw that they were glazed over. She wasn't really there with me. The pain was overwhelming, but I felt the need to be strong for her. I had to hold myself together for Ami's sake.

At the end of our hour-long visit, something happened to break the spell. When we walked to the balcony of the building, which faced the street where

I parked my car, Ami saw my car and saw her grandma there. She lit up and began screaming out as loud as she could, "Grandma! Grandma! Please, I want my grandma!" This was the most normal reaction I had seen out of her. Bob told her she couldn't see her grandma right then, and she began jumping up and down, her feet leaving the ground. My mom got out of the car, but Bob motioned for her not to come in and told her to wait downstairs. He would have to get approval first. I looked at him, incredulous. Approval for what? The judge had not said that my mom couldn't see Ami. Ami then went to the corner of the room, faced the wall, and began to cry. To that point, I had not seen a tear. We went downstairs so she could see her grandma for a minute before the visit was over.

That would be my status from that point on: a single hour of visitation a week, every Wednesday after school at 4:00, with someone supervising our every move. But not only that: I was allowed only one phone call a week, and for only ten to fifteen minutes while her father listened in on us. Wasn't this incredible? The pedophile could listen in on our phone conversations. During these conversations, sometimes Ami would sound pretty good; other times she was very sad and withdrawn. She would try very hard to be happy. She would say something about us, become very sad and quiet, and then she would try to laugh. It was all so heartbreaking.

She would ask me to come to her school and see her, and I would tell her I couldn't, but I was not allowed to explain to her why. I didn't know what sick "supposed" professionals as Dr. Adams, her dad, Leona Kopetski, and these people had told her, except that we could not see each other because her mom and dad fought. After my second visit, I took Bob Hovenden aside and asked him if I could tell Ami the truth, that it was not because her dad and I were fighting—it had nothing to do with how her dad and I were getting along—it was because the social workers, judges, and psychologists didn't believe her and didn't believe me. Bob said, "That is your side of the story. Their side is that you have coached her." With that, I saw that he wasn't a neutral social worker looking out for the best interest of the child. He had already made up his mind not to believe Ami or me and to go with anything the others said. This was truly a corrupt industry. And the guardian ad litem, the one person who was truly supposed to look out for

Ami's best interest, was again just a pawn for the social service gang. In two years, Paula Tomko had seen Ami and me together just once for fifteen minutes. She had spoken to me once for five minutes and never returned my phone calls. She had seen Ami three times, each time with Derek. Once during these supervised visits, when Ami begged Bob Hovenden if she could please go home to my house, Bob told her he'd have to talk to Paula Tomko about it. Ami had said, "Who is Paula Tomko?" However, she was in the court continually filing motions for her fees to be paid by the courts or our taxpayers' money.

After I filed motions pro-se to get permission for a year, Bob was able to get permission for my parents to visit Ami, and when we showed up on a sunny summer day, Ami was waiting for us on the terrace outside Bob's office, three stories up. When she saw her grandma and grandpa with their basset hound Beau, she started jumping off the ground and screaming out, "Grandma! Grandpa! Oh!" We all had a great visit together, although this prison like confinement was difficult for my parents. When it came time for Ami to leave, she shut down—no tears, no emotions. She just walked out. I saw that she was protecting herself. Her grandma and grandpa had been two of the most important people in her life, providing her with unconditional love since her birth. My mom turned to me and said, "What has he done to her?"

On another visit, when we were reading books together, Bob suggested to Ami that she read the books on the bottom shelf. "They are about feelings," he said.

Ami said, "I don't like books about feelings. I don't like to feel anything."

I pulled her close to me and just held her tight. In one of Bob's reports he states that Ami is clearly upset that she could not have more time with her mom (e.g. "I miss my mom, I want to go to your house. I want you to be my first-grade teacher, I love you, I really miss you, tell the police to come and get me; I'd like to judo chop the judge; it doesn't feel good seeing you for only two hours").

As the visits progressed, she started coming out of her shell a little more. We hugged each other tight every time, so glad to see each other and then so sad to leave. She would ask why she couldn't come home with me. She wanted to see her room and her house. She told Bob that she only wanted to be with her mom and she only liked her mom's kisses and no one else's. Once she held up a dandelion she had picked, made a wish, and blew on it. Her wish was that she could always be with her mom. When I bought her an American Beauty Doll she had been wanting for some time, she said it was in her basement and her dad had destroyed it and the head was off her doll. I had a wonderful picture of her and her cousin Ryan on the beach in Hawaii when they were both holding hands. I had it made into a poster for her room and had it professionally framed. It looked like a post card and was expensive to create, just as her doll was expensive to purchase. She told me he broke it putting it into the car.

During one visit she said, "My dad told me that you tell me to say bad things."

"Ami, honey," I said, "have I ever told you to say bad things?"

"No!"

"Just keep telling the truth, honey."

Two weeks after that, Ami pleaded with Bob for him to leave us alone together. When he refused, she asked him why, and he answered, "Courts and judges."

"I don't like the courts and the judges," Ami said angrily. "They are bad. I hate the judge. The judge is bad and stupid." By this point, I always had a wire on me, so when my local news station later ran a story on us, this and several other parts of the tape were played.

At the end of that visit, Bob told Ami to kiss her mommy good-bye, and Ami threw a fit. "I am not leaving here with anyone but my mom," she said.

During another visit, she told me she was going to whisper something to me on the phone. The next time we talked, she whispered, "When am I coming home?" Derek, listening in on our conversation, immediately yelled at her and frightened her and hung up the phone.

On other visits, she began to show more emotions. In fact, she would sometimes regress into a baby state and ask me to just hold her. She would get very angry and say, "I only want to be with my mom! Mommy, will you carry me in?" She was now a tall five-year-old and a little difficult to carry. But this was what she needed, so I let her regress and just went along with it wherever she was.

During some of my visits, I had started to notice that she was grabbing at her crotch area, a familiar sign to me. Then on one visit, she told me in a quiet voice, "Mom, I have my discharge."

In a very alarming voice, Bob said to her, "Should I tell your dad?"

Ami's eyes widened, and she suddenly became very frightened. "No!" she screamed.

After the visit, I said, "Bob, why would you do that to her? She is frightened. If she starts to open up why would youshut her down like that?"

"Well," he said, "I didn't tell her dad. I told Gail."

"My God, Bob, that is the same thing as telling her dad." Could he really be that ignorant? After the visit, I asked Bob how much contact he had with Derek. "Once a week," he replied. And I immediately knew that he, like everyone else, was being manipulated by my ex.

On another visit, as we were walking over to the grocery store—with Bob walking on the side where the cars were, as if I were a criminal and might run away with her—out of the blue Ami said, "Mom, I have little red bumps down there on my pee-pee." Ami didn't think Bob had heard her, but when she saw that he had, she quickly covered up for herself. "I think I fell and hurt myself," she said, "but I don't know when." This incident was relayed to Gail, who in turn relayed everything to Derek.

After every visit, Derek picked Ami up and made sure I saw him, letting me know he was there as if to say, "Look, Maralee, I have your daughter." After one visit, I came out about fifteen minutes after he had left Bob's office with Ami. As I was crossing the street to my car, I felt a car approaching close behind me, slowly, as if to touch the back of my knees, and I turned around. Sure enough, it was him, smirking. I looked right through him and waved to Ami.

On the freeway, on the way home, he would drive very slowly, as if waiting for me to catch up to him. He would go as far as to pull onto the side of the road and drive approximately fifteen to twenty miles an hour. One day, I had a friend's car, and as he had pulled off the shoulder of the road to wait and watch for me, he did not know I was in another car. I drove right by, watching him look in the rearview mirror and pulling to the shoulder to wait for me to approach. All I could think of were the times Ami would tell me he'd pull over to the side of the road and touch her while she was in the car. The visits were pure torture for both of us. When we had to leave each other, she would hug me so tight, and we could not let go of each other.

In the meantime, I had been contacting as many people as I could who might be able to help Ami and me. I worked all day every day, trying to rescue Ami from her situation. I talked with attorneys who were familiar with these kinds of cases and what was happening in the court system. I met with a Colorado congresswoman, with Governor Romer's wife, with Marilyn Van Derbur Atler—who had known about my case for quite some time—with D.D. Harvey, Dan Schaeffer, and the Attorney General's office. I met with anyone who could have some influence on my case. I met with attorneys from the most respected law firms in Denver but couldn't find anyone to take my case pro bono. Most were simply not interested in taking on a case having to do with child abuse. I even contacted the famous lawyer Jerry Spence from Wyoming. I thought since I had grown up in Wyoming, that might help my cause, but he told me he didn't handle these types of cases. I even set up a meeting with Walter Girash, another big-named lawyer, only in Colorado, and tried with every ounce of persuasion I had for him to take the case, but to no avail.

So I decided to go public.

CHAPTER 27

Congress and Media: Giving My Child a Voice

I was watching 60 Minutes one night when I saw a mother named Evelyn Hayes who was going through the exact same thing I was. I called CBS to find out where she lived, and that evening, I got a hold of her. This was the first time I could talk to and cry with someone who understood my pain as well as I did. We did not have the internet to network like women do today. We both yelled and cried and had exactly the same emotions. We were dealing with the same outrageous injustices. We kept in contact, and Evelyn introduced me to Dr. Amy Neustein, another mother fighting to protect her little girl from sexual abuse from the father. After talking with Ami several times, she asked if I would testify before Congress on this issue. I immediately agreed and testified with about ten other mothers from all over the United States. It was an amazing experience.

I decided that since the courts hadn't helped, and the system was completely biased against me, I would go to the media with my case. I contacted Linda Castrone, the reporter from the Rocky Mountain News who had been at my hearings two years previous when I had lost custody. I told Linda what had happened since then and that I wanted her to do a story with her. I gave her all the reports, and she went to work. At the same time, I began soliciting the help of Channel 7 news through a reporter named Julie Hayden. Julie said the station was interested in doing the story and that she would come and interview me at my house.

When Julie arrived, I had all the reports and tape recordings organized. I was nervous but done with the court system and very ready to go forward. The cameraman and reporter listened to me intently, with tear-filled eyes. These people dealt with all kinds of criminals, and yet this seemed more painful for them to hear. They came back a second time to do the actual filming. I was nervous, but the interview went well. At one point, I mentioned the tape recordings I had made of Ami's nightmares, and they asked to listen to them. I had not listened to them since I had taped them two years earlier. Since no lawyer or judge had ever allowed them in the court room, I had just put them away. I had forgotten how horrible her cries were, and when I played them for the reporter, the pain and the memories came rushing back.

On one tape, in her sweet little voice, she kept saying, "Mommy, you're not going to get lost, are you?"

I said, "No, Ami. Mommy is not going to get lost."

Then she repeated the question over and over again, so I said, "Ami, Mommy is not going to get lost! I told you that. Why do you keep asking me? I told you, you and I will always be together, always!"

I did not remember that tape. When I heard it, I began to cry.

"I told her we would always be together," I said through my sobs. "I've let her down." As the reporter listened to Ami's cries, her face turned red, and she began to cry. The cameraman also had tears in his eyes.

They copied the tape that recorded Ami saying, "My dad does this." I remember that night vividly. After I had picked her up from her Dad's, she got into the car and said that her dad had touched her again. I asked, "Honey, while I was gone?"

"Yes!"

In the tape, I told her I was sorry, I was doing everything I could to stop it, and I did not know what else to do. The cries and detailed information in those tapes is excruciating to listen to.

When the reporter and cameraman asked to film Ami's room, I led them upstairs and looked inside with them. The room was filled with things she loved, her stuffed animals (including Benna, her favorite), her rocking horse, her ballet slippers. Her beautiful antique bed that was her Grandma's and mother's, handed down to her, canopied in white lace, covered in a white-and-gold comforter, set up against the window, which had white lace curtains. Her room was a princess room, so pretty and filled with memories of a little girl's dream world. And now it was so still, so quiet, full but empty.

The cameraman went over to her large wooden rocking horse. On top of the leather saddle sat a doll with a bunny coat just, like the one Ami wore when she was a year old. My mother had bought it for her. It was a replica of Ami when she was little. He filmed the doll and then went over to Ami's music box and turned it on. The ballerina popped out, and it played the song Ami and I used to dance to: "I could have danced, all night. I could have danced, all night."

I had to leave. I couldn't bear to watch, knowing she was no longer in this beautiful room, safe and peaceful, with all her belongings and her mommy close by. It was like a death.

When they finished, the reporter told me that she knew this was very hard for me and that they both empathized. She said she had a daughter the same age as mine. After the story aired, Julie Hayden and I became friends.

As it happened, the two stories—the newspaper article by Linda Castrone and the television report by Julie Hayden—came out in the same week. Both were extended reports lasting several days. The newspaper full-page article and the Channel 7 story both ran for a week.

On July 7, 1992, the morning that newspaper article came out. I was so afraid to read it. It was a huge article with the headline, "Whatever Happened to Ami?" They used our first names, since I had to be careful what was printed, but it definitely got the story out. And when Channel 7 News aired that night, the station's phones began ringing off the wall. The public was outraged. The calls just kept pouring in to social services and the district attorney's office, which wound up spurring them to re-open the case. The news blocked out our faces so as to not identify us.

When I saw the news, I was somewhat in shock. When I heard the tapes of Ami's voice, and when I saw her empty bedroom, I began to cry. I thought, maybe now justice will be done.

Later, Julie Hayden told me that Derek called her afterward to scold her for the report and to tell her that his daughter loved him, and he loved his daughter. Linda Castrone told me that he called her too and then tried to manipulate her editor, who made Linda go over everything she had written and make sure it was accurate. Derek went to see Linda Castrone's editor to try and sway her. His manipulation continued on every front.

My mom wrote a letter to the editor and stated, "We want to thank The Rocky Mountain News for the article on our sensitive and sweet granddaughter Ami, even though as shattered as our hearts have been the last three years. This is the most horrendous nightmare grandparents could imagine or endure. We have been in this child's life daily since the day of her birth. Many mornings our first early telephone call of the day was Ami. Now all we hear is our daughters heart breaking and have heard her father is looking out for her welfare. He refuses to let us talk to her or to go see her when her mother has supervised visits. He has taken her from all of her family. Don't you think that this child feels pretty much abandoned by everyone she trusted? Help us fight to rid the system of this cancer that is destroying babies and families." My mom's letter writing campaign continued to the U.S. Attorney, Department of Justice, House of Representatives, and any one above our defunct judicial system. She never gave up day after day with just a typewriter. Bless her heart.

At this point, Ami had been away from me for five months, and her preschool had still been filing abuse reports to no avail. I later found out in court, through Ami's teacher's testimony, that Ami was telling her that her dad put a "hard rock" inside of her and hurt her and that she was afraid to sleep in her bed at night. Social services still refused to respond or do anything, even though a police report had been filed. They did not even go out to see my child. The school was furious.

CHAPTER 28

Seeking Criminal Prosecution

Social services did absolutely nothing, but the DA, Bob Gallagher, said they were going to investigate. He promised that if the judge didn't do anything about my case, he would. One day, I had wired myself before going into the D.A.'s office and entered the building with my attorney, wearing a gray pinstriped suit and a crisp white shirt, a man's tie, my hair up with my big black legal binder book with all pertinent information inside it. I felt by looking more like a man, they might find me more credible. Not understanding gender- bias at the time. When I set off the detector, I lightheartedly joked that it must be the underwire in my bra and proceeded through with a slight laugh. While in the office with the D.A. Bob Gallagher, I handed over my big black book and went through evidence of the abuse, emphasizing key points. I then asked Gallager, "How can you not prosecute this case criminally when you have more evidence here than I'm sure you do in most of your child abuse cases?"

"I believe Ami has been abused," he said, "and if Judge Bieda takes this child from you, we would step in and do something." My attorney Mike Scott was with me. When we left the D.A. and were outside I pulled the wire out from my shirt. My attorney, astonished, looked at me and said, "Geez, Maralee!" with a worried look and then said, "Good!" This tape aired on Channel 7 news. It would take Gallagher eight weeks to begin the investigation, and when he did, the detective assigned to the case, F. H. Parker, was the same one who had done nothing when Humana Hospital reported an expected child sexual abuse, and when Tim King had filed his seven-page police report as well.

Two days after the Channel 7 news report (in which Arapahoe District Chief Judge Stuart, whom I had written letters to, commented that Judge Bieda "better have a good reason" for this long delay), Judge Bieda called a hearing to remove the temporary order that had taken Ami away from me. The news media showed up, and the judge closed off the courtroom once again to the public.

Michael Scott had volunteered to represent me pro bono for this hearing. He was a good friend of the Fowlers and was Congresswoman Pat Schroeder's brother. The other side did not expect me to have any representation, and Mike blew Steve Calder, Derek's attorney, away. For the first time, Calder was stumbling and turning red.

The day was taken up with the testimony of Ami's therapist, Gail Adams. She admitted on the witness stand that she would believe Ami when she told her about her father's sexual abuse and that she would even call social services. When asked what kind of relationship Ami and I had, in one breath she stated that we had a very close and loving one, and in the next she said that I should not be allowed to see my child again.

I sat there stunned. I stared at her in disbelief with her shallow demeanor as she talked about Derek, her eyes lighting up as if she were in love.

When the hearing ended, Calder was nervous that the judge wanted to continue it the next day—he knew he was up against a good lawyer and not prepared. He found excuses for not making every court date the judge put in front of him. Judge Bieda said he would rule later on the new hearing date.

Little did we know that months would pass before we were to get another day in court.

CHAPTER 29

Coping Mechanisms

The days were long, but I never stopped fighting. I was in constant contact with people who could somehow free Ami, who was about five years old, from her bondage. I viewed her as a prisoner of war, not knowing how long she would have to endure that type of life or what type of torture she would have to endure in the upcoming days.

On the days we got to visit with each other for an hour, sometimes she was distant, barely connecting with me, and other times she was just gone, with a chilling, blank stare. That is what hurt the most. Her eyes told me everything. She used to ask me who the people were that were trying to help her because she couldn't see that anyone was. I couldn't let her give up hope. At first, she asked questions and shared with me some details about her days, but she had been trained on what she could and couldn't tell me. So after a while she sometimes grew afraid to tell me what she did and just shut down. And as for me, I wasn't allowed to ask her how she felt.

One time she lay on the floor and said she didn't have a head. I tried to play with her to get her out of this state. I got on the floor and said, "Of course you have a head," and touched her head.

"I can't see you," she said, keeping her eyes closed. "You can too see me," I said.

"I just want to die," she said.

By this time, I was tape-recording our sessions with Bob surreptitiously—due to the wire—and on the advice of Diane Baird of the Kempe Center, having Bob film us with a video camera. I had asked for Diane's advice because I was having trouble reaching Ami when she blanked out during our visits. It was Diane's expert opinion and recommendation that we document what was happening so she could watch the video and see what Ami was doing. (Diane once arranged with Bob to come in on a session so that she could observe Ami firsthand, but after it was set up, Derek came in and demanded that she leave.)

One day, while Bob filmed us, Ami and I made up a mermaid story that she loved, called "The Little Mermaid Movie." It went something like this: We had a cave on the beach where we sold mermaid tails in all different colors, and the only way her friends could come and be with us (since we were mermaids) was to wear one of her magical tails to come to the bottom of the ocean with us. When Ami told this story, she concluded by saying that men were not allowed. "We can swim with all my friends and have a wonderful life. There's a ship, and we all go in, and there's a beautiful little girl's room there." She described the room as if it was hers. In the closet were beautiful dresses, as there were in her own closet, before she was taken away. As she spoke, her voice was dreamy and captivating; it was as if she was actually down on the bottom of the ocean, safe with all the people she had chosen to be around her.

She then stated that the little girl was missing her doll that was left on the bed, so we must take her doll to her. As we swam to the top of the water, she looked out at the beach and saw the little girl, who she was sure was the little girl from the ship, and yelled, "Little girl, little girl, your doll! I found your doll!"

When asked why there were no men there, Ami said, "Ariel's father died. He's dead."

◆ ◆ ◆ ◆ ◆ ◆

Each visit, I tried to stay as close to her as I could and reach her. Some visits were very hard. We both were hanging on tight to each other, clinging close, neither of us wanting to leave. Most times when I left, I cried all the way home, and when I got home, I threw myself on the bed and bawled. I just wanted to die. Ami seemed to be getting worse every week. Her hair had been falling out, and now it was breaking off to the roots. It was very thin and colorless now, even though she used to have thick, long, dark hair. Her eyes sometimes had deep circles under them, and she would say, "I cried and I cried for you all night long, Mommy. I threw up in my bed." And even though she had a tiny build, she was now overweight.

I had recently gone to Washington DC to attend a conference on child sexual abuse. Glennie Rohelier, the founder of Alliance Rights for Children, had hosted me during the conference. She gave me a beautiful ballerina outfit that had belonged to one of her granddaughters. When I showed this outfit to Ami, she put it on, very excited, but then looked in the mirror and exclaimed, "I'm so ugly! I'm so ugly!"

"Ami, come here!" I said. "You are not ugly! You are so beautiful, inside and out."

"No!" she cried, "I am ugly. I have an ugly body and ugly hair!"

This is a child who used to know she was a doll and could not wait to put on a new dress and look at herself in the mirror. Now she could not even look at herself. Her father was not only raping her body, he was raping her self-esteem.

Usually, before I got to see her, my day had already been shot. I couldn't function; I felt numb and anxious at the same time. After the visit, the pain was intensified. How did we cope? One day, Ami cried when she left me and said, "It's too hard to say good-bye. I don't think I want to come here anymore." How I wished someone would help us. No wonder mothers give up on their children, the pain is unbearable.

I was beginning to feel it would take an act of God to change our situation. We were both just trying to survive. A couple of times, I drove one of my girlfriend's trucks over to Ami's school to watch her play at recess. Even though it was a very cool, cold day, she was wearing a sleeveless dress. I looked at the other little girls playing together, and then I looked back at Ami. She looked like an orphan. I wanted to hold her and tell her everything was going to be okay. I told myself that I would get her home someday. I would protect her from her father.

There is no way for me to describe what it feels like not to protect your daughter and to be punished for trying to do so. Imagine that your daughter was kidnapped by a pedophile, and you knew where the kidnapper was and what he was doing to her, but you were unable to rescue her or find anyone to help you. In fact, instead of helping you, everyone was criticizing you and telling you what a wonderful man the pedophile was. You did not have police helping you or the public rallying around you to find your child. That was my situation.

Every night I went to bed thinking of my poor little girl. Every morning I was awake by three or four in the morning, unable to sleep any longer. I felt her pain. I felt my own pain. It was truly unbearable. I would jump out of bed, run to her room, and throw myself onto her bed. I felt that I would just die without her.

Mike Scott had agreed to represent me for that hearing, but I was on my own now and needed help. I couldn't afford an attorney who wouldn't take my case pro bono. At this point, I was depleted. I had given my home to an attorney, sold my engagement ring, the rest of my jewelry, my furniture, and my car. I had gone through all my savings, had liquidated my retirement account, and spent all the money I had put away for Ami's college education. I was paying Ami's rapist $800 a month for child support and paying $400 a month for my supervised visits. I was court ordered to pay his attorney's fees of $12,000 and they had garnished my bank account with judgments to pay the G.A.L.'s attorney's fees, and garnished my wages leaving me no monies to even live.

◆ ◆ ◆ ◆ ◆ ◆

I went to DU law school and met with a professor there by the name of Penny Bryan in family law. I was told she could be of some help, and I knew that if I had to represent myself, I would need help. After telling her my story, she seemed unsurprised by what had happened to me, but she would later tell me that she wouldn't have any advice on who could represent me. But she did have an idea: she wanted me to come and speak to her domestic relations class. I was flattered and surprised but told her I wasn't really a very good speaker. She said that her students would learn a lot from me. They were studying child-abuse issues and looking at Richard Gardner's theory of parental alienation.

I thought about it for a minute and then asked, "How big is this class?"

"About 150 students," she said. 150 students! I said to myself. I can't do it.

"You'll be great!"

I agreed to speak, and it went over very well. One of the law students wrote a letter to me, stating:

> *Thank you for your voice in a world of silence. Thank you for standing tall when they tried to make you invisible.*
>
> *Thank you for speaking for those with no voice. Thank you for standing firm when your knees must have been shaking.*
>
> *In law school, we learn about contracts and property. We read about faceless people in faraway places and analyze the rationale that justifies their fate. We study and prepare to protect the interests of our future client. After meeting you, I understand the reality of that future and faraway client.*
>
> *I would like you to know that your story has made a difference in the way that I will practice law. I am making a commitment to myself to protect my clients from the system. After receiving my JD, I will have the ability to contribute positively to the legal system. After listening to your plight for only one hour and thirty minutes, I realized the nightmare could happen to anyone. As a future attorney, I have a responsibility to my profession and the children not to let this kind of abuse reoccur. Your story will not be forgotten. It is forever in the hearts of everyone who hears you. You have forever affected me and has re-sparked my sincere ambition of why I wanted to become an attorney since I was a girl.*
>
> *Love, Linda Fine*

This experience inspired me to do more of the same—to spread the word of what had happened to Ami and me so that society would become more aware of what was happening to mothers like me and to children like Ami. Through a lot of networking, I began speaking all across the United States.

◆ ◆ ◆ ◆ ◆ ◆

Earlier that year—April 20, 1992—I had, the invitation of US Congress, traveled to New York to testify before a Congressional subcommittee on child sexual abuse. This was after Judge Hickman's ex parte ruling when I lost Ami. While at the Congressional hearing, I found out there were mothers all across the country going through the exact same situation. I no longer felt so isolated, and I began to understand that the problems in our social-service system and judicial system were widespread. I guess you could say I was being empowered. I was so angry at the system that I felt determined to do whatever it took to educate people, and most of all, whatever it took to free my child from the abuse by her own father. I started to feel that I could make a difference by educating people on something they had no idea was going on or that could go on. I now knew that my case was not an isolated one.

This was happening to children and mothers all across our nation.

The laws were there to protect the children; however, the system was skirting those laws and avoiding the abuse issue. The laws couldn't protect children if judges avoided dealing with their abuse and refused to educate themselves on child sexual abuse. For a year, I worked on a committee to help rewrite the laws for the Colorado Children's Code and saw that judges everywhere would rather believe a mother was a vindictive ex-wife than believe a father would molest his own daughter.

CHAPTER 30

Your Child's Best Advocate

At the continuation of the July hearing, Mike Scott once again volunteered to represent me. In his opening statement, he mentioned that his sister, a congresswoman, was very aware of this case.

Mike brought out the sexual abuse evidence more than any previous attorney had and emphasized that there was physical evidence to prove the abuse.

At one point, Derek took the witness stand, and Mike questioned him on his abuse of Ami. When Derek didn't answer him, Mike said, "Mr. Walker, can you explain why your daughter said that you licked her pee-pee and moved her tongue in and out of her mouth at the age of three like this?" Mike then motioned his own tongue in and out of his mouth. Mike then entered into court records the reports from Children's Hospital and from the child advocacy and protection team, along with the Humana Hospital report, and Dr. Marion's report from Kaiser, stating that there had been sexual abuse, and the police reports verifying abuse only to have Judge Bieda throw them out, stating that it had all been litigated in the past hearings. Up to that point, I had felt that there would be no way this judge could continue to ignore three different doctors' reports and two police reports.

All these reports were new, and the court had never admitted them into evidence. I thought they would return Ami to me and realize what a mistake had been made. How could I still have been so optimistic? How could I have still believed in the system?

After this, six months went by without a ruling from Judge Bieda. I had called Linda Castrone, the reporter from the Rocky Mountain News, and told her I was going back to court again and hopefully this time the judge would listen to the evidence. She wanted to do a follow-up story on my case, and I asked her to wait to see what Judge Bieda's ruling was first. After months had passed, I called Julie Hayden, the news reporter who had covered our story on Channel 7 News and told her what was going on. She quickly aired a report on the delay, asking why the judge was sitting on a case with so much evidence of child abuse. Immediately after that program aired, a hearing date for the ruling was scheduled. Meanwhile, I called the Children's Hospital abuse team of doctors and told them that Judge Bieda was going to make a ruling within the next day or two. The doctors got together and felt it imperative to write a letter to the judge, expressing their concern about the evidence of abuse. They asked for Judge Bieda to please contact the child's advocacy and protection team at Children's Hospital before making a ruling on this case.

The doctors were never contacted.

The hearing was scheduled for March 16, 1993, at four o'clock. My mother flew in to be with me for it. We thought for sure that I would get Ami back home.

I had previously set up an appointment with the police department to meet with Detective Perry and another police officer, one who had gone out to Derek's house after Doctor Marion had notified the police of her sexual abuse. I wanted to ask them why no criminal charges had ever been filed against Derek. This meeting took place in the early afternoon before the hearing.

My best friends Kim and Liz, who had witnessed Ami's behavior many times from age two to five years of age, came with me to this meeting. They are both professional, low-key women, but as the officers explained why no charges had been filed against Derek, my friends grew angry and started to raise their voices. One of them said, "Remember, we pay your salaries! What kind of a job are you doing in this case!" Their anger became so intense that they were asked to leave so the police could just deal with me. I had learned control from the day they took Ami away from me when she was two. One of the officers was so uptight that when he heard a shuffling noise out in the hall, he opened the door and yelled out, "Arrest those women!" However, my friends were not doing anything wrong. They were just quietly talking with the chief of police about my case.

As soon as Kim and Liz left the room, the police said, "Do you mind?"and put a tape recorder on the table in front of me. I responded, "No, not at all!" then shifted a little bit, calmly pulled a wire out from underneath my bra, and placed my tape recorder next to theirs. "Do you mind?"

They thought they could intimidate me. But I was a mother fighting for her child, and nothing could intimidate me at that point.

It was a grueling conversation. I had never met the other officer, but Perry was a different story. He had interviewed Ami when she was three, and his report alone should have put the father away. Two years after I had seen him at Target, and he couldn't look me in the eye. I was now sitting across from the sexual-abuse specialist who knew better than anyone that my child was being abused.

I said,"Perry, remember my little girl and what she looked like?"

"Yes," he replied.

I pulled out recent pictures of her that I had taken at our supervised visits, showing Ami, now with hardly any hair, her face in a moon shape, as when I had shown the picture recently to Dr. Krugman who was now the President of University Hospital said to me this child is sick she is on steroids. But he didn't want to look at them. I shoved them on the table in front of him and said, "Perry, look! Look at my little girl! Is that the little girl you remember?"

He exclaimed, "Maralee, there is not a day that goes by that I do not think about this case!"

"Then why is no one doing anything?" I asked him. "You know the truth, and criminal charges were supposed to be filed."

Perry explained that after he had interviewed Ami that day, he had thought our case was headed for criminal court. He didn't know why it had been locked up in family court.

For two hours I sat there with them, telling them all that had transpired. What I had on tape was incredible and I definitely held my own up against these two. The other cop was very defensive, as if he knew he had screwed up. Finally, I told the detectives I had to go, because I had a meeting at three o'clock with Susan Dycus, the new guardian ad litem. I had also set this meeting up long before this surprise hearing was scheduled. But Perry told me she had probably cancelled, since she had been at court all day. They had closed the courtroom to discuss my case. I guess this was Perry's way of helping me and giving me a heads up.

That was the first I had heard of that. The hearing was supposed to be at four o'clock. Why was everyone there without me? My mom was here, and I made phone calls to everyone I could.

When I got there, my family and friends were already there. It wasn't supposed to be a hearing about abuse, so it was open to the public. The reporter Julie Hayden was there as well but had not been allowed in the courtroom. Judge Bieda spent the entire time chastising me for having gone to the media. I sat there feeling doomed. They had closed the courtroom and had been meeting all day without me. After seeing a horrible document placed before me, I leaned over my shoulder and told my brother-in-law, "Tell the reporter, Julie Hayden, it's really bad; tell her to stand by to cover this." And that's when the judge imposed a gag order on me. I was not allowed to discuss this case anymore to anyone. If I said anything about Ami or Derek, I would go to jail, never to see Ami again. He wound up writing a nineteen-page opinion dismissing all investigations prior to this date, prohibiting any further investigations, and gagging everyone involved. The GAL wanted to confiscate all my records, which they had talked openly about in the courtroom, but Bieda's response was that it would not be legal and that it would look bad to the public. They then discussed taking the case numbers off all the files so that no one could get into them. The nineteen-page report was unconstitutional and alarming to say the least. It once again took every bit of power I had left in me not to just scream! He quoted Kopetski's cross-examination by the new GAL that the mother would abduct the child if given the opportunity. Kopetski also noted she did not entirely rule out the possibility of sexual abuse from another source, including the mother, and that the focus "on her genitals" could be a form of sexual abuse. She also opined that the mother was very controlling and that the father was not controlling. Then Judge Bieda said, "The materials submitted are without foundation, are unauthenticated, are hearsay, and have no legal basis." 1.

The mother and her counsel have admitted no credible evidence that the father has abused his daughter. In fact, the overwhelming weight of the evidence is to the contrary. 4. Provisions of 14-10-129, C.R.S., which provides that visitation rights of a parent may be limited if it would "endanger the child's physical health or significantly impair emotional development." It would be in the best interest of the child that visitation with the mother continue to be supervised as previously ordered by the Court. Such supervised visits shall continue indefinitely, until the mother can demonstrate to the Court's satisfaction that she is no longer a danger to the child and that she has recognized the harm she has done to the child and the damage and expense that she has caused the father. (See Judge Bieda's Order, Appendix D.)

Unless people were there at the court that day, they would find it to be unbelievable. My brother-in-law was there and high up in the military and he had never seen anything like this.

At the end of the hearing, Derek was escorted out through the judge's chambers while they escorted me out by thepolice, as if I were a criminal.

Julie Hayden was just outside the courtroom doors and had already heard the bad news as I came out the doors. With concern and tears in her eyes, she said, "Maralee, I am so sorry." I told her that I could not talk to her, due to the gag order but that she should get a hold of my attorney, who could speak to her. She told me that she had reported on murders and other horrible crimes in Denver, but she had never felt as sick as she did when she reported on this case.

I was trembling as I left with my brother-in-law on one side and my mother on the other. I had no chance of winning anything. Everyone was against me. I ran for the bathroom and tried to vomit, but I had nothing in me, just dry heaves. I barely made it out to the car with my family holding me up. Not dead yet, but I felt close.

CHAPTER 31

Working Nationally to Free My Child

While waiting for the next hearing date, I continued all of my outside affairs as quietly as I could. Most of my work was now being done outside of Denver metro area, with the exception of a letter I wrote to the Chief Judge Stuart of Arapahoe County and a grievance filed against Judge Bieda, along with an appeal.

Dear Judge Stuart,

The judge in my case ignored crucial physical evidence from doctors' reports, police reports, and teachers' testimony. The time he took after receiving information and reports on this case to making a final ruling was an unreasonable amount of time.

He relied on expert testimony or a report written by Leona Kopetski, MSW that left out all doctors' reports' and police reports regarding abuse. I find it alarming that the personal opinion of Kopetski (with no medical credentials) should supersede the findings of medical doctors.

The judge chose to ignore the counsel of the Children's Advocacy Team (medical experts in the child sexual abuse field) to review relevant facts pertinent to this case. (See attached letter.)

The judge determined that this evidence was to be omitted on the grounds that it had been previously argued. All of the information in question was new to the court and had never been presented to the court.

The judge's bias was most evident in his greater concern for his public portrayal by the media than for the best interest of my child. This is best illustrated by his forty-five-minute dissertation of the dangers of "too much press" before the final ruling in this case. It was further demonstrated by the ending of his five-month hiatus without a ruling, only after your televised comments, "That he better have a very good reason for the delay." He was clearly influenced by the fear of "the power of the media." He openly discussed in the courtroom of how to confiscate all my records.

In closing, Judge Stuart, this ruling is clearly puni- tive to the petitioner and severely deficient of factual evidence and is solely based on the opinions of incompetent opinions of Leona Kopetski and Claire Purcell when the physical evidence that stated sexual abuse of my child should have taken precedence. If Judge Bieda was uncomfortable with the subject matter and wasn't able to remain objective throughout the proceedings, then he should have removed himself from the case. This type of case demands expeditious and protective rulings because childhood is precious and fleeting, and every child deserves the best start in life as possible and, most of all, protection and safety. I have a great deal more of the documented facts that support these accusations, and I anxiously await the opportunity to present them to you. Thank you for your consideration.

Sincerely, Maralee McLean

I really began networking outside of Denver again, and I came into contact with John Shield, the chief executive officer of the Barbara Sinatra Children's Center. After I spoke with him on the phone several times, he asked me if I would come to Palm Desert and speak to the board of the Sinatra foundation, adding that they were very influential people. He then told me he would pay for everything and put me up in a nice hotel. He really wanted me to speak, and I liked John even without meeting him, so I agreed. John and his wife were good friends with the Sinatras. When I arrived, he and his wife took me out to dinner and kept telling me that they knew I would do an incredible job. The center was incredible. Children were running through the beautiful building hallway, holding hands, laughing, and off to the side was a professional examining room, clearly placed to make a child feel comfortable. There were psychologists helping the children that were drawing their feelings on posters. Some of the drawings were quite telling. Trained professionals were everywhere. It was truly a safe place for children who had been abused. I started to cry as I walked through the hallways, looking at all the children and wishing my little girl had a place to go like this. Just knowing there were other children going through this nightmare, and she would not be all alone, would have brought so much comfort. I spoke before the board and John felt I had done a really great job.

On another day at a rally for mothers of incest victims in Washington DC. I went to Capitol Hill and lobbied for the rights of abused children. I spoke at conferences for women's groups in Texas, LA, and Indiana, including the very influential Women of Washington, and I spoke at classes at DU Law School. The time and energy I expended on this issue would take years, and it was helping other cases, but meanwhile, months and years were passing by, and soon Ami's childhood would be gone forever. Though I felt then, and still feel today, that her innocence and childhood had been instantly stripped from her the very first time her father had molested her.

During this time, I was lobbying on the hill in Washington one or two times a week. I would work as a flight attendant on flights to DC, get in late at night, and then wake up at six o'clock the next morning to take the train into Washington, where I worked with the law firm of Verner, Lipfert, Mcphereson, and Hand. I would wear my suit on the train, wheeling my luggage through snow and ice, so I could come back to the law firm and change into my flight attendant uniform to work the flight back to Denver. Spending two trips a week like this was exhausting. They had put together a memo regarding child abuse cases that went to Janet Reno and would set up my meetings on the hill with specific Congressional representatives. I would spend the day lobbying and telling the stories of many mothers and children out there suffering due to the injustice and incompetence of our judicial system. One time, after spending an exhausting day, Marilyn Van Derbur-Atler's daughter, who was getting her law degree and working with the firm, watched me speak all day. Once we got back to the law firm, she followed me into the bathroom as I changed back to my uniform. She said, "I admire you so much and can't tell you what a good job you did today." As tears welled up in her eyes she said, "Watching you made me hate my grandmother."

CHAPTER 32

Free Our Children

Realizing now this was going to take years, my only option was still the very same court system that had proven to be incompetent and inextricably corrupt for me. I had vowed never to step foot into civil court again, but I had no other choice. I was now bankrupt and could not afford to hire another attorney. The money it would take for an attorney just to read and understand my file would be close to fifty thousand dollars. Besides, at this point I no longer trusted an attorney to do a good job. I knew my case backward and forward, and I had a great memory for dates and times—when motions were filed and exactly what went on from hearing to hearing throughout the past eight years. I didn't know the law, but how could I do any worse than what had already happened? Mike Scott did not feel that I could win an appeal and strongly suggested against it. I filed a motion for an appeal, and it was denied. The work just to put together the appeal had taken months. I also filed grievances against Judge Bieda, Leona Kopetski, Claire Purcell, and Gail Adams, all to no avail.

I had met Joan Pennington, a lawyer from Princeton, several years earlier through networking. She knew these cases well and had written an article, "Custody's Hardest Cases." She was incredibly intelligent, well connected, and won Attorney of the Year in New Jersey. We decided to stage a rally at the capitol building in Denver. We planned the rally over the phone and decided on a date that was six months down the road, July 10, 1992, which happened to be about three weeks after I lost Ami to supervised visits. We notified all the mothers we could think of, and using my passes from the airlines, brought in the most educated attorneys in this field. I called MASA—mothers against sexual abuse, a large organization out of California—and spoke to the director, Claire, whom I had met at a conference in Washington. She brought in a lot of people, and the directors for the Alliance Rights for Children came as well. We lined up keynote speakers—authors, mothers, the director for domestic violence in Denver—and Joan invited three great professional vocalists. This was big and lots of work. I had to find places for everyone to stay. Every room of my house was full, and I asked my neighbors and friends to take some people in.

I needed a table to put the authors' books on, Joan had invited Louise Armstrong, the author of "Kiss Daddy Goodnight", so I called Continental and asked them to bring a big table to the capitol on July 10th. I had purple helium balloons with gold-sparkled lettering with the name of each child that had been victimized and taken away. Everyone was to wear purple. I talked a flight attendant friend into carving 4-inch, large solid hearts out of gold metal and strung them with thick purple ribbons for the mothers that had the courage to stay in there and fight. Before the rally, I had a supervised visit with Ami, and I gave her a necklace with a large gold heart and thick purple ribbon. I put it around her neck and told her that it was very special; someday it would have a lot of meaning for her. I told her to hang it on her bedpost and keep it close to her.

The preparations were endless. A company donated port-a-potties, and I talked a concession guy into putting up a tent for food. Another company donated a sound system, and I found some men to help put the large speakers and equipment in the trees and on the capital steps. I typed professional press releases to give to the media, and all the news stations showed up. I had obtained all the permits for the rally at the capitol.

The morning of the rally, I thought I might throw up from the pressure of everything going as planned. As the rally got underway, I was on the top of the steps when I saw my sister Leslie comes running up to me. "Derek is here," she said in a shaky voice. I asked her where, and then I saw him moving through the crowd toward the steps with two large black men. He had a fanny pack on the front of him, and I thought for sure he was there to kill me. I quickly moved over to Julie Hayden, the news reporter, with my heart racing and said, "Derek is here!" She asked, "Where?" and I pointed him out. He had purposely walked right in front of my mom, dad, and family. Then he disappeared.

It was a sunny, blue-skied Colorado day. Joan Pennington kicked off the rally with a great speech. At the end she said, "We have all come here today due to the hard work of a mother who fought to protect her child. We are collecting a list of judges in this corruption and the first name on the list is that of judge Michael Bieda, who has sentenced Maralee McLean's child to a life sentence of abuse."Just then she lifted her arm forcefully in the air against the blue, blue sky with the capital in the background and yelled, "This is for you, Ami!" It took them 20 years to listen to domestic violence we do not have another 20 years for them to listen to this issue.

She then asked Judith May, who is a survivor of childhood incest, the first singer, to come on the stage, and she sang with the most incredible voice a beautiful song called "Little One Heal the Broken Wing."

Little one, I see you in the night
holding fast and holding tight
Hold on to your dreams

Little one. I'm coming as fast as I can
to be your guide, to take a stand
I am on my way.

I can't get to the shore without you,
Sword at my side,
I am on my way.

After the most crushing, heartfelt song that any of us mothers who have lost their children could hear, Joan asked me to come up and speak. I had been working so hard on organizing the rally that I had not really prepared a speech, so I used one of my old speeches and ad-libbed where I could. I felt this empowerment—not my own but of God! My voice was not my voice. I felt as if God was speaking through me. I was so strong, and my voice was so powerful. My first statement was, "**Whyare mother's going to jail to protect their children? Why are they going into the underground? Why are mother's committing suicide? I know the answers to these why's! The pain is unbearable! Our children's prayers have been turned into fear and their dreams into screams. It is time to listen to the children. This is like the Civil Rights Act of the 60's this is the movement of the 90's.**"

Afterward, a man got on his knees in front of me and said, "My God, you can speak! You've got to continue to speak." Joan had brought in professional singers who sang in between speakers. After all the professionals and (most importantly) the mothers spoke, we got in a circle and held the purple balloons with gold strings with the names in gold of their children on the balloons. Then we released the balloons atthe same time, saying quietly, "Free our children." We watched, looking up at the blue, blue sky until we couldn't see any of the balloons anymore.

◆ ◆ ◆ ◆ ◆ ◆

For the next six months, I began pulling my case together. First, I filed for a hearing date, and then I began plugging away at the many files I had collected over the last seven years. I had learned how the system worked from being in the system. The challenge was if they would kill me in the legal arena with the abundance of statutes and laws I did not know.

Prior to filing these motions, I needed to first request more time with Ami. In the process of seeking help for my cause, I had met a prominent retired federal judge in Colorado named Hilbert Schauer. After reviewing my file, he had been shocked and disgusted by the actions of the professionals in this case. Following that, I had shared with him bits and pieces of my case over the years because I knew that getting too much information at once tended to overwhelm people, even people who were well-educated in the judicial system. It left most of them dismayed and shocked. How could this happen?

I wrote my motions but then had my friend and confidant review them to assure that I was doing everything properly so the case would move forward. Needless to say, I was sending a message to Judge Bieda that I meant business. I'm sure the judge was quite surprised at the professionalism of my work. The courts never found out who was helping me.

The preparation took quite some time. Then it was time to decide what tactic I would use in order to get my child back home with me. Obviously the courts were not going to listen to the abuse issue. I had spent close to seven years now studying my case along with many other cases like mine, and none of the mothers had been able to release her child from this ongoing torture or protect his or her child from the continuing abuse. Most were now excluded from their children's lives. Of the hundreds of cases I was aware of and the moms I personally knew and came in contact with from all across the country, all of them had limited supervised visits. **In fact, they were limited to fewer visitations and were under closer scrutiny during their visitations than convicted felons.** It was no wonder that mothers tried to run away or wound up killing themselves. One mother, an attorney, Marcia Rimland, had seen no other option but to take her own life and that of her five-year-old daughter. Most mothers found it agonizing to deal with the pain of one-hour visits once a week for years, and that, coupled with the money it cost them to pay for legal representation, left some so depleted and depressed that they simply could not cope and wound up losing all their parental rights and visitation privileges. Others, like me, hung in there for the most painful and humiliating experiences a parent would ever want to endure.

Perhaps the most humiliating aspect of this whole ordeal was the nature of the supervised visits. At times, I felt that I would suffocate during them. The subjects of our conversation—the words my child and I spoke to one another—were severely curtailed. The supervisor observed everything we did, listened to everything we said, following us closely, jotting down everything on his yellow pad.

Bob Hovenden was not a therapist but more like a nazi prison guard. We were never to mention the abuse. Even when Ami would bring up things to do with the abuse, I was not to respond to it, and such moments were the only ones Bob wouldn't record on his yellow notepad. For instance, when Ami told me she had her discharge again and red bumps "down there," this was never discussed nor mentioned to anyone. It was as though they wanted her to forget all of her family on my side and forget that her friends even existed. I was not allowed to bring up our memories of her childhood or show Ami any pictures of our past or my family or sing old songs together because then she might get upset and miss home. And if she did get upset, I was not allowed to ask her what was wrong.

◆◆◆◆◆◆

Derek was thirty to forty-five minutes late on some occasions, which just killed both of us. Ami and I lived for these meetings. She would get very upset with her dad for that, and the psychopath thoroughly enjoyed the control he was exerting. In one meeting, Ami acted out her frustrations by beating up on an air-filled toy man in Bob's office, yelling out, "I killed him! He's dead! He's bad!" Bob looked on, seemingly unconcerned about what this represented about her anger toward him or her father. Nor was he concerned when she said, "I cry all night for you, Mommy, and I throw up in my bed. I come to your window at night, I am a fairy, I am on the window sill, and I am always with you, Mommy. I don't think I even live in Denver anymore. Every time I'm with you, it's like a dream." She pleaded with us to take her home. "Tell the police to come get me!" she cried out one day. On another day, she had a new idea about how to get us some more time together: "I want you to be my first-grade teacher!" she told me.

On the occasions when we were finally allowed to go outside of the office, there were even more hidden rules. Bob walked on the outside of the sidewalk in case I would jump into a parked car and run away with my child. He never let me out of hearing range of Ami.

One day on a visit when she was five, I told her she was never alone, that God was always with her. "You need to pray to God," I said. "He is always there, and he will listen to you. Talk to him before you go to sleep."

She turned to me and said, "Mommy there is no God, only Greek gods!" Afterward, I was told by Bob that I was not allowed to pray or mention God. A couple of visits later, when we were outside in the park, Ami whispered, "Mommy, I prayed last night!"

"Good, honey," was all I could get out before Bob was there, hovering over us.

Once when we were all in a car going to the park, I asked Ami, "Pretend we're in an airplane and you could go anywhere you wanted to go. Where would you like to go?" I expected her to say Disneyland or Hawaii, but instead she said, "Oh, Mommy! Let's go home!"

Once we walked by an apple tree. Ami and I both loved green apples, so we reached for some and picked them off the tree. Two years later, we walked by the same tree and I exclaimed to Ami, "Look how large the tree had grown!"

"Maralee," Bob said, "by the time you get out of supervised visits, you will not be able to see the top of that tree or reach the apples."

CHAPTER 33

Coping with No Christmas

Another heartbreaking moment was at Christmas when I was not allowed to take Ami to our home where I had put up all our Christmas decorations in the hopes of being allowed to have her for part of the day. For each of the three years before that, our Christmas visits had taken place in Bob's office several days before Christmas—not a very special occasion for Ami. Every Christmas we hoped in great anticipation for a home visit.

I had to try and do something special for my little girl. I approached Bob with the idea of taking her to The Nutcracker ballet in Denver. Ami loved the ballet, and I knew it would be a memory for us to hold on to. She was almost eight years old by this point.

I asked him way in advance, knowing that it would have to be approved by the so-called professionals and by her despicable, sick father. I waited patiently, hoping that we could have some kind of special time together. At our next visit, Ami told me not to count on us getting to go to the ballet. My poor little girl did not want me to be disappointed, as we both had been so many times.

Finally, Bob informed us that our plan for TheNutcracker had been approved. However, I was to buy a ticket for Bob and pay his hourly rate so he could come with us and supervise.

On the day of the performance, I hauled all of Ami's Christmas presents to Bob's small office, where we opened them up in an atmosphere not remotely pleasant or festive. I had spent much of the night before going through Ami's room and finding her favorite outfit for the holidays: a long, royal- blue sweater dress with a large Santa on the front with a white fur beard. I grabbed her white tights and looked for her little blue gloves with white fur around the wrist and gold bells that hung from the top of the gloves that chimed as she walked. At the top of her closet, I found her gloves, along with the blue- and-white fur hat that matched her dress. I daydreamed for a moment how precious she looked in that hat, surrounding her beautiful little face with white fur. I held her clothes to my chest and smelled them, envisioning her with this outfit on.

When she was little, Ami's favorite dress of mine was an elaborate peach sequin and chiffon dress with beads. When she was only three, she would put it on and say, "I want this dress someday, Mommy! Mommy, wear this now to the grocery store!"

I would laugh and say, "I can't wear that to the grocery store, but I will wear it sometime for you."

Needless to say, that day, I wore that dress.

Ami's hair was now pretty much gone. It had fallen off or broken off; I had no idea what had happened to her long, thick gorgeous hair. She was terribly upset about it. The hat I brought would cover her hair.

As we walked into the entrance hall of the Buell Theatre, people turned and exclaimed, "Look at that little girl, isn't she darling!" just as they used to when she was little. Ami began to beam. It had been a long time since people had noticed her, and she loved the attention. Bob, who was not someone I would ever date, was all dressed up; he seemed to be gloating over the fact that he was with us, pretending he was my date. I was repulsed, and he loved every minute of it.

As we walked into the theatre itself, something happened I will never forget. Ami ran toward the front part of the balcony, exclaiming, "Mommy, I want to sit down there by the music!" I explained that our seats were the only ones I could get and told her to move away from the balcony rail. She was a few feet away from me, and I could not get close to her, and Bob was uncharacteristically trailing behind us. I said sternly, "Ami, get away from the railing. You are going to fall off." She was jumping with her foot on the first rail and hanging over the rail. My heart was pounding. Any time in the past I ever so much as raised my voice, she always listened and responded, but this time she didn't.

I started to push people in front of me out of the way, trying to reach for Ami while still telling her to get awayfrom the terrace. But she wasn't listening to me. She seemed to be in a trance-like state. "Ami!" I yelled. "You are going to fall off, and you will die!" Quite a harsh statement, but I felt that I had to reach her.

She said, "So. I don't care if I die. You go with me!"

"I do not want to die!" I said. I knew I had to do something to get through to her, so I yelled defiantly, "You are not my little girl! You are not the little girl I know!"

That did the trick. She turned and yelled very loudly, "I am too your little girl! I am the only little girl you will ever have!" Then she immediately got off the railing and came toward me. I grabbed her in my arms and held her as tightly as I could, telling her over and over how much I loved her. Later I wondered what other people must have thought of me, but I didn't care. They had no idea what this little girl was going through.

◆ ◆ ◆ ◆ ◆ ◆

Worse than the humiliation of the supervised visits was the loneliness and pain of my house without Ami. I often felt compelled to go into her beautiful room, all canopied in ruffles and lace. Her ballet shoes hung next to a painting of a ballerina on her bedroom wall, and all her stuffed animals lay on her bed, even the big white polar bear I had bought her before she was born. As I looked around her room with all her belongings, I began to cry out in insurmountable pain, like a mother lion calling out for her cub. I threw myself in her bed and lay there, crying for hours until at some point I cried myself to sleep. One time when I had a Miami layover and I could not sleep as most nights I could not stand the pain willowing up inside of me and I just had to release it. I went to the balcony of my hotel room overlooking the ocean in the middle of the night and screamed as loud as I could, "AAAAAMMMMMiiii, AAAAAMMMiii!" As the moon glistened over the water and the waves crashed I knew she could hear me and God and obviously everyone else did too.

After seven years of this living death sentence the judicial system and the so-called child advocates had bestowed upon us, we were in a living hell, a kind of spiritual warfare against evil. I felt that I had truly come up against evil and often wondered where God was in the midst of all that had been visited upon an innocent child.

CHAPTER 34

A Dream Given, Then Taketh Way

I was still searching for a firm that would take my case pro bono, spending long hours and many exhausting meetings explaining our case and literally begging for help. Finally, I was referred to a well-known firm, Lozow and Lozow, to take my case.

My new attorney, Kerry Rohweeder, was young and cocky and worked diligently. He found it amazing that it took over a month for the courts to allow him into my files and that my records were so tightly sealed. He found this to be very strange behavior of the court. But once he had access to them, he scheduled a deposition of the father within a month. He brought me to his office to role play for our pending motions for our next appearance in court.

The day Derek's deposition was scheduled to take place, he clearly had none of the pertinent information that had been deposed—information on his taxes, evidence of his income, and so on. But Rohweeder didn't let Derek get away with his usual games. He grilled Derek until the atmosphere became extremely uncomfortable. Susan Dycus, the new guardian ad litem and yet another woman infatuated with Derek, stuck up for him at every turn. The temperature of the room became very cold and once again I felt evil surrounding me.

◆ ◆ ◆ ◆ ◆ ◆

At about this time, Bob Hovenden told me he was going to recommend changing my visits to unsupervised. At last. I had been filing motions in court pro se to get this to happen, but finally the guard was starting to see that it made sense to do so. Even hardened criminals, once they establish under supervision that they can follow the rules and consistently act in a way that's beneficial to the child, eventually graduate to unsupervised visits, and here I was stuck in supervised visits for years!

Duane Mullner, my therapist of three years, had a lot to do with this development. He had been meeting with Bob and Derek to move the visits to unsupervised. Bob had finally agreed and told Duane he would approve. (This was a big deal for Bob, who was a total wimp when it came to going against Derek's wishes—he stuttered and turned red whenever Derek talked to him.) Duane then wrote a report, stating the child and the mother need to be together. (I only recently learned that Derek filed a grievance against Mullner for this and won $20,000 from him. Duane was so kind he didn't tell me about it at the time.) He and his wife were afraid they may lose their house.

The first step would be to let my little sister supervise our visits. Judy and her husband had moved from New York to Colorado, and they were living with me while they looked for a home. Derek was apparently greatly alarmed by this suggestion. My little sister and I look a great deal alike, and Ami and Judy have always been very close.

Months earlier, my sister had been the only person in my family allowed to see Ami, with Derek supervising at all times. This was because Ami kept pestering him to see her aunt Judy, and Derek had finally allowed it. Ami treasured those visits. She would call my sister out of the blue while she was at work and say, "Aunt Judy, can I see you today?" I know Ami felt as though she was getting a part of her mother from being with my sister.

For their first visit, I was told they had met at the museum, where Ami sat along with Judy, having tea. I was surprised to hear he had left them alone for even a moment. As they sat down, Ami immediately told Judy, "You know, Aunt Judy, we cannot talk!"

Judy said she could tell that Ami was referring to her abuse; she was afraid Judy was going to ask her about it and that would be the end of their visits.

"I am not going to talk!" Judy said.

"And I am not going to talk!" Ami said back.

Judy was quite shocked at how frightened Ami was but let her know she understood exactly what she was saying.

During this stretch, Ami's spirits had improved immensely. She was so much happier. I could see it in her eyes. What a relief and blessing it had been for my sister to move back to Denver and live with me! I could not wait to see my sister so she could tell me even the smallest detail of anything about Ami. Derek had always liked her. In fact, he sometimes introduced her to his friends as his sister-in-law, even in front of his girlfriend. (This gave Judy the creeps, and not just because he and I had been divorced for years.) Sometimes he would discuss with her incidents from when we were married, maybe about a painting at a museum or some trivial event and considering everything that has happened between us and what he has done to his daughter, that also made her feel extremely uncomfortable. Sometimes Judy felt as though she would throw up having to be around the sociopathic father, but she would do this for Ami's sake.

One day Ami was in the athletic club after a swim meet, which Judy was allowed to go to. (I was never allowed to go to any of her activities, whether ballet recitals or swim meets.) Judy told me that Ami got very upset this particular day because she wanted Judy to put her hair in a high ponytail as I used to do, but her hair had fallen out. It was maybe two or three inches long now and very fine. Ami threw a tantrum and threw the hair brush, which broke my sister's heart. She was six years old at the time, and my sister later told me that when she took off her swimsuit, she was developed way beyond a typical six-year-old.

One day, as Judy was leaving a visit, she said she saw Ami's eyes turned distant. I had seen this quite often in Ami's eyes. They were not the eyes that used to dance when she was a child, the half-moon eyes that drew everyone close to her. These eyes were stone cold. Judy said that she sat on a brick wall and kicked rocks as hard as she could, staring far off.

After finding that Derek was becoming too informal with her, my sister decided to tell him she was not present to be his friend but only for Ami. I guess he thought he could work my sister the way he had worked every other woman, but she would have none of his manipulation.

After this meeting, Derek told Judy she could no longer see Ami. Plus, he had heard of Bob Hovenden's suggestion that we move gradually toward unsupervised visits, with Judy supervising the visits in the interim.

But soon afterward, Judy and her husband had to relocate back east and move to New Jersey. So for our new interim supervisor, we were assigned a nice elderly lady named JoAnn Thorstad. It was such a relief to be out of Bob's office and away from his super controlled treatment. For four years he had not let Ami come to her home. We were allowed after several years of supervised visits in his office to finally go to the park a half a block away from her home, which was torturous to Ami. She would meet her cousins there (Leslie's children), and they would all wonder why they couldn't just go over to Ami's house and play. Now to get a visit with Ami at home after all this time, it was decided that Bob and the Susan Dycus, the new GAL, would both have to come on a visit to see if this could be approved. (I guess they needed two people because I was such a dangerous mother.)

The visit was on December 17, 1993, from 2:30 p.m. to 5:30 p.m.; Ami was seven years old. Before it happened, I needed to agree to the following rules:

1. I would be responsible for paying $160, and at any visit from then on, I'd pay $60 per hour for two staff members.
2. I could discuss no future visits at my home.
3. Nobody else (except my roommate Connie) could be there. If anyone came to the door, I was to tell them to come back at 6:00 p.m.
4. I was to take no phone calls or call anyone during the visit.
5. I was to make no comments about how everyone was "pray- ing for her to come back home" or to sing "you and me against the world." Any comments made to Ami that sug- gested she did not want to live with her dad and/or would be better off living with me, and the visit would be immedi- ately terminated.
6. If there was something I was concerned about, I would com- ply with Bob's suggestion. (Although as stated above, I never metioned she would be better off living with me. I was not allowed to say anything.)

7. I would not make derogatory comments about Derek, the courts, Gail, Paula Tomko, or Bob. (Amazing, like I was ever allowed to say anything. I guess the father was writing this.)
8. I would not allow any doors to be closed and/or locked during the visit. Bob and Ami needed to be in the same room at all times.
9. No media representatives would be present. No pictures or tapes of the visit would be provided to the media, or my visits would be suspended for a year.
10. There would be no photographs of Ami larger than 9x12 inches. There would be no evidence of articles on sexual abuse in the house where Ami could see them.
11. If I became emotionally upset, I was to leave the room until I could compose myself.
12. I would take the time necessary to assess how many things Ami and I could realistically do in three hours. I shouldn't try to do too much.
13. When there was a half-hour left, I would inform Ami that it was time to start getting ready to leave.

While most of the rules were strange, the one about picture size was put in so that I would have to take down a large, beautiful portrait I had on the wall of Ami when she was three. I nonetheless agreed to their demands and anxiously awaited this visit. It had been years.

I completely decked the halls for her visit. I put up little white Christmas lights everywhere, including around the pine tree in the front yard.

The inside of the house looked wonderful too. I put her gifts under the tree, hung her stocking on the staircase, put on some Christmas music, and made sugar cookies. I decorated the tree, leaving off Ami's favorite ornaments so she could put them up herself. I wanted everything to be perfect. You would think I was having a huge party, but it was just for Ami and me.

When 2:30 p.m. finally came, I put on "I'll Be Home for Christmas" and eagerly awaited their arrival. When they didn't show up at first, a familiar anxiety kicked in. What if she didn't come? What if Derek had found a way to cancel it?

What if they had no intention of bringing her? But then they showed up, and after Bob came into the house first, to make sure I was in compliance with the rules, he went back out and got Ami.

All our neighbors kids gathered outside, and when Ami came out they all cried out, "Ami's home!" They ran up to hug her and asked Bob if she could play with them.

"Not now," he said and brought Ami to the front door.

As Ami entered our house, I watched her eyes dance once again. Her long-awaited dream had come true. As she had said to me many times, this was the only home she had ever known. She ran throughout the house and quickly proceeded up the stairs to her beautiful room, canopied in ruffles and lace. She sat on her bed, looking like she was in heaven, and then lay back with all her stuffed animals and just stared around the room. Her eyes took in every picture, every decoration, every doll, and trinket, even the wallpaper with the rocking horses in pink and powder blue that we used to count when she was little, her big polar bear, her favorite stuffed dog, Benna, named after Aunt Judy's dog that she loved so much, and the cradle in the corner with the Cabbage Patch doll that Kim had given her.

I stood for a while at her door and just watched her. We were both so happy. The dream to be together at home, we had both longed for many days, weeks and now years. It all seemed so surreal. I went to her, held her tight, and said a prayer in my head.

"It's exactly how I remembered it," she said. Nothing had ever been moved or changed in her room.

She quickly jumped up and began running throughout the house again, from room to room, checking everything out, wondering why the big portrait of her wasn't up anymore. I had to ignore that question. I watched her and ran with her and tried to explain everything she asked about.

My God! My baby was home!

◆ ◆ ◆ ◆ ◆ ◆

After several more weeks and visits, Ami could come home for regular visits. JoAnn Thorstad was our regular supervisor, and everything went smoothly. Soon I would get to have unsupervised visits. As we got closer to a hearing date to determine if we could go in that direction, Derek began imposing stricter rules. He would not allow Ami's cousins to her birthday party, and no one in my family was allowed to be around her at any time. He knew I would probably be granted my request for unsupervised visits, so he was clamping down. My sister Judy flew out for a visit for that Easter weekend.

I was told that she couldn't be in the house when Ami came for Easter Sunday, our first Easter visit at our home. Ami and I had both been excited about the holiday, especially since she would get to see her aunt Judy. Derek prohibited, but he was still pathetically exerting control in order to feel powerful. I was not about to remove my sister from my own home because of this sick man's control issues, but my attorney suggested I go along with his wishes, since we were so close to a hearing date. I was adamant however. There was no court order keeping Judy from Ami. It only hurt Ami. "Just go along with it," my attorney Kerry said, "and have your sister out of the house for that time period."

So I reluctantly told Judy what was going on, and she was very upset but agreed to leave the house before 9:00 a.m., when Ami was scheduled to arrive.

That morning, before bringing Ami to my house, Derek called to make sure my sister wasn't there. I told him she had a friend picking her up at 8:45 a.m.

He showed up early, just as my sister was leaving. From her seat in Derek's car, Ami stared at her aunt Judy through the window and put her hand up to the glass. Judy placed her hand on the opposite side of the glass, and as their hands met, they both began to cry. Judy left, and Ami had no idea why she couldn't see her aunt Judy anymore.

After this, Derek filed for an emergency hearing to end my supervised visits for not obeying his rules and to remove JoAnn Thorstad as supervisor. There is no doubt in my mind that he arrived early, knowing exactly when my sister was leaving, just so he could try and find an excuse to cut off my visits.

Needless to say, I was heartbroken. We were so close to getting unsupervised visits. So now, instead of getting unsupervised visits after four-and-half years, I was looking at the possibility of losing all of my visitation again with no grounds but a true sociopath making all the rules.

Immediately, "the team" went to work. Susan Dycus wrote a motion to end my supervised visits as per Derek's request. The motion was put into effect immediately—no hearing, no court ruling. Just like that, I lost my visits with Ami.

Even after all that had happened to this point, I couldn't believe it. I had abided by all his sick rules, and I still lost my visitation. But in spite of how devastated I felt, I of course felt even worse for Ami. She couldn't possibly understand why her sick father was doing this to her.

The psycho who hardly ever allowed Ami to call me allowed her to call me. "Where are you, Mommy?" she whined when I answered the phone.

I could only imagine him smirking in the background.

CHAPTER 35

Beaten and Abused by the System

I was near the end of my rope, so depleted and devastated that my mom came to Colorado to get me, insisting I go back to Montana to be with my parents. I had no more strength to fight. I felt completely depressed at having been so close to moving forward and then cut off for no other reason besides the father's control. My visits with Ami had been completely stopped, and I couldn't see any way to get them back. This unilateral move by Dycus the GAL and the sick man she had aligned herself with left me bewildered and spent. Their behavior was absolutely cruel and ruthless! Kerry, my pro-bono attorney, set up a meeting with Dycus and Derek for visitation. At the meeting they wanted me to admit there was no abuse and I could get my visitation back. Unbelievable how stupid did they think I was? My attorney withdrew.

But after a few days of rest, I returned ready to fight back again. With Judge Schauer's help, in March 1995 I filed a lengthy grievance against Kopetski and Purcell and started filing motions in Arapahoe County Court to try to get my visitation back. I was going to do this myself.

And I started getting more creative with my earnings. A year earlier Continental had closed its base in Denver, and I was given a choice: to commute to New Jersey or take a leave. I took a two-year leave so as not to have all my wages confiscated anymore by Derek for his child support and by Kopetski and Purcell for back money I had owed. Plus, I didn't want to commute, so I could reach my goal of freeing Ami from the pedophile's clutches. So my brother, who owned a car dealership in Montana, suggested I work at a dealership completely on commission. That way I would show no income when the courts wanted to see it. On the months I would have to report my income to the courts, I would cut back on my sales so they would not confiscate all my income.

I was able to schedule a hearing for May 31, 1995. When the date approached, as he often did just before a hearing, Derek did something dramatic. He filed a motion for a restraining order against me. Given that I no longer had visitation, I was doing anything I could to see Ami. One day I drove by her school, just to watch her playing at recess. This was not illegal; all I was doing was looking at my beautiful daughter at play. During our phone call that evening, I told her I had seen her playing. She told her father about it, and he then filed for a restraining order against me, claiming that I was likely to flee with the child, as I had done before. (He was referring to the times I had been given permission by the police to go to Vail with Ami to protect her from her father.)

Then, a week before the trial, Susan Dycus tried to thwart the case by drawing up a motion to force me to undergo another psychological evaluation. I knew that this would only delay the hearing for months, and as it was, I was not getting to see my little girl at all.

It was clear to me that I needed to be proactive regarding this demand for an evaluation. Otherwise, the hearing would begin with Dycus's insistence that I get one, the hearing would adjourn, and then we'd have a lengthy delay. I knew their tricks now. So I moved quickly to have it done before the hearing. I was told of an evaluator in Boulder with a great reputation, one who was highly respected in the courts. His name was Dr. Monty Atkinson. I contacted him immediately and explained my situation, praying that I could get an appointment to see him very soon. He agreed to do the evaluation, and I met with him within a couple of days. By that point I didn't trust any therapist, but I had to have an evaluation done so the GAL and Derek could not use this tactic to delay this case any further. If Dr. Atkinson was as good as his reputation, then hopefully he would see through all the injustice and write an evaluation that spoke the truth. I went to the appointment, and we spent several hours talking and testing. I brought in my big black book with the evidence from doctors', police, and therapy reports. The black book was somewhat of a learning tool for professionals to better understand what happened in this case. It also consisted of a study done on these cases, a summation of Gardner's theory of "parental alienation," transcripts of congressional hearings, and newspaper clippings about my case. This book took many months to put together, and I left it with Dr. Atkinson to review.

CHAPTER 36

Becoming My Own Attorney

Two days before the hearing, Dr. Atkinson gave me the evaluation to take to court. I was so nervous to read it. After reading it, I just started crying. The report was truthful and informative. It showed my character as well as my psychological well-being. What a breath of fresh air. I needed this for court, but most of all it gave me strength to endure the hearing.

My little sister Judy flew in from New York to be at my hearing with me. Since the hearing was not on abuse, I hoped that the judge, Judge McCrumb, would not seal the court room. I had all my exhibits numbered and in order and had several witnesses that I had subpoenaed for the hearing. Friends had also shown up to support me. However, the judge sealed the courtroom and asked everyone to leave. Bob Hovenden was now testifying in my favor, as well as Duanne Mullner my therapist, Dr. Carole Jenny who is from Children's Hospital Child Advocacy and Protection team. Dr. Jenny is one of the top experts in the nation on abuse and highly respected. It was amazing she was going to be my witness since I was not an attorney. Dycus had a fit and began raising her voice. She would not allow any of my witnesses to testify and immediately went out of the court to call Dr. Carole Jenny and tell her not to come.

I had all my questions ready, my exhibits and I was prepared to question all witnesses including their witness Dr. Adams. Since none of my witnesses were allowed and I did not know how to fight this and the judge was going along with the G.A.L. I had no other alternative. When I questioned Dr. Adams with great questions I was standing near the podium. The judge told me to sit down and direct my questions from the table. I was not hostile or threatening, but my questions caught her in several lies and made the witness very uncomfortable. It threw me off because I think better on my feet.

This hearing was unproductive, and when I went out of the courtroom, my sister and Duane begged me to give up and let him have Ami; it was going to kill me. Just give her to him! It was May 31, 1995. I was now at the trial table as my own attorney. On the other side was Susan Dycus and Derek. The guardian ad litem, as usual, was representing the father and not the child, as per her job description. No accountability for G.A.L.'s.

My heart was pounding as the trial began. Right off the bat, their first motion was to seek a psychological evaluation of me. It was exactly as I had thought: they would use this to detain the hearing for at least another six months. For some reason, even though my motion for immediate visitation with Ami had been filed six months earlier and the GAL's motion for evaluation of me was filed only a week before the trial, the GAL's motion took precedence. I was not an attorney, so I didn't know why this was the case. It had been over five years, and nobody had asked for an evaluation of me, and now Dycus was demanding one. Well surprise, surprise, I was one step ahead of Dycus. I introduced into evidence Dr. Atkinson's evaluation as Exhibit A.

Dycus freaked out. She ranted about me and my character, but I rebutted point by point what she said, exposing her lies and backing up what I said with proof. I explained to the judge that the evaluation had been done by a reputable therapist in the Denver area. This would save the court time, and we could now move on to the more pertinent motion of unsupervised visitation, the motion that had stood before the court for over six months, whereas the Dycus motion had appeared a week ago. I had Bob Hovenden, the supervisor, ready to testify that this needed to move forward, that we were ready for unsupervised visits.

Dycus was shocked that I had moved so quickly and objected strenuously to the evaluation. Some legal maneuvers I did not understand stood strong, and the judge ended up rejecting Dr. Atkinson's evaluation. Dycus then went on a rant, stating that the evaluation should be done by Kopetski and Purcell. The mention of these two women's names sent chills down my spine. They were the same people who had crucified me four years earlier. I felt sick all over but knew I had to pull it together and think about how I was going to fight this. As we were battling back and forth in the courtroom, I politely but emphatically asked the judge, "Your Honor, may I speak now, please?" repeating "Your Honor, may I speak now, please?" insisting that I be heard on this issue because if the judge went with Kopetski, it was all over for good. I remained calm, even as I felt my heart race and my palms sweat.

"The only reason I am here today," I told the judge, "is to ask for unsupervised visits with Ami. We need some normalcy brought back to our lives. I want to be a mother to my little girl. In the best interest of the child, my daughter desperately wants to be with me. We need some quality time together. Ami so desperately wants to be with me and is upset with a supervisor always being there. Miss Dycus has brought up this evaluation as a ploy to keep this case going on for months and to make sure supervision continues."

The real problem here was that Susan Dycus had never drawn up a parenting plan for us, which normally happens in these cases. Typically, the visiting parent has scheduled supervised visits, and if all went well after a certain amount of time, it moved to unsupervised. For over a year Bob had tried to move the parenting time to unsupervised visits or to allow my sister to do the visitations for a couple of months and then move to unsupervised, but Derek and Susan Dycus had not cooperated. When meetings had taken place, the plan to do what was best for Ami was set aside due to Derek's anger and his fear of being found out. He had to protect himself at all costs.

The GAL once again stepped forward to ask for Kopetski and Purcell. "Your Honor," I said, "I have no problem going for another evaluation; however, I will not go to Kopetski and Purcell. Their evaluation bared no truths in this case and left out all pertinent information on my child."

The judge then stated, "The Petitioner refuses to go to Kopetski and Purcell; therefore, she would not give a true evaluation."

"Your Honor! Once again, I will go to anyone else."

Names were then thrown out, so in the middle of all the shouting, I yelled out the name of Dr. Van Scoyk, the doctor who had recommended Monty

Atkinson to me. I don't think Dycus heard where the name came from, but when she did, she jumped on it even though Derek was yelling out Kopetski's name.

I was privately beaming because I now would have a true professional looking at my case with some common sense, not someone like Kopetski with her MSW riding on the coattails of Dr. Purcell, both earning lots of money by making carbon-copy evaluations of the mothers and always siding with fathers using the PAS label. Oh! How many times these two therapists—or should I say hired guns for the court—had done this! They were known throughout the state of Colorado for siding with the male and never finding abuse. They were disciples of Richard Gardner, the man who wrote that, "All of us have some pedophilia within us. It is good for little girls and little boys to be sexually abused because it makes them better sexual partners as adults… We need to have more pity for the pedophile than scorn… Western culture is ignorant in this because this has been an acceptable behavior for centuries."v

I told the judge that I would like to respond to Miss Dycus's suggestion of Dr. Van Scoyk. "I have no problem with Van Scoyk," I said, "or whoever you recommend, but I will not see Kopetski and Purcell."

At that moment, the judge entered an order for Dr. Van Scoyk. I was so happy. This was truly a milestone, but I knew not to show any emotion, for then Derek and Dycus would surely fight against Dr. Van Scoyk. I asked the judge if the respondent could be responsible for payment to this therapist since it was his motion for the evaluation. I had already paid for an evaluation, I said. Dycus insisted that I pay, and the argument continued.

In the middle of this, Derek argued that he wanted to see Dr. Van Scoyk as well. I knew what Derek was up to. He needed to get to this evaluator to manipulate her. I said, "Your Honor! This evaluation or motion that they have filed is holding up Ami and I from having a quality of life together that she deserves to have with her mother. This is damaging to the child; she is suffering! The motion was filed to have an evaluation of me, so I see no need for Mr. Walker to have any access to my evaluator if the evaluation is to be done on me." Judge Post ordered that the evaluation by Van Scoyk start within the next two weeks and ordered Dycus to arrange this to take place immediately. She then ruled that Derek was to have no contact with the therapist. My gosh! I had won! This was big! No control by Derek. He wasn't even allowed to call her. This was the first time anything had ever gone my way! The judge was listening to me, and I was doing a good job. She then ruled that the money paid to the therapist was to be divided equally by both of us. But I no longer cared about the money. I just wanted to move quickly with another evaluation so as to get back into court with the motion that I had filed more than six months earlier for more time with Ami and unsupervised visitation.

Even though my motion had not been taken up and my witnesses had not been allowed to testify, I knew I had been heard that day and left the courtroom feeling good. It was the first time I had been able to have any kind of control and have a voice. I felt I had done a better job that day than my previous attorneys had during any other trial I had been through.

The evaluation was set up for two weeks later, at the very limit of the court's recommendation. Meanwhile, both Susan and Derek did their best to get to speak with Dr. Van Scoyk. Derek called repeatedly so he could talk to her or set up a meeting with her, but he was not allowed to do so. Susan Dycus tried to set up a meeting between Dr. Van Scoyk and Derek, to no avail. I am not sure if no phone calls took place, but I know he did not get to meet with Dr. Van Scoyk. It was clear this was to be an evaluation of me and that there was to be no contact by the father. The manipulation was difficult for him this time.

I eagerly met with Dr. Van Scoyk and gave her any and all the information she needed. We set up a series of six meetings that would last about a month. I had nothing to hide and desperately was seeking to have time with my little girl. Dr. Van Scoyk was very professional. In the back of my mind, I knew that it might not work. But being the optimist I am, I believed that this evaluation would influence the court to let me see Ami again.

After a delay because Dr. Van Scoyk went on a two-week vacation, a new hearing date was set, and I couldn't wait to get back into trial. I had not seen Ami since Easter, even though on May 31 two years later, Judge Post had ordered the evaluation so that I could resume visitation with Ami quickly.

On August 7, 1995, still working pro se, I filed a notice to re-set a hearing to push for unsupervised visitation. In response, Derek, working through his loyal partner Susan Dycus, filed a motion worse than any visitation motion of the past six years. It was more or less written by Derek, stating that no one in my family—including Ami's cousins, aunts, and uncles—could ever be around Ami. Moreover, none of my friends or anyone who had helped me through this difficult time, such as D.D. Harvey, Diane Baird, and a long list of others—in other words, anyone who knew about the abuse—was not allowed to be around Ami.

I saw through all this, of course. If he were to catch me with anyone in my life, even accidentally, around Ami, I would lose all visitation rights altogether.

Following this, I received harassing phone calls from Ms. Dycus at my workplace, which left me screaming into the phone, my voice shaking. My office partners could hear my pain through the glass of my office. The next day, August 9th, she showed up at the car dealership, dressed in baggy shorts and flip flops, very unprofessional, and approached me with a document she wanted to bring to my attention. At the moment, I was in the middle of closing a $60,000 deal. She hadn't called; she had just barged in. Surprised to see her, I politely asked why she was here. She then held up a large envelope and said, "I have some documents I need to discuss with you!"

"I am in the middle of closing a business deal," I said. "You will have to wait."

I showed her to my office.

Later, when I sat down with her, she took out a document and proceeded with her bitchy attitude to tell me to read and sign it. I began reading at once, and to my amazement, it was taking away more of my time with Ami. We were going backward after five years of supervised visits. Once again, I was being treated like some kind of criminal. It was a good thing it was not during the time of the Salem witch hunt days or surely I would have been burned alive at the stake.

I was stunned at the further restrictions of family and friends and now less time together due to the child molester's fear of being found out. I seethed with anger. I felt like a volcano about to erupt. I was not in a court of law and sick to death of this disgusting woman's face in my face and sick of her not doing her job, which was to represent Ami's best interest. I looked at her with total disdain and said, "Absolutely not! Under no uncertain circumstances will I sign that document! Your behavior is out of line, and we are not going backward. This document is sick!"

"If you do not sign it," she said, "you will never see your child again!"

"If I sign that document," I said, "I will never see my child again. It's written to set me up for failure. No one could abide by all those rules. I will not sign it, and you need to leave. I have work to do!"

She walked out, threatening me that I had just lost my child.

She left the document with me. After she left, I could feel my heart racing and felt short of breath, as though I was going to have another anxiety attack. I had several anxiety attacks in the past where I had driven myself to the emergency room sure I was having a heart attack. I learned to ignore the severe pain racing through your heart, knowing now it was just an anxiety attack. I began taking deep breaths and broke out in a cold sweat. While I was in this state, one of the guys from work came into my office and asked, "Are you okay, Maralee?"

"I'll be fine," I said.

"How can they harass you like this?" he said. "You need to file a law suit against her!"

Yeah right, I thought. Then I would be in the same league as my psychopath ex-husband, who sued everyone.

Immediately I called Hilbert Schauer, the retired federal judge who had been helping me since I had started representing myself. He told me to sign the document and write "under protest" beside my name. So I did what he told me. Then I told Dycus that I had filed it with the court.

When she found out that I had signed under protest, she was livid. It was now apparent to me that Derek's goal was to end my parental rights altogether. Lots of the mothers I had met in my talks and travels had lost all of their rights, but none of them had gone through seven years of supervised visits. They could not withstand the supervised visits. They became like zombies afterward, numb to the world around them. I was now starting to feel this way, so I knew how and why they had given up. The pain was unbearable! I had now been in this for years and did not think it possible to withstand any more abuse by the system and for the system to allow the abuser to continue abusing both of us. This had gone way beyond what was humanly possible to endure.

CHAPTER 37

CNN International News Becomes a Powerful Voice

For months, I had been working with CNN on a story about my case. I had contacted them after the hearing when Judge McCrumb had denied the witnesses I had subpoenaed to testify and had once again sealed the courtroom. Finished with their lies and tactics, I had no other alternative but to hope to get responsible and respectable news coverage by the best. Undoubtedly to me that was CNN. Ami was nine years old now. She and I were never going to be together again unless I took drastic measures. I knew that going through the courts was not the answer. So once again, I was in a catch-22 situation. I might have lost her for good or I might have gotten her home.

I called all my closest friends and asked them what I should do, but they didn't know. It was too big, they said. I weighed my decision back and forth, as CNN continued to move with the story. A lot of investigating needed to be done, and after nine years, there were volumes and volumes of files to go through. It would take them months to understand this case.

I found it absolutely impossible to make this decision, so I put my faith in God. I prayed that God would choose and leave the door open if this was to go forward or close this door if it was not meant to be.

On a trip to Dallas to speak before a political women's group, I had met Kathryn Andrews, a mother who had lost both her son and daughter around the same time I had lost Ami. She had all her parental rights taken away not long after supervised visits started. After my talk, she had approached me, and when our eyes met I immediately knew her pain. It was as if her pain flowed from her veins into me, continuing into my heart, and my own pain seemed to transfer back to her. We embraced with a feeling I have a hard time describing. Maybe it is what it is like when parents of children who have been kidnapped and possibly killed. No one can understand that pain but someone who has been through it.

The moms I had met at conferences, or by word of mouth, or who had been selected with me to testify before Congress—all of these women throughout the years had been close and in contact with one another. For some reason I really connected with this woman.

CNN did both of our stories. In her interview she said, sobbing, "I am not a mom anymore." In my interview, while crying, I said, "I am not allowed to be a mom."

I kept my knowledge of the CNN story very quiet as I waited for the hearing with Dr. Van Scoyk evaluation.

Meanwhile, I knew I was going to need a lawyer to represent me, because I had violated my gag order with CNN, and I would certainly go to jail if I didn't get one and more than likely with an attorney I would still go to jail. After meeting with several female attorneys, I came across the name of Jeanne Elliott, a lawyer who had a reputation as a bull dog. When I entered her office, I found her confined to a wheelchair. I later found out that she was the attorney who, eight years earlier, had been shot in the courtroom by a policeman, the husband of a woman she was representing.

Because she had been in the military, she had rolled to protect her vital organs, which may have saved her life.

The first words out of my mouth were to inform her how difficult this case was and that I wanted to actually do all the speaking because I knew every motion and order that had been filed for the past eight years. However, I was obviously not an attorney, and the GAL and judges had pulled many illegal tactics in the courtroom. I needed someone who knew the law, who could redirect and object.

Most lawyers would have of thrown me out of their office or thought I was an arrogant wacko. If she did think that, she never let on. Instead, she asked me to tell her as much as I could. After a couple of hours of giving as much information as I could, I was exhausted. She listened intently, asked me questions, and then told me to bring her all my files.

"You want all my files from home?" I asked.

"Yes," she said, "all of your files!"

I looked at her skeptically. Surely she didn't know how many boxes of files that I had. She then told me to bring the files to her house and that she would take the case.

I felt good about her the minute I met her, but I worried that she would never have enough time to be brought up to date on my case. We were pressed for time. I knew I would soon be summoned to appear in court for contempt. However, I felt for the first time that I had the right person to represent me. She was intelligent, and most of all I really liked and respected her immensely.

The next day was a weekend, and she wanted to get started as soon as possible. When I arrived home, I put all my boxes together. Some were so heavy I could not carry them to my car, so I got my flight attendant luggage wheels out and put the boxes on the wheels. One box was so heavy I still do not have a clue how I lifted it into the car.

Jeanne lived in a beautiful condo in a great location. She lived in a secure building due to her circumstances, never knowing when the domestic abuser man who had tried to kill her would get released from prison. The doorman rang for Jeanne and told me what apartment to go to. As the door opened, there was another woman with Jeanne. She introduced her as Judge St. John. I knew this name well. She was a very respected judge in the community. Both women opened their eyes wide when they saw my files. I said, "I told you!"

Jeanne smiled and said she would get back with me. I felt like a ton of bricks had been lifted off my shoulders. I smiled as I walked out, feeling confident that she would do a good job. It felt good to have the files out of my sight.

◆ ◆ ◆ ◆ ◆ ◆

At the hearing for the renewal of my visitation with Ami, Dr. Van Scoyk testified to the relationship of mother and child and how shocked she was to find that the GAL Susan Dycus was looking at ending my parental rights. She was astonished, she said, that the GAL could even recommend such a thing. "Especially in this case," she said. "Maralee represents nothing of a mother who would lose parental rights. She does not have any mental disorders, any drug or alcohol problems. She is a mother who was desperately trying to be with her child. The only problem Maralee has at this time is severe depression." Susan Dycus pulled her usual tricks and accused me of all kinds of terrible things. Jeanne was pretty shocked at the extent of her lies. But we won back supervised visitation nonetheless.

Meanwhile, the CNN coverage was moving forward. I had kept it very quiet until the week they flew into Denver to interview me. Only my closest friends and family knew. During the weeks leading up to the interview, the CNN lawyers had been going through the files given to them by an attorney from Florida. She had got my name from a firm in Washington DC who was working on legislation—the same firm who had set up my lobbying meetings on Capitol Hill. She was an attorney in the same situation but in the beginning stages of this nightmare. I had advised her to get Allan Rosenfeld from Vermont to represent her. Allan had the knowledge to represent her and understood the corruptions in the system.

I was to be interviewed by Kathy Slobogin, the reporter from CNN. She called me shortly after receiving the files and asked many poignant questions, to the extent of drilling me. At times I felt angry at her questions and told her to read the files and the reports. It always took people time to understand and a lot longer to just process the injustice and harm the system had done to a child and her mother.

In October 1995, CNN arrived with their camera crew and lighting equipment. That's the day I realized it was really happening. I was so scared at the outcome and of the unknown. My heart raced as they emptied all the equipment out of a plain white van, so no one could track who they were. As they entered the house, everyone was friendly, but I was still feeling nervous. God! Are you with me on this? Please stay close to me! I need you with me.

I was told not to prepare for anything to say but to just respond to Kathy's questions. Once the producer and the cameramen got the room and lighting under control, we began. I had been on television before, but not internationally, and the last time I didn't have a gag order. The interviewwent well,and theywanted to do three more days of taping. The rest of the time they spent investigating and interviewing doctors, police, Ruth, Ami's preschool teacher, and numerous others involved in the case, including the team at the DA's office, the DA, and all the specialists involved. The list went on and on. Kathy and her producer, Leanne Schoff, had obviously done their homework. They were a truly professional team. They knew exactly who they wanted to see and who they needed to contact.

On the second day, they wanted to film me outside at the park on the corner of my block. We had called this "Ami's Park" ever since she was a toddler because whenever we drove by she could not understand why other kids were there. "That is my park, Mom!" she'd say. "How come those kids get to play there?" So many, many times we treasured being at that park together. I had our dog Rustle back at my house—Derek had had someone dump him off at my door when he had moved—and now I was walking him down to the park, remembering the past.

The next day they filmed me baking chocolate chip cookies, which I often made for Ami. Something about the smell of fresh chocolate chip cookies baking in the oven with a glass of cold milk made me feel cozy and nurtured. My mom always baked cookies, so I guess I was continuing the family tradition. Ami and I loved to bake cookies together, especially on a cold winter day.

When they were finished filming, they told me that the piece would air on or around January 22. I now felt confident I had made the right decision to go forward with CNN, although I would waiver a great deal between then and the time the piece actually aired. Would I get Ami back? Would I go to jail for violating the gag order? The threat of jail never deterred me, only the prospect of never being able to see my child again. I knew this was where Dycus was heading. It was so unjust that I felt the world needed to hear my story. The public needed to be aware of how our court system could fail our children so miserably. Most people would never guess that judges such as Michael Bieda would so willingly ignore a father's sexual abuse, causing so much pain to an innocent child, or try to confiscate all my files and records to hide what the court system had done. Most people didn't know what drastic measures were taken to gag or lock up mothers for trying to protect their children from one of the most hideous crimes known to man: incest by a father.

Then I heard that the CNN piece would air for sure at 7:00 p.m. eastern time on January 21, 1996. I called family and friends to notify them of the exact time it was to be showing and to give them a phone number at CNN they could call after watching the program.

At the time, Ami and I still had supervised visits, even though the rules were becoming harsher because of the GAL's and Derek's schemes. Back when I won back supervised visits, Susan Dycus had picked a law student to supervise my visits with Ami. This particular supervisor would sometimes call right before a visit and cancel. Ami and I would be heartbroken and simply devastated after we had waited all week to see each other. Last Easter, she had cancelled our visit an hour before Ami was to arrive. I was furious. She obviously did not have a clue how important these visits were. Easter had been an important day ever since Ami was two years old, when we had made a tree with a branch from a lilac bush and placed it in a beautiful bowl with a floral arrangement. My mom had once again started the tradition. Then we dyed eggs pale pink and purple and all pastel colors. We poked holes in each end of the eggs and blew the egg yolk out into a bowl. Ami was the best at this. She would blow and blow her full cheeks puffed out and her little face reddened, but she would not give up until all the egg yolk was out, which cracked us up. Then we would decorate each egg, gluing on pearls and old jewelry, and finally hand hang each on the "tree" with a different pastel-colored ribbon. Ami loved our Easter-egg tree, and she loved hunting for eggs in the backyard and the house. And of course, we would go to church. However, now, in keeping with her father's demands, we were not allowed to go to church, nor was I allowed to ever say a prayer with her.

When the supervisor called and cancelled, I had been furious. I said, "How can you do this to her? Ami was counting on this and so looking forward to coming home for Easter. This is not acceptable, and I am not going to be the one to tell her. You will break her heart. This is not a babysitting job. If you cannot be more dependable one day a week for a couple of hours you should not have ever taken this job." The supervisor had then called to tell Ami she had to cancel, and Ami cried so much and was so upset that the supervisor decided to make the visit after all.

A few days before CNN was to air the story, Ami and I had a visit together, and CNN was showing previews of what was to air on Sunday night. I did not know that CNN was going to run previews of me like this until my mom called me and told me she saw this woman on TV, never registering that it was her daughter until she heard my voice.

The next supervised visit Ami and I had together, we were walking to the park from our house when a neighborhood kid, not knowing what the piece or the preview was about, said, "Maralee! I saw you on TV." My heart sank, and I ignored him, hoping no one had heard. That Sunday, just before Ami's tenth birthday, I went to the Fowlers' house to watch the program with Kim and Pat. I had invited only my closest friends to view it with me. I had never seen any version of what they had done and had no idea how it would look. The piece was called "Parental Alienation Syndrome," and it was excellent. They interviewed the Child's Advocacy and Protection Team from Children's Hospital, among many other people. They exposed the flaw in the theories of Richard Gardner, who was responsible for having propagated the idea of the parental alienation syndrome that was being used all over the country to protect pedophiles and send moms to jail. They even showed the check the court had paid Gardner for his advice. (See Appendix D.) The show was an hour long. It told the complete story. As I watched, my heart ached as I thought about all the children not being protected. I felt a huge lump in my throat and cried while watching the program. It seemed unbelievable that this was where my beautiful little girl, and my life, had gone. It was surreal, like an out-of-body experience. We all listened to each word so carefully you could have heard a pin drop in the room, trying to grasp it all and at the same time wondering what the outcome would bring.

During each commercial break, we would all evaluate what we had just heard, but I kept reflecting on how much time had passed and all that had happened to my little girl. It was so far removed from the life I had dreamed of for her.

After the program was over, we all hugged. We agreed that CNN had done an excellent job, but we immediately began to worry about the consequences. I now had violated the gag order, and my story had become international news. How soon before I would be summoned to court? The thoughts raced through my head. Would the courts do another ex parte hearing without me present and put me in jail? Or maybe there would be enough public pressure now to scare Arapahoe County and the judges enough to get Ami out of thesituation and put her back with me.

My friends suggested that I stay at Pat and Kim's house, but I wanted to go home. But then my anxiety started to peak, and I began to fear what Derek might do to me. One of my friends mentioned that Derek was such a lunatic he could actually kill me—something I had been afraid of for years. Kim and Pat decided to stay with me. Just before walking out the door, Pat, who is a doctor, a logical man with quiet mannerisms, stopped dead in his tracks and said, "Wait, let me get my gun."

We lived through the night. However, the next morning, the dining-room picture window had been broken out. A huge rock had been thrown through it, though everyone had been asleep and hadn't heard it.

During this time, I returned to flying and was commuting from Denver to Newark to fly my international trips. A month later, when I was working out of state, I got a call from Kathy Slobogin, telling me that Derek was suing her, her producer, and CNN. I was not surprised. I had told her beforehand that he would probably sue them, because he sued everyone. Kathy was not worried, just surprised he had the gall to do so. "We made sure we had all our ducks in a row," she said, "before doing this story."

I told her I was worried that CNN would settle with him, but Kathy said, "I will fight this, don't you worry." I told her that if he actually made money from the story that had implicated him as a child molester, I would wish I had never done it. If CNN paid him off rather than standing by the truth, it would go against every grain in my body and would be worthless to the cause and set a terrible precedent for every pedophile.

It was now February, and I was still waiting for the blow from the courts. Would they admit their mistake or just put me in jail for contempt?

Then, while at work, I got a call from my sister, telling me that my mother had suddenly taken very ill. Since I had been on leave from Continental, I had no flight privileges and no money to get to Montana to be with my mom and dad. It was a dire time for me financially. I had holes in my shoes and in the linings of my coats and was paying the pedophile and the system thousands of dollars a month. When I went to the airport, I talked to a ticket agent, trying to get an emergency fare. I was thinking, I can't lose my mom right now. Please, God! I couldn't get an emergency fare I could afford, but when Leslie and her husband met me at the airport, the airlines they talked to gave them a good fare, so they got me a ticket too.

We spent three days in Billings with my mom in terrible condition. She had suffered an aortic aneurism seven inches in diameter from her upper part of her chest down. The hospital was sending her to Houston to the best heart surgeon for her condition.

I called Continental and talked to one of my friends. This was an emergency, and I had to be in Houston with my mom. She had done so much for me my whole life and she was a huge part of my life and we were so very close I wouldn't make it if I lost her. It looked like I was going to lose her. My friend got us all passes. Meanwhile, I made all the hotel arrangements in Houston for us.

While on the way to Houston, we stopped in Denver. I had arranged for a visit with Ami and her supervisor, the law student, to see her grandmother at the airport on the way through to Houston. Since I had lost an hour of my visitation, I was owed one, so I convinced the law student to make the arrangements. Ami had always been so close to her grandmother, and she was now excluded from her life. She might never see her grandma again. Judy thought it would be too hard on Mom to see Ami, but I knew it would be all right. The supervisor brought Ami to the Red Carpet Club at the Denver Airport.

They had a short visit, hugging and kissing each other, but at least they got to see each other, and it was so wonderful to see Ami and my mom together after so long. My mom was in Houston for nearly two months. During this time, I slept in her hospital room to help take care of her, watching the strongest woman I know suffer tremendously. She had two major surgeries, aneurisms (one aortic and one in the back), a staph infection, and a heart attack. At one point, she slipped toward death, but I called out to her, "Mom, you stay in here and fight! You've come this far; stay in here and fight!" and I shook her until she came back.

Although this was a great hospital, my mom would not have made it if we hadn't been there by her side. She needed more care than the nurses could possibly give. My dad was with me the whole time and would only leave in the evening where he would go to the hotel to sleep.

In May, while in Houston, I got a call from my attorney, Jeanne Elliot, that the courts had scheduled a hearing for my gag order in ten days. I would have to leave my ailing mother to attend that hearing, which was bound to be bad for me.

When I arrived back in Denver I was exhausted, emotionally depleted, and had lost between fifteen and twenty pounds. I talked with Jeanne on the phone, and she told me not to worry, everything would be all right. She would meet me at the court at 7:00 a.m.

CHAPTER 38

Contempt and Jail Time

When the alarm went off, I was already awake in my bed. I had gotten very little sleep. I felt numb, almost paralyzed. This would be the day I would go to jail, but I was too exhausted to care. Leaving my house, I felt incredibly alone.

As I approached the courthouse, I had flashbacks of all the horrible events that had happened there. Suddenly, my breathing was shallow, and I could feel a panic attack coming on. Immediately, my body was overtaken by it. Breathe slowly, breathe slowly, breathe slowly, breath slowly. I felt chest pains again as well. I can't go in this place! God, please stay with me. Breathe, breathe. Whenever I felt this panic attack I would always pray to God and that was the only way it would be released from my body.

I got out of my car and began to walk up the same walk I had walked so many painful times, having flashbacks of Judge Bieda's punishingly sick court order, after which I could hardly walk out of the courthouse, and the many more punishing rulings that came before and after Bieda. Fortunately, he had since been removed from the bench—one of the only judges in the history of Colorado removed from the bench for delivering punishing court orders to women and being a sexist, biased judge.

When I entered the courthouse, I saw that the docket had been cleared for the whole day, just for a hearing on my gag order. I was scared to death. This should be a quick hearing, I thought. Why the whole day?

Jeanne hadn't yet arrived, so I looked frantically for a phone, called Judge Schauer, and told him what was going on. He told me it looked like I was going to jail and that I should call CNN. They had told me they would help me if I went to jail because of their story.

Just then, the automatic doors opened, and Jeanne Elliot entered in her wheelchair, wearing a beautiful pink and gray suit. I had never seen her so dressed up; she looked so professional. Her curly hair bounced as she talked with another attorney entering the building. I was amazed by her bravery. This woman had to repeatedly reface her fears, coming into the very courtroom where she had been shot. That is why we have metal detectors today going into courthouses.

I greeted her, told her she looked great, and told her how scared I was that the judge had cleared the docket for the day just to cover my gag order. I told her Judge Schauer had told me to call CNN, and she thought that was a good idea too. I scurried back to the phone booth to make that call, and I reached Kathy Slobogin's voicemail. I left her a nervous but pleading message to help me. I was more than likely going to jail today, I told her.

We entered the courtroom, and the hearing began by citing my constitutional rights. Jeanne was incredibly well prepared. I had never seen a judge and attorney go back and forth on legal tactics so much, mainly on my civil rights. The judge, Cheryl Post, was also prepared for Jeanne's tactics. They both recited law statutes back and forth. It was far more impressive than anything I had ever seen on a lawyer show. The CNN tape was played several times, and as they played it, I thought, how could this judge watch this tape and not have any questions about the abuse and how Arapahoe County had mishandled my case?

It was now time for me to testify. The father had the GAL as his attorney helping him out, and he was representing himself. How wonderful, he was going to be asking me questions. I approached the witness stand and was sworn in. Derek began his questioning, his face animated. He was loving every minute. He started by asking me, "How did CNN get reports on this case?"

I responded, "An attorney from Florida gave them to CNN."

He looked disappointed. He was sure he had me on that one. Then he started asking me to tell the court about all the organizations I was affiliated with or working with on abuse. I thought to myself, "Go ahead, you idiot, keep asking me about who I have been affiliated with. It will be good for the judge to hear. I want it to go on record for Ami to know how hard I fought to protect her."

Straightening my shoulders and lifting my head, I cited all the organizations I had been affiliated with in the last eight to nine years: Alliance Rights for Children in Washington DC; The National Center for Protective Parents; Women of Washington; the law firm of Verner, Lipfert, McPhearson, and Hand in Washington; the governor's task force in Colorado to re-write the Colorado Children's Code; and DU Law School, and I had testified in New York before a Congressional hearing, etc. When he asked why I had been affiliated with a law firm in Washington, I told him that this law firm had set up my appointments on Capitol Hill with senators, and they had put together a memo showing cases across the U.S. where the system had totally failed the child when the father was a molester of his own child. The memo was with Janet Reno, and she was now looking into the problem. I loved getting all of this on record and noticing the judge's reaction out of the corner of my eye.

Derek then asked me, "You believe I abused Ami?"

"I believe Ami!" I responded.

"So you believe I abused Ami?" he repeated.

Once again I said, "I believe Ami!"

He brought up the CNN piece and how damaging it was to him and his career. This almost made me laugh out loud. First of all, this man had no career; second, he had never been identified in the CNN story. Ami was not identified either, and my name had been changed. Furthermore, you would never know I was her mother, for I was not allowed to go within a 100 feet of where she was at any time without supervision.

Later, when Derek was asked how many times he had seen the tape, he said, "At least twenty-five times."

I found that just a little obsessive—to have watched a one-hour tape twenty-five times—but the judge didn't seem to pick up on it.

By the end of the day, I was exhausted. Jeanne looked at me and said, "Every time I go to court with you I feel like I have a big red X on my butt!"

The judge announced her ruling, beginning with five contempt citations. My attorney asked the judge for "work release," and I panicked, thinking she was referring to prisoners who wore those orange uniforms and picked up trash. I quickly argued with Jeanne that I didn't want work release, I would go to jail, but Jeanne repeated what she said to the judge and told me to shut up or I would go to jail. I thought work release meant I had to be out on the sides of the roads or in public with orange prison uniforms, picking up trash. I would rather be hidden in jail.

I ended up sentenced to 30-day jail sentence and then got probation with a stern warning that if I met again with any news media whatsoever, I would receive an immediate jail sentence. Neither party involved was to talk about this case any further and was not to address any media entity. The gag order would stay in effect until the child was eighteen. I was so relieved I didn't have to go to jail.

◆ ◆ ◆ ◆ ◆ ◆

The next day, I had a visit with Ami, and she told me that her dad was going to marry the woman he had been dating for a short while and that they were going to have a baby in a couple of months. I began to think, "What is he going to do?"

He was going to leave the state, since his girlfriend didn't live here in Denver. My heart racing, I calmly asked Ami, "Are you moving?" She was eleven years old, and I had been working so hard to be with her. I was terrified it would all fall apart and she would be moved out of state. But she told me they would be staying in Denver. More than relieved, I sighed. "Oh, good!"

But immediately I began thinking of his wife and future child. She was from a wealthy family. She had no idea what she was in for. But maybe this will help me, I thought. He could devote his sick attention somewhere else for a change.

Meanwhile, my mom was getting released from the hospital in Houston, so I had to go back there to get her. My sisters were too afraid to bring her back by themselves.

My mom and dad then went to my sister's house in Loveland to stay. My sister Leslie was a nurse, but she was very nervous to take my mom because she was still so frail, but the important thing was that my mom had survived. We had all survived. For me, it had been an amazing thing to watch the love my parents had for each other. It was beautiful to watch, and painful as well, since for a long time we hadn't known if she would make it and had left it all in God's hands.

◆ ◆ ◆ ◆ ◆ ◆

Once my mom was in Colorado at my sister's, I went back to work on my case. With the help of Judge Schauer (a retired judge), a meeting was set up with two new judges and all the involved parties, the supervisor, the GAL, attorneys, and of course the pedophile and myself. Susan Dycus had still not set up a therapist for Ami and me even though it had been court ordered for several months. The two new judges were trying to determine how to move this case forward. The other federal judge, a friend of Judge Schauer's, said he would like to talk to the father alone. As he left the room with Derek, he touched my shoulder, as if to say it was all going to be okay. The female judge who stayed in the room talked about how we would have to take "baby steps" to move this case forward for the child to be with the mother.

I couldn't believe what I was hearing. After all we had been through, we were now going to take baby steps? What did she think I had been doing for eight years?

"Baby steps!" I said. "You've got to be kidding!" I looked around the room, incredulous. Are any of you mothers in here? You can't possibly be a mother and be saying this."

I was so worn down from the emotional drain of taking care of my mother and the pain of not being with Ami that I felt as though I was going to have a nervous breakdown. I was beyond depleted and tired of never showing my vulnerability. I got up out of my seat, thinking I was going to pass out. My attorney grabbed me and held me steady. I then felt my legs weaken and began to tremble, crying so hard I thought I would never stop. I left the room and collapsed outside the door, sobbing. After a few minutes—I have no idea how many—I pulled myself together and headed for the elevator to leave. Just as I entered the elevator, so did the federal judge who had been assigned to the case. He looked at me and said, "Stay strong. It is going to get better!"

The baby steps began. First, a therapist named Julie Lee Richter was assigned to our case, "to help bond mother and daughter." Once again, more money was being charged so that I could "bond" with my child. Only this time, she was to help us become reunited. What a game this all was. How much more money could they get? As if this woman was going to help Ami and me bond. We had never ever lost the bond between us; we just needed to be together.

For the first couple of months, we had weekly visits, and we played games that were put out by the therapist. But all we wanted to do was to be together in a natural situation and be able to talk. This game playing in front of a therapist was anything but natural.

In the meantime, we needed a new visitation supervisor. JoAnn Thorstad, the elderly woman who had been doing it, had been removed after the Easter debacle. After her, the law student had been horrible. So Jimmy Schauer, Hilbert Schauer's wife, offered to be our supervisor. Incredibly, before the court would allow the wife of a respected, retired federal judge to do so, she and Judge Schauer had to meet with Judge Post in chambers first, to be approved. Judge Schauer was appalled by this being a federal retired judge, and Judge Post had been before him as a new attorney, but they both went through with it for Ami's sake.

Then, for the first time in eight years, a parenting plan was put into action. Baby steps were now transforming to more baby steps, but at least now I could see the roadway and knew that it led very slowly to more and more time with Ami.

After three or four months, the time came when I got to have a visitation to be alone with Ami. I was to take her in my car from the therapist's office to the mall, for one hour. It was all arranged. Derek would meet us at the mall after our hour was up. Ami and I were so excited to be getting time alone together that we left the office walking on clouds. Once we were outside the building, however, there stood Derek, next to his car. He demanded for Ami to get in the car.

"Ami is to be with me!" I said.

He viciously yelled, "Get in the car, Ami, now!"

"She is not going anywhere with you!" Ami instantly got into his car, and he drove off.

I went back to Dr. Richter's office to tell her what had just happened. The therapist was with another client and happened to come out of her office as I entered her waiting-room area. She was puzzled that I was back. Distraught, I told her what had just happened. She was upset too but instantly saw Derek's unwillingness to cooperate and his need to control. She told me she would handle this and would let the GAL know what was going on.

Afterward, all I could think about was the fear in Ami's eyes and how quickly she had moved to do exactly what her father had told her to do almost robotically. Derek now knew he was losing control and that I would at some point have unsupervised visits with Ami. So he set up a meeting with the therapist and the GAL to try and win over Doctor Richter. Later, I found out from the therapist that he brought a bra of Ami's that he said I had bought her, which he found inappropriate. He pulled out of his briefcase a lacy lilac bra and began to explain that I should not buy such sexy bras for Ami. At first when the therapist brought this up, I could not figure out what she was talking about. I would never buy Ami anything like that. Then I remembered that Ami had changed her shirt during one of our supervised visits, and her bra was so dirty I told her I would wash it for her and gave her one of my old bras to wear. By the time she had left, I had forgotten all about it. I couldn't believe he had actually brought a bra to a meeting with our therapist, and I was disgusted to know he was carrying one of my old bras in his briefcase. I explained to the therapist what happened, told her he gave me the creeps, and to please not tell him it was mine.

By this time, my little girl was eleven, and she was graduating from elementary school. Dr. Richter had arranged for me to attend the ceremony.

The last time I had been to Ami's school was when she was in first grade in the morning, before school had started. At the time, Derek had told me that I couldn't come to the school, but there was no court order and Ami told me she wanted her crown she was mayor for the week and would I bring it. I told her

I would bring it before school. Entering her room, I had looked at the artwork with little kids' names on the wall, looking for Ami's. On Martin Luther King Jr. Day, the teacher had apparently asked each child to write what they wished for. Ami had written, "I wish there were no more rules!" I stared at her writing for quite some time. Then I went over to the long table that was titled "Mayor for the Week," and it had Ami's name on it. I smiled as I walked toward the table and placed her crown next to the dirty stuffed animals she had brought from his house. Then I looked inside her desk, at her papers, and as I did, I realized how much of her childhood I was missing out on and started to cry. Then I had the idea to leave her a note in her desk, since I knew that anything I sent her in the mail as cards and letters had never been given to her. In the note, I told her how proud I was of her for being mayor for the week and how much I loved her. Then drawing a few musical notes, I wrote the song out from Annie that we used to sing together: "The sun will come out tomorrow! Bet your bottom dollar that tomorrow, there'll be sun." Just as I had finished the note, the principle had entered the room and began to yell at me in an angry voice I was not allowed in the school. I was quite shocked and told him there was no court order saying I couldn't come to the school. He threatened me angrily and told me to leave or he would call the police. I told him I had every right to be there; there was no court order telling me I couldn't go to her school when she was not there. In fact, I paid Cherry Creek school taxes, and her father didn't. He replied by telling me that Derek was the custodial parent and repeated his threat to call the police then walked away angrily.

I never forgot that day. I was Ami's mother, and yet I had been treated as a common criminal. Now, entering the school more than five years later, I was still viewed as a hostile intruder. When Ami spotted me, she ran up to me and pulled me in line with her. I noticed I was being scrutinized by several of the teachers. I could see their eyes on me as they said hello to Ami and as Ami proudly introduced them to her mother. I could tell I was again being viewed as a criminal. These people had no idea what she and I had been through. Okay! Maralee, hold your head up high. You know who you are, and these people have not a clue and are too ignorant to understand the pedophile profile.

By the end of the ceremony, with the school packed with fifth graders, parents, and teachers, I heard a familiar voice coming over the microphone from the stage. Yes, it was him. The pedophile was up on the stage, giving a speech thanking all the wonderful teachers and staff at the school where his daughter had attended since kindergarten. Oh! If these people only knew how sick he was. A pedophile expressing his gratitude to some of the people who had helped him to keep his secret. Just then, the policewoman who had supervised our visits at one time walked up to us. She had been at the graduation ceremony because of her child. She looked me in the face and said, "He is so sick. How are you two? I think of you so often."

I replied, "We're hanging in there." She knew what was going on and always really liked Ami and me. She saw through Derek.

As I got up to leave, I saw him standing at the back of the room where I would have to exit, talking with several other parents and holding his new baby girl in his arms. He was a stay-at-home dad now while his new wife worked around the clock and paid all their bills.

When I had first heard that their baby was a girl, my heart had ached for her. Once a pedophile, always a pedophile. They do not stop their behavior, and there is no cure. Now, seeing the baby, I wanted to see this little sister of Ami's. As I was walking by, I said hello, and he introduced me to the people he was talking to. I love babies, and the impulse came over me to ask him if I could hold her. He quickly pulled the baby away from me, and with his scary blue eyes and tightened lips loudly said, "No!"

Everyone instantly looked at me as if I were evil and dangerous. It was humiliating.

The next week, before therapy, I called Dr. Richter to tell her how the graduation had gone and how the school and Derek had treated me. Dr. Richter was now starting to see the picture.

Dr. Richter was really trying to help us and was doing her best to stay out of the crazy politics involved in my case. The best thing she ever did for me was call me at work before a therapy session to warn me that at our session later that day, Ami was going to recant the abuse. Dr. Richter wanted to be sure to prepare me. Derek and Susan Dycus had told her Ami was recanting, and Ami had done so herself to Dr. Richter. I wondered how she had gotten this information. The therapy sessions were designed just for us, so why and when had Derek and Dycus brought Ami to her? But I didn't even ask because I felt a huge lump in my throat. Why would Ami do such a thing? Did she really not remember? Was she dissociative? I begin asking Dr. Richter the same questions, but she said, "Maralee, I just wanted to let you know where Ami is at, so you would not get upset."

I thanked her and got off the phone.

Driving to the visit, I replayed what Dr. Richter had said to me on the phone earlier that day. When I got there, the door closed, and Ami was excited to see me. Then she sat across from me in a chair, instead of sitting where she usually would, as close as she could get. Dr. Richter said, "Do you have something you want to tell your mother?"

Ami acted very nervous and finally said, "Mom, my dad never did anything to me! You need to admit when you are wrong!"

I just stared at my nervous little girl. I gently told her I believed her when she was young and that I could not forget or pretend, but I would try to understand. I felt myself begin to tremble. If Dr. Richter hadn't warned me, I don't believe I could have held it together.

She then said, "Mom, don't you want me to come home and be with my kitty?" In other words, she was telling me to shut up about the abuse, so we could be alone together again. I took deep breaths, my heart aching. I felt as if my own daughter, the child I had given my life to protect, had just kicked me in the stomach and left me breathless.

During my drive home, I remembered the conferences I had attended in Washington DC on dissociativebehavior. Experts had spoken on this issue, and sexual abuse victims had described how their pain had been so unbearable that they actually left their bodies when their father was abusing them. It was as if it was happening not to them but to someone else. Did Ami now not remember any of the abuse? She had her mother beside her, fighting for her. I had hoped this would help her to deal with the abuse, since a lot of these children didn't have any parental support, given that the non-abusive parent was often in denial or refused to believe their child.

I called Duane, my therapist, to ask him how this could have happened. He explained to me that Ami would not have survived had she not dissociated. This was not a neighbor next door, he said. This was her dad, a trusted parent. "Be glad she was able to do this," he said. "It will save her. She can't deal with this until she is safe and no longer under her dad's control."

CHAPTER 39

Dissociative Behavior

It was now 1998, a year after the CNN show had aired. I was getting Ami for five hours alone, twice a week. It had seemed like such a long process to go through all the baby steps to get to this point. We had both been constantly afraid that at any time they would separate us and deny us our time together. We had both been so programmed it was as if we were prisoners who had been granted furloughs and were anxiously questioning if our freedom was real. The first time we rode in the car together and went to the grocery store, we both looked over our shoulders as if we were doing something illegal.

As Christmas approached, I was excited that I would have Ami overnight for Christmas Eve. This would be our first Christmas together since she had been taken away from me when she was four. Now, she was twelve. I begged all my family to come to my home again, eight years later. My mom was still weak, and it would be difficult for her to make the trip with my dad, but she exclaimed, "We will be there with bells on!"

And she was! She literally tied red ribbon with gold bells to her cane, and she shook it as she came off the airplane entering the terminal.

I wanted Ami to have the Christmas she had been hoping for all these years. The alienation of all her family had been harmful to her, and now we would be all together again. It felt like such a healing was taking place in Ami, and in all of us, at the same time.

My father's eyes sparkled with joy when he saw his granddaughter at her home. We all watched old home videos of my family at Christmas, and the grandkids got a real kick out of seeing their moms and dads as kids at Christmas.

As we sat down for Christmas dinner that evening, the table was set with all my mom's china and crystal. It looked beautiful. Everyone was starving, but all I could think was to thank God for this Christmas with Ami and family. My prayers were now maybe starting to be heard. Yet I felt anxious that her father would find a way to end it all.

The next morning as the sun came up, the kids began waking up all the adults. Santa had come, his cookies had been eaten, and the glass of milk was empty. We began passing out the Christmas presents, which seemed to go on for hours. Ami and I enjoyed every minute, but the clock was ticking. I saw her become quieter and quieter as the hour approached for her father to pick her up, and my heart ached for her. She didn't want to leave. I became upset for her that she couldn't just enjoy her family for the whole day. His own family was so broken that he didn't even get together for the holidays.

When Ami heard her father's car horn honk out front, she looked down as tears welled up in her eyes. She went straight to Grandpa, got up in his lap and hugged him. She went around the room then, hugging and kissing all of her family good-bye. Once she left, I just wanted to sleep away the pain of her tearful departure, the memory of watching her slowly approach her father's car with head hanging down, then turning and waving good-bye to me.

For the first few months of time we had alone together, it seemed almost surreal. We never wanted anyone else with us or even to come over to visit because our time together was so important. Sometimes Karen, Ami's best friend, would come over and end up staying too long. Ami would start to get grouchy toward her at first, and then later come right out and say, "I need time with my mom now."

But once we settled into our visitation schedule, we started to share and adjust to a somewhat normal life. We now were making up for lost time that we could never get back. To really be a mom and tuck her in at night and talk for hours like we used to was so wonderful. I can't even begin to describe how happy I was to have my little girl home. No, she had not been protected from her pedophile father, though God knows I tried, but at least we could be together now. I now had a chance to have a life with my child and to be a normal mom and give her a normal life. I helped her comb the knots out of her hair and helped her with her school projects. I was so proud of her when she won first place.

That summer when she was twelve, we got to live the life we had always fantasized about. We went to my parents' fiftieth wedding anniversary that I had planned and organized for months at Red Lodge, a magnificent mountain resort in Montana. It was a wonderful celebration with family and friends. We visited her aunt Judy in New York, her aunt Leslie in Loveland, and she got to have her friends stay overnight at our house.

And we took a trip to Hawaii again! The first time we got on an airplane together, we were both so excited. Since I was back with Continental at this point, we could fly for free. Walking through the airport with her, I was fearful I would run into a lot of people I knew, and someone might say something inappropriate like, "My gosh, is this Ami? You got her away from her dad?" I also was anxious that at any time I would say something that someone in the airport could overhear and just like that, my visitation rights would be taken from me. So when I saw people from the airlines that I knew, I looked away, for fear that they would say something. They would mean well, but it might make Ami uncomfortable.

As we got to the ticket counter, we were very excited, but it still didn't seem real. The agent handed us our tickets, and we were in first class. As we walked down the jet way, I found myself looking over my shoulder and becoming very anxious, worried that this was just a game and they would find some excuse not to let us go. When we got to our seats, we both kept looking over our shoulders. Until that plane lifted off, we both felt like it would not happen. We did not smile or relax, waiting for the unknown terror that they could bestow upon us next.

I loved every minute of that trip. She remembered so many things from when she was a little girl. She remembered when she got up on the stage and sang with the band. She wanted to stay at the same hotel we had stayed at when she was little. She wanted a floral lei with candy when we checked in and when we got to the pool. She remembered how she had almost lost Benna, her stuffed dog that Aunt Judy had given her.

Back home, I realized that Ami was no longer a little girl, and I could now get rid of all her baby clothes. I had kept everything all these years, holding on to the memories. But now I could let go, so we had a big garage sale and sold all her old stuff. Once school started, I didn't see her as often, so I spent a whole week fixing up her room, making it more grownup. I put up new wallpaper and curtains, bought new sheets, drilled holes in her dresser to install china knobs, and even turned the ceramic horse we had made together when she was five into a lamp. I stayed up until two in the morning then went the next day to pick her up from school. She was in middle school now, and it was the first time I got to do this—to be a normal mom and pick up Ami from school.

◆ ◆ ◆ ◆ ◆ ◆

Still, Derek's imprint was everywhere, and she was still living with him and developed a loyalty to him. She lived in two different homes now, she said, and she liked them both. One day, when we were driving to a museum in Denver, we passed the building where we had supervised visits with Bob. "Every time I go by that place," I said, "I get sick. Don't you?"

"I never let myself think about it," she said. For the most part, we could act freely with each other, but there were still restrictions, and there was still an underlying fear that it could all be taken away at any moment. In my garage, I had a lot of posters on the walls from the rallies I had attended or spoken at, with headings like "Remove Judge Bieda, Judge Jails Mom and Gives Baby to Baby Rapist" and "Free Sarah!" (which was the pseudonym used in the media reports on Ami). When Ami started coming back home for visits, I had taken them down and put them away, but when we drove into the garage together, Ami said, "You better get rid of those posters, Mom. We're not safe yet."

◆ ◆ ◆ ◆ ◆ ◆

Now that we were together again, it was hard for me not to feel bitter about all the years of hearings, legislation, all the motions, phone calls, harassing letters, calls and visits, sleepless nights, anguish and heartbreak, only some of which I've documented in this book. It was hard just to forget it all and enjoy my time with Ami, and not dwell on all that I had lost—her entire childhood, just about—due to her father's selfish, disgusting unthinkable behavior, and the incompetence of the judicial system. But I had to, for Ami's sake, and for the sake of my sanity.

◆ ◆ ◆ ◆ ◆ ◆

In general, we never talked about the abuse or the disturbing events of the past. However, there was one time when I just could not understand her relationship with her dad. She had come home from school, and I was looking at her homework when I came across what she had written about the summer. I began to read, eager to see what she had written about our first summer together in years—about our family reunion in Montana or about our trip to Hawaii. But it was all about her summer with her new family. I was just mentioned as her mom, Maralee. Immediately I felt a lump in my throat. When I asked Ami why she hadn't mentioned any of what we had done together, she responded, "Mom! You know how much I love you!"

"That's not the point," I said. "I guess I just don't understand the relationship you have with your dad."

"We have a good relationship," she said. "I love both my mom and dad. You need to put the past behind you and just remember the good things like our trip to Honolulu together, and only look forward, never look back." Sniffling a little bit and biting my lower lip I thought, This is a twelve-year-old girl. God! How profound!

"Ami, are you safe?" I asked her. She didn't respond. "Ami," I said, "would you tell me if you were not safe?"

"I don't know," she said. "I just want to have a normal life."

My little girl's knowing blue eyes stared into my soul as if she wanted to grab all that mess inside of me and throw it all away. I looked at her and said, "I can't forget, Ami! I would have to get a lobotomy!"

At the time, I wished that I could have Ami's attitude. Instead, I was having the opposite experience: I felt haunted daily by all that had happened. I should have gone in front of the camera that day in the back of the courtroom after they took her from me, showing my face and speaking my mind. To hell with the gag order. I should have told the public what Judge Bieda had done—how he had torn a daughter from her mother's arms, how he had ignored reports from doctors and police officers with firsthand evidence that this little girl had been molested by her father, how he had forced me to pay $1000 a month child support when I wasn't even seeing Ami. I would have gone to jail, but so what?

And I felt bitter and vindictive, too, determined to get back at everyone who had acted so terribly. I fantasized about planning a big class-action lawsuit against everyone, not for the money, just to make them pay. I wanted to file a lawsuit against everyone involved in the case.

I begged God to release me from my outrage against these people, to let me be more like Ami and dissociate myself from the whole nightmare. I couldn't help but melt into tears whenever I thought about it. I never let Ami see this emotion. I wasn't sleeping well, and I was distraught so often. I needed help.

CHAPTER 40

New Lies and New Targets

I wish I could say that with a new wife and a baby at home to take care of, Derek was leaving us alone, but amazingly, he somehow found the energy to try to control our time together. Susan Dycus had decided that Ami's activities took priority over our visitation time, so Derek scheduled her activities on the days that I was to be with her. He was the group leader for Odyssey of the Mind, so he scheduled their meetings on the days or evenings I was to have Ami. He signed her up for ski school on every Sunday, the only day of the weekend I had with her. We had to get up at 6:00 a.m. and drive to a parking lot where the bus would pick her up. Although I wanted her to ski and loved the idea she was learning, it was difficult to always be giving up my time due to his manipulation and control.

Around her twelfth birthday, Ami had a ski day and was looking forward to her birthday party we had planned together when she returned home. There was a really bad snow storm in the mountains this particular day. After I went to her pick- up destination where the bus would arrive, Derek called meto tell me she would be arriving a little late. He had the phone numbers of the individuals who were in charge of the trip, the people who knew when the bus would actually be arriving, but he never allowed me to have those numbers. So what he knew, but I didn't, was that the bus was four hours late. He let me sit in my car for that whole time, calling me every hour to tell me that the bus would be arriving in twenty minutes. It was absolutely freezing out, and I had to keep turning the car on and off to keep warm.

When Ami arrived, she was exhausted and very disappointed that she had missed her party and the only time she would have with me. By the time she got home, our visitation would just be ending, so Derek came to the drop off spot to pick her up.

When Ami climbed off the bus and saw her dad, she said, "What are you doing here?" with an angry look on her face. She ran to me, threw her arms around me and began to cry. Seeing this, Derek threw her skis in the back of his truck and angrily yelled at her to get into his truck now.

Months later, I asked my new attorney Gary Johnson to file a motion with the court for fifty percent of the time. Ami and I both wanted this. We were dying to have more time with each other. Having to go back to court was traumatic for me, but now I naively believed they could no longer say anything negative and it would be a simple short hearing. Once again, I was wrong. Derek told the court a string of lies until I finally couldn't hold back and called out to the judge, "He is lying!" Finally, I was called to the witness stand to testify. The information and schedules I had with me at court proved that Derek was lying. By the end of the day, the judge ordered that Ami and I were to have fifty percent visitation. Now, eight and a half years later, Ami had helped our cause by actually getting to meet with the judge in chambers and asking him for more time with me.

After that, Ami and I settled into a normal routine together. She had half her time with me and half with her father. We had so much fun together, just laughing and carrying on like we had never been apart. It was so wonderful to actually be a mom, having her friends come over and taking them to all their activities. Our house became the house all her friends wanted to come to, and we had great times and special birthday parties. Most of the time I would find myself giving her too much, but I didn't care. The idealistic life I had envisioned for her had been tainted for good, and she had been through a living nightmare. She was going to get spoiled for a while. But still, I tried to instill in her all the appropriate values and as much normalcy as possible so that she would be able to thrive as a teenager and as an adult.

Still, I felt haunted by all the past memories. When in New York, I found myself calling literary agents to see if I could get my book published, and I wanted to make phone calls to Court TV. I thought of my own pain and what so many people involved in this case had done to me emotionally. I wanted to stop this corrupt system from ever doing this to another mother and child. Before, I had been movingforward with only Ami in mind, trying to accept and survive all the painful things they did to me, ignoring my own scars. Now the wounds had resurfaced. Why now? I asked myself why I couldn't accept what I had now. I had Ami half the time, and she was on her way to a healthy life. But was her father still abusing her? Once a pedophile always a pedophile?

Maybe I couldn't settle myself down because I had never lived in lies and denial, pretending all was well. Her father belonged in prison. But Ami seemed to accept things the way they were. It made me sick! I didn't know if he was still abusing her. I knew by the things she said to me that she remembered some of her past, but under no uncertain terms did she want to deal with it and had told me so. She told me she would deal with it when she was an adult.

One day on a lay-over in Sao Paulo, Brazil, I tried to rest in my hotel room. I had flown all night and only had a few hours to sleep before I flew back to the States. But my body seemed not to want to sleep. I would sleep maybe three or four hours, and then I was just fine, ready to get up, raring to go. This couldn't be healthy. I begged my mind not to go there—no more torment or vicious memories of the past. It was over as much as it could be, and I had done all I could. I told myself, Rest, Maralee, please let yourself rest. But then I thought back with a pang of regret. I should have gone on the news the day Judge Bieda put a gag order on me and told the public about his ludicrous ruling. Let the public see my face and tell them how he ignored all doctors' reports and police reports of evidence, how he had put a gag order on me and wanted to confiscate all my records. I could have said it so well. So I would have gone to jail, so what? They weren't going to give me Ami anyway.

I decided that when I got home, I'd call Tom Kelly, the CNN attorney, and tell him I wanted to file a class-action or a civil lawsuit against all the people or so-called professionals involved in my case. I didn't care about winning any money—Tom could have it all. There just had to be some kind of justice here. As I thought about the people I would sue, the tears began to flow, and it seemed as if they would never stop. I begged God to release these memories and guide me forward to what I need to do. I needed inner peace and couldn't stand the pain of having been silenced. God! Oh, God! Please help me. I was overwhelmed by how hard I was crying and wondered where it was all coming from; I hadn't cried that hard for quite a while. My last thoughts were that I should either get heavy-duty therapy or begin lawsuits andgrievances because something had to give. The pain pierced me every day.

◆◆◆◆◆◆

For the years she had been with her father, Ami had been unkempt. Her clothing was torn and dirty, and most of the time she looked like an orphan, and not because her father didn't know how to dress. He himself dressed in fine clothing. Things would be different now, with Ami with me half the time. We began with the basics of learning ways to do her hair. From age five to ten, she had lost a lot of her hair. At one point, she was nearly bald. Now, her hair was starting to look healthy again. We shopped 'til we dropped, buying pretty outfits for her, and we had a ball. Ami was now overweight, and I minimized it, knowing that most child-abuse victims had eating disorders. My main fear had been that she would become anorexic. We found beautiful and fun clothes that looked great on Ami and could camouflage her weight gain. Every time we went shopping, I would find something that looked great on her. Her self-esteem was so important; she had been feeling that she wasn't pretty any more. I didn't know it at the time, but I was creating a monster clotheshorse, who today can't stop buying clothes and jewelry! However, she has excellent taste and pulls looks together that are very creative.

◆◆◆◆◆◆

The following spring, I was to have my first spring break with Ami. I worked my month's schedule around Ami's spring break, hoping to do something special with her, like go to England together or just hang out at home. My lifestyle as an international flight attendant allowed us this privilege. We were both really looking forward to it. Then, I received a phone call from Susan Dycus notifying me that Derek wanted to switch fall break with spring break so he could take Ami to England by himself. I felt very frustrated with this. It was just another tactic for him to control our time together. He had been married for six months, and he was going to England not with his new wife, but with his twelve-year-old daughter? I felt sick to my stomach that they allowed him to do whatever he desired and changed our break time so thathe could take her to England.

Now I had two weeks off with no Ami. Plus, I was worried about what he would do with Ami on this trip. His wife had no clue about the kind of man she had just married. As Kim said to me, "That poor woman, she is in for a lot of heartache. Someday she'll be at your door with questions."

When Ami returned from England, we picked up where we left off. I had become the social director for her and her friends. I loved every minute of it, knowing this phase would last only a short while before she would become more independent.

◆ ◆ ◆ ◆ ◆ ◆

For the next few years, we did a lot of traveling together. We went to Rome, and immediately upon our arrival at the hotel, we dumped our luggage and rushed out to get something to eat. Then we rushed to the Vatican and spent hours there at the museum. After the Vatican, we head toward the Spanish Steps in the evening to enjoy dinner at an outside café. The only table available was with four other women, so we joined them, and struck up a very interesting conversation. Two of the women were from Iraq and in their early twenties, intelligent and quite attractive. The other two were mother and daughter from Norway. Once we got to talking about the differences in our cultures, the conversation took on a life of its own, as we joked about how men behaved in each place. Our subtle laughter turned to roars, and Ami was so delighted with the interaction, listening intently to the women speaking in different dialects and enjoying the fun we were having.

The next day, we shopped, ate, and went to the Trevi Fountain. Years earlier when working trips to Rome, I had gone to this fountain many times, feeling lonely and full of despair, and I had made a wish that I could protect my little girl and get her home, away from her sick father, dreaming of a day we would come to Rome together. Now, Ami and I went to Trevi fountain. When she saw it, she ran excitedly toward it to throw a penny in and make a wish. We stood next to one another in the very spot I had made my wish. I looked over at Ami, she was concentrating very hard on her wish. Since she was little, she always took her wishes very seriously before tossing a coin in a fountain or blowing out her birthday candles. I remembered that when she was four she had made a wish before tossing a coin in a fountain, and when I asked her what she had wished for, she had said with a sad voice, "That my dad would stop touching me."

She closed her eyes tight, and after taking what seemed to be an eternity, she kissed her penny and tossed it in the Trevi Fountain.

◆ ◆ ◆ ◆ ◆ ◆

Even though we were happy we were together, there were still rough times to go through. Derek and his wife very quickly had more kids. His wife still worked round the clock to support him and the kids, so Ami wound up doing a lot of the childcare. When I picked her up from school for her overnights with me, she would be exhausted from her stay at her father's house. Her hair was dirty, and and she looked like she just got out of bed. I asked her what was going on, why she looked so tired, and she said that she had to get the kids ready in the morning, so she didn't have time to get ready for school. And whenever I called to talk to her on any given day, I could hear the kids in her room screaming and crying.

Her grades began to fall. She couldn't study at his house at all. The kids were so out of control that I could not even talk to her on the phone.

Ami's friend Karen told me that Ami's dad never slept with his wife but prefered sleeping on the couch. I hoped that this meant he was leaving Ami alone. How sick! She also told me that sometimes Ami would go upstairs and sleep with him on the couch. Later I confronted Ami—did she sometimes go upstairs and sleep with her dad on the couch? "Yes, sometimes," she replied.

"Why would you do that?"

"Well, sometimes I get lonely," she responded.

Times got rougher over at her dad's house as he began to fight with his wife, and Ami told me it was getting hard to be there. When she confided in me that his wife had a bad temper, I could not help saying, "Don't blame her. She probably has her reasons." So while his wife worked, Derek had lots of free time. Of course, he did not do housework or yardwork but instead worked out at a gym and hit on other women.

Three or four years went by, and every year he needed a vacation by himself to get away from the kids. His wife bought him a ticket to Venice, Italy, for a couple of weeks, and he brought six other people with him to stay at a beautiful home. Of course, Ami was included, and her best friend, Karen. Amazingly, after working hard all year, his wife would take her vacation looking after the kids while he was away.

The next summer, he took his kids and Ami to Paris for a month. I flew to Paris later so I could see Ami there. When he brought her to my hotel with his little children with him, he told me proudly that everyone had thought Ami was his wife. Ami was thirteen. How could he be proud of such a thing?

Karen told me that when she babysat his kids, the house was filthy, and she was uncomfortable there. Ami's room was in the basement, and her father kept her separate from his wife. Ami ate dinner not with the family but alone in her room.

He seemed not to want the wife and Ami to get close. He took Ami to movies, theatre, and lunches, just the two of them. Karen told me that Ami didn't like to go to lunch with her dad because people thought she was his wife.

Sometimes when I picked up Ami at his house, there would be a strange car there. One day, just out of curiosity, I asked whose car it was. Ami said it belonged to a woman Derek used to date who now had AIDS. When I asked if her stepmother knew this woman came over, Ami said no.

Derek took another trip to Paris, this time supposedly alone. Ami told me that they had been fighting a lot and that his wife had a broken arm. Ami also told me of another woman in her father's life, a French teacher who had come to her class that day to observe. Afterward, the three of them had gone out to lunch together. He was now with another woman in Paris on his wife's money, and she was at home with a broken arm and her little babies.

I had never spoken to this woman, except to say hello, and I knew she was so manipulated and controlled by him she would not have listened nor heard anything I would have to say to her. Now I felt she needed to know I was there for her if she needed me. So I called her up and let her know that I had heard she had a broken arm, and if she needed Ami or me to help with the kids, we would be happy to.

On the day her dad returned from Paris, Ami told me he had obtained a court order to remove his wife from the house. I said, "Ami, there is no way your dad could get a court order like that in a day." She then told me he had been working on it for months.

When his wife came home from work that evening, he had the police there with a court order blocking her from going within a hundred feet of her house or her children. I was so sickened by this I couldn't sleep for a week. He knew that the court would keep the mom and baby together if the mom was still nursing, so he had waited until she was done nursing the baby that month so he would get all the kids. He filed charges that she had abused him. This was a man who could dead-lift 500 pounds, and she was about five-foot-two and 110 pounds, plus she had a broken arm. I found out she was staying in a hotel, and he had her house and her babies. At the same time, she lost her job. She was from a wealthy family and not hurting financially, but still my heart went out for her.

Their custody battle began, and I saw that she didn't stand a chance. He was way ahead of her, and she didn't even know what hit her. I told Ami that what her dad was doing to her was horrible. I thought to myself, "Please see through your dad and realize what cruelty and evil he is capable of."

I was told by his wife that she was ordered to pay Derek $6,000 a month and pay all his bills. This man had never worked a steady job in his life, and he now had $6,000/month, her house, a brand-new SUV she had paid for, and her kids.

Not long after this, I got a phone call from her, asking me to lunch. I told her I didn't want to be seen with her, but I would help her if she came to my house.

When the doorbell rang, I looked out the leaded glass door window and saw that she looked distraught and thin. As she entered the house, I grabbed her and hugged her. She was not very social and kind of cold, from what Ami had told me, but I still hugged her.

The first words out of her mouth were "What is he, a psychopath or something?"

I had wondered when she would catch on.

I invited her in and let her vent. For a while, I just listened, and then I gave her advice that it had taken me years to learn. I told her that he was way, way ahead of her. He had been planning and strategizing for months, possibly a year, how he would do what he had done. I told her that she should have no women involved in her case—no female evaluators and no female therapists or GALs. He would and could manipulate any of them. I told her to make sure to get a "man's man" to do any evaluation. If he was wimpy, Derek would work him. Before they appoint a GAL, I told her to let me know who it is and do not agree until they have been checked out. The GAL would carry 90 percent of the weight in her case, I told her; she—or hopefully he—would make or break whether or not she got her kids back. I told her to never allow him to go behind the scenes to talk to therapists or evaluators. He made lots of private phone calls and would even appear in the clerks' offices, just to talk to the clerks of the presiding judge. Since he had labeled her an abuser, I said, she needed to prove what he had done to her.

She then asked me, "Did he ever choke you?"

I responded, "No!" and looked at her with concern. She went on to say he choked her around her chest to cut off her air supply so he would leave no marks on her neck. He had done this several times, until she had almost passed out. Maybe because he knew she had asthma, she said, and it was a great fear of hers not to breathe. She said he would only do this if she went into the basement, where Ami's room was.

With that, my heart tightened. I said, "Is this not your home? You can't go in the basement of your own home?"

The other time he hit her, she said, was when he was going down to the basement right after he had showered, wearing only a towel, and she had said, "Do you think you should be going to the basement like that, with the allegations that were against you?" She went on to say that he kept all his clothes in a closet in the basement, even though there were at least three empty closets upstairs. Not wanting to hear anymore, yet still curious, I wanted to know what she had thought when he had taken Ami and not her on European trips, to movies, and to dinner. Why couldn't she see? But I decided not to go there for two reasons: one, my gag order, and two, she seemed very shaky, and it was possible that she would go back to him.

She then brought up the affairs he had during their marriage and asked me, "Did he do this with you?"

I told her that when I was pregnant he had slept with at least five of my friends or acquaintances. One of them, I said, was the woman she had Thanksgiving dinner with every year. She said that Derek had told her that I cheated on him when we were married. I said, "I am not that kind of a woman, and, no, I never had an affair."

I told her that she needed to get the best attorney to represent her, and I knew some good attorneys I could not afford. I told her to let go of the affairs he was having; the courts didn't care about them. They didn't care about fidelity, about morals, or about values. If she brought them up, it would only make her look like an angry, vindictive woman who was being abusive to poor, pitiful, Derek.

She left with a head full, and I prayed that she had listened closely.

A few weeks later, I got a call from her sister, who was an attorney in New York. She told me she had been unable to access my case—it had been sealed as a sexual assault case. However, she did get into my divorce file. "Did you think your daughter was sexually abused?" she asked.

"Absolutely," I said. "Without a doubt. I lived through it with her. I have tons of proof the courts never allowed— doctors' reports, police reports, teachers' reports, therapists' reports."

"I'm worried about my niece," she said.

"I wondered when someone was going to worry."

"I was told he sleeps with your daughter in the basement," she said, and I felt instantly sick to my stomach.

"He's a pedophile," I said. And I asked her why his wife couldn't see that.

Her sister said that his wife had had a difficult time as a child. She hadn't been very social and she was pretty insecure. Their whole family, she said, was upset. Derek was after their estate.

It seemed incredible to me that Derek could actually get their family estate, but anything that pervert had set his mind to, he got. I was told that Derek would have to be disabled in order to get to the estate money, so he then claimed that he had to have both his shoulders operated on. However, the doctor refused to allow the surgeries. The judge ordered he not do any surgery until after the final decision and after the last court date.

Before the next court date, he had both his hips replaced at the same time and came into court with a walker. It didn't work. Knowing how he worked the system, I told Barb Glagowitz, the attorney for Children's Hospital what Derek was up to now. She asked me, "When is his next hearing? I would like to be there." I told her I would find out.

A few weeks later, his wife called me. Glagowitz had shown up at the hearing, and she was grateful that I was helping her behind the scenes. Derek was fighting for custody of their children now. You might wonder why a lazy man would want to have so many children in the house with him, but you have to remember that first of all, he would get a hefty child support payment from her (in addition to the one I was forced to send him once a month), and second of all, it was about control. It was a battle, and his wife was losing, so I gave her some advice: He would manipulate and work behind the scenes. He would contact the therapists and other social workers involved in their case. Once again, I told her to make sure she got all male evaluators and to not allow any outside phone or personal conversations.

To that point, it had been going badly for her. In the initial hearings, Derek was clearly winning what he wanted. But once she put a stop to all his private phone calls and private meetings with the so-called professionals, her case began to turn around.

She ended up getting the kids, and he got visitation. Of course, he moved on to another victim—with kids—and rarely showed up for his visits with his own kids. Thank God! She got the kids, and although they still had problems, they were doing much better with her.

◆ ◆ ◆ ◆ ◆ ◆

Karen had become like a second daughter to me. As Ami accumulated more friends, Karen became more like her sister and started to stay over at our house more and more. She didn't seem to be comfortable in her own home, and at the time I didn't know why. As the years went by, I found out it was her brother she could not be around. He wasn't sexually abusing her, but he was abusive, and her father didn't seem to protect her.

I was now raising two girls, and Ami was home. During this time, I became the girls' social director and taxi driver. I did everything I could to make home the best home it could possibly be and just fun. We had a great time together and even better talks. I loved taking them shopping for clothes and accesories and fixing Ami's hair when she would let me because I knew that soon she would be an independent- minded teenager, and she wouldn't let me do such things for her.

When school started, they both joined the cross-country team and the basketball team. It was great to watch them participate. Being able to go to functions at the school and actually be a part of Ami's life was so refreshing. Yet the pain of all the past memories continually haunted me, especially when Ami had to go back to her father's. The questions in my mind ran like a vicious cycle, and then I would have to let them go, for we were together, and no other mother in my situation that I knew of had even got their children back. I would tell myself to just enjoy this time because in the near future she would be graduating, and this would be all I had left of her childhood.

Ami still refused to discuss the past. When Karen asked her about it, Ami's response was "We'll tell you when you're an adult." She seemed to remember everything but didn't want to go there. I told her that under my desk were the files for her case, and that if she ever wanted to know anything, it was all there. I told her I had tape recordings and proof of everything, from doctor reports and police reports to a book I was writing that would prove everything.

◆ ◆ ◆ ◆ ◆ ◆

Two years after the CNN Presents had aired, I got a call from Tom Kelly, the CNN attorney who I had come to know and respect from the years of knowing him. He had all my files and was sickened by what had happened in the court system. He had been very prepared to take Derek's lawsuit to trial, but CNN had been released from the claim—it was focused on Children's Hospital now. He told me he felt like a heart surgeon who never got to do the heart surgery.

Just before Ami and I were about to go to Hawaii again, Ami told me that the lawsuit trial was scheduled for the same time period as our trip. Ami had been listed along with her father as a plaintiff in the suit, and that had caused a rift between us. Now I was so angry about it that it had to be written all over my face. One day I could not bear it anymore, and I said to Ami, "I can't believe you went along with your Dad on this lawsuit. If you had any idea of the blood, sweat, and tears behind all of this, you would never do this. These people are the very people who tried to protect you! Do you think these doctors are going to want to protect other children when this is what happens?"

Ami rarely showed any emotion, but at this, she started to cry and said she wished she had never done it. I reached over and just held her as tight as I could. I was so sick of holding everything in; I wished she could remember everything so we could move forward with therapy, but she couldn't do anything until she was on her own and released from her father's control.

For those two weeks, instead of being on a beach in Maui with Ami, I sat at home, waiting to be called to testify. When I was called in, I came into the courtroom only to see Ami and her dad leaving together. I was not called to the witness stand, and since it was a jury trial, I had wanted to testify. I had never had the opportunity to testify before a jury. The abuse of Ami was not to be a part of the trial; it was his suit against Children's Hospital for giving out medical evidence without his consent since he was the custodial parent.

However, when I saw the list of Derek's witnesses, I could tell what he was up to. He was going to prove he never abused Ami, but he wouldn't have to defend himself against any evidence that he had abused her. I tried to warn Barb Glowgowiz and the attorneys from Children's that they were not prepared for where the father was going to take this. I told them they needed to bring in some expert witnesses like Richard Ducote, an attorney from New Orleans who knew about these kinds of cases. I gave them a list of experts then called Tom Kelly and told him that Children's was going to lose, that they weren't prepared for what Derek would hit them with. "Maralee!" he said. "Barb Glagowitz is an excellent attorney. She can handle it. She worked under me for years."

I then called Allan Schuchman, the other attorney for Children's, and told him where the father was going with this case. He reassured me that they had everything under control. I never did get to testify. A couple of months later, I received a call from Mr. Schuchman. "We just got the verdict," he said, "and we lost. We should have listened to you. You were right all along. I'm so sorry."

Feeling the tears well up in my eyes, I tried to keep from screaming. My whole insides ached, my heart was pounding, and I felt breathless. This was so repulsive. This sick man had won again. I told Alan I felt sick. "How much did she get?"

"One point two million," he said. "And Derek got around $525,000 for his pain and suffering."

"I've got to go," I said and hung up the phone.

All that money given to Ami's father to compensate him for the pain and suffering he had endured. It was all so unbelievable. I turned my head toward the window and let my tears stream down. How could this happen?

Two weeks later, Derek went to the newspaper and tried to clear his name. I knew this was exactly what he would do.

I was outraged. First of all, Ami had won the 1.2 million, and second, it was not a trial over whether or not he was falsely accused, only about whether Children's Hospital should have legally given out Ami's medical records without the father's approval, since he had custody.

And that wasn't the end of it. He filed a lawsuit against Dr. Carol Jenny, who was released from the lawsuit and was paid $30,000 dollars for her attorney fees. Dr. Jenny was head of the Children's Hospital Advocacy and Protection Team and considered to be one of the top doctors in the nation on child sexual abuse. From what I was told, she had moved out of state when the money was awarded, and the court ruled to give the money to the child since she was not there at the hearing. I never really understood this maneuver. Donna Nelligen, who was a nurse practitioner and worked for Dr. Jenny, was told to speak to CNN on this issue, since the team had all seen my child and believed my child was being abused. She was held in the case and not released. My understanding was that she was not allowed to give out medical advice of the minor child without the perpetrator or father's permission since he had custody. Since the opposing side had not won anything with CNN, they had to find a way to litigate against Children's, and I guess Donna Nelligen was the one they needed to keep the lawsuit going.

Ten years later, after CNN had aired the story on our case, by complete coincidence I was the only one on a ski bus at Winter Park ski area when a woman got on that I recognized. The woman reacted to me in the same way and said, "Are you Maralee Mclean?"

Stunned, I said, "Yes! Are you Donna Nelligen?" We both had tears in our eyes. We had never officially met. Back when the lawsuit was going on and Tom Kelly had called me about the case, I begged him to help Donna Nelligen with attorney fees, and he said they were. I was later told by Allan Schuchman, the attorney for Children's Hospital, that Donna was going through a very rough time. Now that we had met for the first time, I looked at her and said, "I am so sorry!" My apology came from deep down in my gut. She told me that Derek had gone after her house on a personal lawsuit and never stopped. Her friends and professional counterparts could not believe what she was going through. They all would tell her this couldn't happen, words I had heard for so many years, and still do. The nightmare never seemed to end, she said. "While in the parking lot at the trial," she said, "he approached me and threatened to kill me."

One time, she'd been so upset at home with her five kids that she started having chest pains so severe she thought she was having a heart attack. She said, "I deal with heart attacks all the time and had my kids call 911. When the ambulance arrived, I was sure I was dying." I flashed back to how many times I had driven myself to the emergency room, sure that I was having a heart attack, only to find that it was severe anxiety. I looked at her face reliving the pain and thought,this evil man has tried to destroy so many people all for his own gain and game. "It was a nightmare," she said, "what he put my family and me through, and it was years of threats, so my husband said, 'Let's just give him the money. I want my wife back.'This was the money for my children's college education," she said. As she told me about it, she began to cry, and I cried with her.

"I tried to call you," I told her, "but you never returned my calls."

"I called you once," she said, "but I was afraid, so I hung up."

"Please," I said, "if you ever need to talk or want to share anything with me, I will be there for you. I wanted to testify in the case so bad, and I know I could have shed some light on the case and helped you, but I was never called." I told her how hard it was for me and Ami now, and how I had confronted Ami. "Do you think any other doctors are going to want to protect the children out there if this is what they get?" I had asked Ami. "This lawsuit is against the very people who tried to protect you." I told her how Ami cried and had wished she had never done it.

Anyway, when I saw the newspaper article, I was boiling mad. How could a newspaper print these lies? I got a call from Tom, the CNN attorney, telling me how sorry and upset he was. "How can the newspaper write what he says to write?" I asked Tom. "I've never filed a lawsuit, but I am going to now. This is sick."

"Don't get down in the gutter with Derek," he said. "I really care about you, Maralee. For your own sake, let it go. I have to tell you, I represent the Denver Post. So let it go."

That day, I received calls from many friends who couldn't believe how Derek continued to lie his way out of everything. When Ami came home from school, I saw she was angry too. She had seen the article and was very upset with her father.

We sat in my office upstairs on the leather couch, where we could talk. Karen was home, and my mom was visiting. "Have you seen the paper?" I asked her.

"I have," she said, "and I told my dad that's it. I told him to leave you alone, and he is never to contact you again! 'I mean it, Dad. Never contact my mom again!"

(After that, Derek never contacted me again.)

It was nice to hear her stick up for me. But, I thought, What about her? No one knew that her father had abused her, except the people closest to her. In the newspaper story I wasn't named, nor in the CNN story. The pictures of her were disguised. But a lot of people at her school knew who her father was. In his selfish desire to lie and clear his name, he hadn't even considered what Ami would have to go through.

Ami and I then talked at length. For the first time, I told her of all the work I had done on her behalf. I told her I had lobbied in Washington DC and spoke throughout the country. I told her about all the hearings and trials. I told her that our horrible supervised visits were all because of her father and not being able to see her family had all been due to her father's manipulation. "Do you understand the control he has on you?" I asked her. "Karen even says you're afraid of him, and whatever he says you should do, you do. Where is your own mind? Come on, Ami, look at this whole thing!"

We talked it out, cried together, and once again hugged and felt close. Nothing was going to strip our mother-daughter bond, nothing. Ami told me she never wanted to live without me. "I can handle anything," she said, "as long as I know you are there."

I call Barb Glagowitz, the Children's Hospital attorney, and told her I needed to see the transcripts to this case. She said she had found the father to be extremely manipulative; it was the worst case she had ever dealt with. "Oh, Maralee," she said, "I am so sorry this has happened!" I told her I wanted to file a lawsuit against the Denver Post but that Tom thought I should let it go and not get in the mud with Derek.

Days went by. I called the newspaper's editor and chief editor but got no response. In time, I listened to Tom Kelly and let it go—although it still bothers me, and I second-guess myself constantly. I couldn't stand the fact that he was getting even a dime, and that Ami's money was Ill-gotten. It was wrong. If anyone should pay Ami, it was the state of Colorado for not protecting her.

CHAPTER 41

When the Dreamers, Protectors, and Warriors Survive

Ami is now living on the East Coast, after many years of attending college I am proud to say she graduated from college. She has had deep struggles to get through life and many challenges, due to the trauma she was forced to endure by our family courts most of her childhood. She is a beautiful spirit and is gaining insights that most of us can't even imagine. Of the $1.2 million she got from the lawsuit, the attorneys, the government, her father got most of it. She took the loss of the money with a grain of salt and told me she would be a better person without it. We are as close as any mother and daughter could possibly be, despite the geographical distance between us and considering all the heartache and separation we had to endure. Ami has proven to be an incredible young woman and she tells me her goal is to make a difference someday for children. She recently sent me a message stating, "I went from 3-4 year-old where everything stopped. I could not access my being until now. I am back! I can't believe it a 4-year-old soul in a 25-year-old body she can dance, sing, swim, she has studied humanity and traveled the world ending by her true love the sea where she gets to be her true mermaid loving her little kingdom by the sea. We did it mom… it is just the beginning so much work to do and I am ready. Thank you for always being on the journey with me, my number one supporter. I am real and solid in a body that is all mine. I have not felt my body in so long the texture of my skin the water on my scalp. Nor have I seen my own shadow, constantly in motion,

I stop for no one, I am a butterfly that disappears just as soon as you can catch a glimpse. I am deep into my spirituality and let go of all that I thought was my existence. I can now access all my powers that have been locked away for so long. There is nothing that will get in my way now as long as I listen to my voice. I made it to the other side. Love you so much."

Another message, "Your baby is alive and feels the beauty of everything that is around her. She just had a major detour… but she is who you always knew she would be… it just took some time… you are exactly who she picked to guide her in her life. Keep doing what you are doing…she needs you to keep fighting… and it is 100% worth it… you are creating a beautiful existence… us in the convertible singing our hearts out… I remember everything and have always been with you… Love you momma and your beautiful soul." All you moms out there that have lost your children due to the courts not protecting your children please know that there is hope.

Karen went to college on the West Coast and is very happy as well. The two of them went to Spain last summer together and remain as close as sisters. Ami is still dealing with being dissociative. She is not on drugs nor an alcoholic, nor has she turned to sexual promiscuity, as so many other sexually-abused children have. Although I know the ACE Research and the Adverse Childhood Experiences and wonder what is in the future for Ami. I thank God for her survival and strength. Ami knows I have been writing this book for years and pushing to get it published. She told me you go for it mom, I just will not read it. This is a poem she wrote at twelve years old, which to me explains where she found her peace.

> "I Am a Dreamer"
> I am a dreamer lost in the world of logic and order. I wonder how big the Universe really is.
> I hear the tinkling of fairies everywhere
> I see an open ocean filled with mermaids diving in and out of the waves.
> I am a dreamer lost in the world of logic and order.
> I pretend to glide in and out of the clouds with a flying unicorn.

I feel that when I enter my world everything is peaceful. I touch the barrier between the dream world and reality.
I worry that someday my special world will collide with the real.
I am a dreamer lost in the world of logic and order.
I understand that my dreams might never come true. I say that my world will last forever.
I dream that I am on a star looking down at the world. I try to keep my two worlds from becoming one.
I hope my special world will never end, for it is my salvation from the troubles in life.
I am a dreamer lost in a world of logic and order.

◆ ◆ ◆ ◆ ◆ ◆

Not long ago, she called me in the middle of the night, crying. I was shocked at the pain in her voice because she rarely let's her feelings out and especially not about her past. She exclaimed! "Mom! I hate my childhood, I hate my childhood!" I heard the pain in her voice. I listened intently. She said, "I did not deserve this! I am not talking about you know what. I am talking about things you do not even know what happened to me. You do not know the things that happened to me! I hate being fat and continuing to sob about being taken away from my family." We were on the phone for at least two hours as she continued to cry out.

I responded, "I know, honey." I could only imagine the other cruel things he had done to her. My heart was aching for her, knowing she was starting to process some of her past with her father. I was crying but never let on to Ami. The next day she called and said she was better. When I told my therapist what Ami was going through, she told me that Ami would start to deal with it soon, or else she wouldn't be behaving like this. She was obviously thinking about it. "She wouldn't be where she is today, Maralee, had it not been for you."

I was frightened, asking myself could she be suicidal? Recapturing in my mind all I have read on child sexual abuse and suicide. This is my greatest fear when she starts remembering the trauma and coming out of dissociation.

We true, natural women cannot live without our children. We had rather die than have them torn from us as your laws allow them to be. Spirit wrongs are the keenest wounds that can be inflicted upon women. When woman is brought before our man courts and our man juries, and has no marks of violence upon her person, it is hard to realize that her whole physical system maybe writhing in agony from spirit wrongs, such as can only be understood by her peers. Spiritual, sensitive women suffer on in silent anguish without appeal until death. Kindly liberate her from her prison of unappreciated suffering.[vi]

As for me, I have dedicated my life to bringing awareness and accountability for what is happening in our courts. I am an activist, child advocate and speak nationally on child abuse and domestic violence. Daily I work on child abuse, protective parent issues, legislative work and courtroom reform. I also work with non-profits writing more articles, speaking and to help educate the nation on protecting our children in family court. "We are ready to live all our tomorrows for one child's life today." I plan to continue to speak at conferences and to make a difference with this book in educating judges, lawyers, therapists, social workers, court appointed evaluators, and the general public to help all sexually abused children and women so they are not victimized twice by the offender and then again by the courts.

"In our civilized society, we have laws against sexually molesting children. There exists a "national double standard" which supports: "sexually molesting children is tolerable, as long as they are your own." It is called "reunification" or "family preservation." This double standard is causing plight of protective parents, requires children to have contact with suspected and known child molesters, through unsupervised or inappropriate supervised visits or actual physical custody. This double standard denies children, who are the victims of incest, equal protection under the law and punishes protective parents who stand up for the children with the law.

"Protective parents," the majority of whom are women, believe their children when they disclose incest and they attempt to secure their children's safety physically, mentally, and emotionally. The plight is not in believing their children, but in believing that there is a system adequately trained and educated to deal with the incest. Sexually molesting one's own child is not treated as a crime but by law is reduced to a family problem, therefore staying in family courts and rarely going to the criminal court system, which requires a burden of proof beyond a reasonable doubt.

However, in civil court or family court, which is your only legal recourse, the crime of sexual molestation is reduced to a custody issue. In family court the child who has no civil or constitutional rights is literally treated as chattel under the guise of his or her best interest. The mother is quickly labeled vindictive, acrimonious and/or unstable—"parental alienator." The father is portrayed as the victim whose life is being destroyed by false allegations.

◆ ◆ ◆ ◆ ◆ ◆

The outcome is tenuous that a child will be believed and properly protected when subjected to the infinite latitude of judicial discretion with all its ignorance, denial, and bias regarding incest. Ironically, at the same time judges inflict "court ordered sanctioned alienation," severely limited or extremely supervised visitation, or termination of all contact between children and their mothers, who are assumed to be "parental alienators."

It is apparent that our laws and court procedures have not evolved to the point to accommodate justice for children. In this country, a father's "parental rights" supersede a child's right to live free from sexual molestation and a mother's right to protect. When the truth and a child's feelings are sacrificed to facilitate "parental rights," then ultimately that child has been taught that he or she does not count, that one has no control over one's own life. This is a creation of a victim or a perpetrator who will reap in life what happened to be sown in childhood, the perpetuation of the vicious cycle of generational violence that will grow.

In this country there are thousands of protective parents—some are living in limbo awaiting final discriminating orders, others have already lost custody, many can have no contact with their children, and others' parental rights have been terminated. Mothers are losing everything, including the very children they are fighting to protect. They are separated, and the child is sent to live with the alleged child molester. Emotionally and financially devastated, these mothers live a tortured existence, ever fearful of what will happen to their children." Every day I get calls from every state with the same outcomes for mothers trying to protect their innocent children.

◆ ◆ ◆ ◆ ◆ ◆

My advice to mothers trying to protect their children in our court system:

1. Hire a good attorney—one who has experience in the proceedings of child sexual abuse cases and domestic violence cases knowing that civil court will make it into a custody issue versus a sexual abuse issue. Most family law attorneys do not have the information required to litigate these cases. This will take a lot of work on your part by looking on the Internet for an attorney who works on domestic violence, and child abuse cases. Make the phone calls and get in the door for an appointment.
2. If you can't afford an attorney, you need to find someone who will do it pro bono. Go to your local legal aid attorneys and ask if anyone can help or if they know of some attorneys who work in this in this type of litigation. You will have to go through several attorneys, but there may be that one that will help. You must have your facts in order and more or less plead for help.
3. Most of these cases are domestic violence cases just know the most dangerous time for women victims of domesic violence is when she leaves.
4. You have access to the computer with a world of information, which can really help. Here are some of the best resources I've found: THE LEADERSHIP COUNCIL on Child Abuse and Interpersonal Violence, www.childabusesolutions, www.childabuseforensic.org, www.usdoj.org which is the U.S. department of justice, www.stopfamilyviolence.org, Alliance University Institute of violence, abuse, and trauma, http://

www.ivatcenter.org, California Protective Parent Association, www.protectiveparents.com, Ducotelaw@aol. com.

5. Educate yourself. Study what is happening in these types of cases. In the back of this book you will find information you can read by professionals who have studied this problem for years.
6. Make sure to get good evaluators who are trained in child sexual abuse and domestic violence. Read Dr. Dan Saunders Research with the Justice Office. Ask questions, as to training, seminars and class hours they have in child sexual abuse. If appointed by the courts this is something that we all have to work on. You may need to educate your own attorney gently on what is happening in these cases. Push for legislation in your state to hold CFI's or custody evaluators accountable and to cap the monies they get per evaluation.
7. If a therapist or evaluator GAL is mentioning PAS (Parental Alienation Syndrome or Dr. Richard Gardner) (Underwager or Wakefield), you will want a new therapist. Removal of GAL once assigned to the case is difficult. You can show them the facts that Gardners Parental Alienation Theory is discredited and stricken from evaluator reports under the relevant evidentiary standards, the courts should not accept this testimony.
8. Do not run. This is not the answer for your child and will be doing more damage. The FBI is after you and the extradition laws will not protect you, and then your child is left with the abuser while you go to prison.
9. Follow all court orders and rules no matter how outlandish they become, and keep it together, and be calm as you can.
10. If the GAL is against you, you will not win your case, so make sure you have a competent GAL, that is not biased, and try to hold them accountable. On the Internet you can find under Richard Ducote, Esq. Legislation 42 United States, Code 5105a. Protective Parent Reform Act. It is a guideline for G.A.L.s
11. Document everything and keep a file together. I suggest getting a legal binder organized with hearings, dates, and times when motions were

filed—all correspondence. Make sure this binder explains your case. If you have therapy reports, police reports, doctor reports, hospital reports with abuse information or physical evidence, place all of it in sequential order. You need to be your child's number-one advocate so you can present professionally and articulate what is happening in your case.

12. If evidence of abuse and proof take it to the District Attorney to prosecute.
13. Write letters to legislature and the Governor asking for citizen oversight of the judiciary.
14. You are not alone there are thousands of protective mothers in the same nightmare. You have the internet to network. Join with other mothers to file a federal law suit.
15. Do not talk to your child about the abuse. Just listen and let him or her know you are listening. If you react, it puts more pressure on them. When they talk, no comments from you on the abuse or the professionals involved will say you are coaching the child so just listen.
16. If a medical examination is required, do not answer for your child. If the doctor or examiner looks to you for an answer, refer to your child.
17. Prepare for torture this is like the Salem witch hunt, so be strong for your child.
18. If you can get media coverage, go for it. You will enlighten more people to what is happening in our judicial system, and now people are listening more. You probably will get a gag order, but you are not sitting back, letting injustice prevail. Use the media as if you are losing all your parental rights. Develop a media package regarding the lack of child protection.
19. If your child cries in the night with nightmares and screams out what is happening to them in their sleep, I suggest putting a voice-activated tape recorder by their bed, just to record the cries for help. This is not admissible now but may be later and you will have proof.

20. Keep your child in an environment with the same surroundings and schools, family, friends. They need some normalcy. And try to keep life for them as happy as you can.
21. Love, love, love with all your heart and soul.
22. You are the one on trial, so affiliate yourself with as many organizations as you can. [I have given you websites to go to for help.] Go to your senators, congressman, the governor, and do not be afraid to state what is happening to your child and how it is being handled in the courts.
23. Have a synopsis of the times and dates, motions that were filed, the outcomes of the trial, evidence of the abuse, all reports, such as medical, therapist reports, and police reports in chronicle order so you can verify what is happening in our court system.
24. Take your legal binder you have put together and educate as many influential people as you can. Once again, you are your number-one child's advocate.
25. Stay calm no matter what you will be labeled with, such as hysteria, so just stay as calm as you can.
26. If you show too much emotion, you are not stable, and if you show not enough emotion, you are considered cold. So try to stay neutral.
27. No matter how painful the supervised visits are, stay in them at all costs. I am not talking money, I am talking the emotional toll it will take, but you can't give up. Stay in the supervised visits no matter how gut wrenching, or they will end your parental rights. Make it a great hour and think quality time is precious time.
28. 115th Congress (2017-2018) Expressing the sense of Congress that child safety is the first priority of custody and visitation adjudications of custody where family violence is alleged.
29. The Joan S. Meier Study PAS and PA. Parental Alienation Syndrome and Parental Alienation: A Research Review.
30. If you can, put together a rally in your city. Pull mothers together for the cause. Believe me, there are many who are too depleted and can't speak and need your voice. If you can lobby on the hill or fight for

legislative issues, demand change. This is not just for your child; this is for thousands of sexually abused children who are handed over to the abuser by our family courts.

31. Try to emotionally and physically surround yourself with a support system from family and friends. This is a nightmare, and if you are in it, you will have to once again stay together, and let your child see your strength.
32. Prayer, prayer, and prayer, and if you cannot sleep, are eating poorly, anxiety ridden, depression, depleted, or suicidal, get help. Be aware the healthier you are, the more you can do to free your child from this nightmare.
33. This will be difficult, and maybe unbearable, but in the end, you will be proud that you stood up for your child and made a difference in the world.
34. My love for your children and for you. God Bless you and keep strong and fight. Never ever give up!

I have been supporting mothers for 25 years. I want you to know I am here to help. Please visit my site www.MaraleeMclean.com to see what we are working on with resources, tips, strategies, and trainings and more connections with other moms.

For protective moms written by another protective mom:

A Mother Who…

- ***Drags herself through months/years of family law court trauma,***
- ***Perseveres through being called a "liar" and "obstructive" constantly,***
- ***Keeps a lid on it while her own solicitor discriminates against her,***
- ***Is bullied by federal magistrates,***
- ***Remains cool when provoked by her x,***
- ***Maintains her sanity through outrageous judgements***
- ***Is ignored by those who should care,***
- ***Looses many nights of sleep but continues to function for her children,***

- *Has little understanding or support from family and friends,*
- *Just keeps her head above water financially,*
- *Buttons it up while court-hired professionals intimidate her,*
- *Is labeled as alienating, unreasonable, or mentally-ill due to trying to protect her offspring,*
- *Gives up everything she has to protect her children,*
- *Continues to love her children like there is no tomorrow despite all of the above, and Still remains standing, Is Not a Bad Mother, She is a Bloody HERO!*

CONCLUSION

Today's women are losing their children to the abuser through our courts in epidemic numbers. We are moving backwards. The trauma and harm to their children, and the women, is beyond belief and should be alarming to all of society.

I have spent over 25 years trying to bring this last taboo to the forefront and bring awareness to what is taking place in courtrooms, nationally and internationally. This is a part of the #MeToo campaign.

Safety of our children and the women is a priority that is not being addressed in our courts. The Best Interest of the Child statute is not what is in the child's best interest when safety is not a concern or paramount.

Approximately 15 million children are exposed each year to domestic violence and/or child sexual abuse or child abuse. Most of these cases are not documented and children are lost in the system with their abuser. Research shows that a child is at risk of increased abuse after a perpetrator of domestic violence separates from a domestic partner. Most of these cases are contested custody cases with domestic violence. Family Courts prioritize co-parenting and paternal access even when domestic violence or child abuse. We have a lack of oversight for the trial courts and need transparency and accountability.

When the courts are using unfounded theories of PAS Parental Alienation Syndrome as explained in my book and the misuse of the theory which is found to be junk science. This theory should not be accepted by the courts it is not approved by the AMA or the APA and is used mostly by abusive fathers to regain control.

The Dept. of Justice's Office on Violence against Women has done in depth Research and Study by Joan Meire Esq. In custody cases where mothers and children report sexual abuse of the child the courts are siding with the father the abuser 81 percent of the time.

Dr. Robert Pearl, M.D., according to Forbes states, "That abused women are 70 percent more likely to have heart disease, 80 percent more likely to experience a stroke and 60 percent more likely to develop asthma than women in happy, normal marriages.

Each year, an estimated 8 million days of paid work is lost in the U.S. because of domestic violence.

Domestic violence costs \$8.3 billion in expenses annually: a combination of higher medical costs (\$5.8 billion) and lost productivity (\$2.5 billion).

Addressing this issue could save thousands of lives and billions of dollars. But as long as the symptoms and consequences of domestic violence with the overlapping of child abuse go unnoticed, overlooked or, worse, intentionally hidden, nothing changes."

Most doctors don't take the time to learn about and use established screening techniques. And unless domestic violence can be identified, we can't help victims deal with the abuse or reduce the long-term consequences.

We have the ACE Research by Dr. Vincent Feletti, which shows how children who have been abused are at increased physical and mental health effects. The childhood trauma and the list goes on and on…

Everyone has a role in curbing domestic violence and child abuse.

While there are significant differences in the roles that court professionals, health care professionals and the public can play, the secrecy of domestic violence and child abuse requires vigilance from all of us.

We need all the judiciary to have further training on domestic violence and to ensure women and children are protected. ie: Saunders Research with the Justice office. A recent research Study for the US Justice Department demonstrates that these extreme outcomes are always wrong (Saunders, et al, 2012). The harm of separating a child from his or her primary attachment figure, a harm that includes increased rise of depression, low self-esteem and suicide when the child is older is greater than any benefit the court believes it is providing.

Improving due process within our courts and getting the professionals adequately trained along with evaluators, and other specialists that lead are placement of our children into the custody of the abuser.

The change of court rules on child contact with violent fathers or male entitlement, and to end the presumption that a father must have contact with a child when there is evidence of domestic abuse or abuse that would put the child or mother at risk. The family courts are relying on the erroneous assumption that there should be contact with both parents at all costs. This practice should be excluded in domestic violence and child abuse cases. If judges were trained effectively they would be aware of perpetrators using the courts to continue their abuse.

The Leadership Council on Child Abuse and Interpersonal Violence, in fact, says that 58,000 times per year judges in American family courts grant full custody of abused children to abusive guardian.

Judges need to be more alert and trained on the tactics of perpetrators of domestic violence who use the courts as a way to continue their abuse. I would like to see the family court judges understand the behavior of sociopath, psychopath and narcissist.

The family court system is designed so judges can rule however they want regardless of evidence, facts and research. Judges are issuing gag orders and threatening women with the loss of their children if they speak out. The media covered my case heavily and that is what needs to happen today so the general public can know about this is a national health crisis as well. We have thought about separate courts with jury trials for these cases. There needs to be due process, transparency and accountability in our courts for all the professionals involved. Society needs to make this a priority before we destroy further generations of children and women.

APPENDIX A

From the Hardest Case: Custody and Incest by Joan Pennington

Protective parents find that simply knowing a child is telling the truth is not enough. These parents have largely been unsuccessful in protecting their children from sexual abuse by the other parent for many reasons.

1. Women and children are generally not believed by the legal system.
2. Focus of the proceedings lies on the issue of custody or visitation instead of the child's claim of sexual abuse.
3. The defendant's due process rights are protected by the Constitution while the child has no legal rights under the law. The courts have abandoned the moral mandate of American law, which requires the court to act as parens patriae to protect the powerless.
4. Defendants are more likely to be men, who are more likely to have the resources; women typically make lower incomes than men and are at a disadvantage when it comes to defending themselves against accusations.
5. Mental health professionals are generally trained to blame the mothers and label their good-faith concern for the safety of their children as fantastic or hysterical. They are generally poorly trained, or not trained at all, in the area of child sexual abuse.

6. Child Protective Services are overwhelmed with their case load and decreased funding, so often they cannot conduct investigations properly and are inadequately trained.
7. Most family law attorneys are not experienced in child- sexual-abuse proceedings and do not have the information required to successfully litigate these cases.
8. When the child describes the abuse, the parent has no idea where to take the child for a valid evaluation.
9. Attorneys appointed to represent the child, the guardian ad litems, are often incompetent, biased toward the father, or passive, and are not held accountable by the system.
10. The protective parent has no resource currently available to obtain information and materials pertinent to their cases, and no local or national platform on which to speak on their behalf in response to the chorus of voices raised against them.

One half of all reported incidents of child sexual abuse are incestuous. According to the American Bar Association, deliberately false allegations of sexual abuse are rare. Judges untrained in the area of child sexual abuse are upset by incest and tend to pretend it is not happening.

The cost to arrive at a judge's decision in custody cases is averaging $100,000 and is rarely overturned by the appellate courts. The cost to our society is astronomical, especially when you add in the psychological costs of the consequential drug use, alcohol addiction, and psychological difficulties. It is estimated that 90 percent of our imprisoned convicts guilty of violent crime are victims of abuse.

Children are encouraged to avoid strangers but are required to be affectionate and submit to adults entrusted with their care. Yet children are three times more likely to be molested by a recognized trusted adult than by a stranger.

In criminal cases, you have to prove beyond a reasonable doubt that a person is guilty. Since almost every juror will have a doubt, it is difficult to convict, and prosecutors don't like to prosecute cases they cannot win. Sexual molestation is the last frontier for prosecutors; they are highly unlikely to take on such cases, especially if it is the child's own father being accused.

◆ ◆ ◆ ◆ ◆ ◆

The key to fair adjudication of custody and incest cases is simply to preserve a uniform standard of fairness toward all of the litigants. A fair system protects the rights of the accused without sacrificing the rights of the victim. No other litigants in the entire legal system are presumed to be lying when they approach the courts for protection and redress, only mothers and children. No other litigants are met with such anger and hostility. It appears that we are not too civilized to continue to kill the messenger who brings bad news. Incest will not go away until the legal system overcomes its own biases and faces it as the crime it is. Oh yes, and in case no one has noticed, mothers are no longer running and hiding. Instead, they are uniting and standing up to the system, demanding equal justice. They are not going away either.

◆ ◆ ◆ ◆ ◆ ◆

Joan Pennington, esq., was abused by her husband. She went to law school 35 years ago due to no protection for her and her five children. She started the National Center For Protective Parents after she received so many calls from mothers all over the U.S. with the problem in our courts, and not being able to protect their children. She testified before congress and was rewarded as the best women attorney of the year for the state of New Jersey. She was in the grassroots effort of fighting for the civil rights being denied protective mothers and their children.

APPENDIX B

Myths and Facts

Myth: Women make sex abuse charges to gain an edge in a custody battle.

Fact: It is only after a woman makes an abuse charge that she "is branded as paranoid,hysterical…and therefore an unfit mother…" and thus becomes the subject of a custody suit brought on by the accused. (Loyola Law Review, Vol. 34, 1998.111-123)

Myth: Women make false charges of sexual abuse against their spouses.

Fact: "Deliberately false allegations of sexual abuse made to influence custody decisions or to hurt an ex-spouse do happen, but they are viewed by knowledgeable professionals as rarities." B. Nicholson and J. Bulkley (eds) ABA Study, "Sexual Abuse Allegations in Custody and Visitation Cases" (1988); K. Faller, Dr. Corwin, and Erna Olafson, "Literature Review: Research on False Allegations of Sexual Abuse in Divorce, "The APSAC Advisor, Vol 6, No. 3 (Fall 1993).

Myth: Sex abuse does not occur with any greater frequency during divorce and separation than when the marriage is intact.

Fact: The occurrence of child sex abuse increases during divorce and separation as a direct result of the loss of family structure, feelings of devastation and loneliness leading to turning to the child for deep emotional support, and greater freedom and access to the child victim. (K. Faller, "Child Sexual Abuse:

An Interdisciplinary Manual for Diagnosis, Case Management and Treatment, "New York, Columbia Press (1988).

Myth: Children confabulate stories of sexual abuse just to win favor with one spouse over another.

Fact: Children are more likely to disclose sexual abuse when the abusing parent is out of the house. "With the breakup of the parents comes diminished opportunity for an abusing parent to enforce secrecy as there is increased opportunity for the child to disclose abuse separately to the other parent." (emphasis is supplied) Dr. Corwin, L. Berliner, B. Goodman, J. Goodwin and S. White, "Child Sexual Abuse and Custody Disputes, "Journal of Interpersonal Violence (Vol. 2) (1) March 1987: 91-105.

Myth: Children are protected from sexual abuse because the courts believe the children.

Fact: "With children six years and under, despite significant psychological and medical evidence of sexual abuse occurring during visitation with a biological parent, 74% of the time the allegations were disbelieved by the systems designed to protect the children." M. Sugarmen, "Sexual Abuse of Very Young Children in the Context of Divorce and Visitation," paper presented at the Boston Institute for the Development of Infants and Parents. Twelfth Annual Conference (1986)

Myth: If the sex abuse really did happen, it can only happen once so there is no risk to handing over custody or allotting liberal visitation (unsupervised) to the accused.

Fact: Molestation recurs at a rate of 57% within one year. The rate of recurrence increases over a 3-5-year span. G. Quick and M Sicilio, "Sexual Abuse Manifestations: A Descriptive Guide" Vol. 29, Consultant, August 1989:120

Myth: If a sex offender is "treated" he has no chance of repeating the crime, therefore it is safe to hand over custody or allow liberal unsupervised visitation to known offenders.

Fact: A conservative estimate is that one in every five "successfully" rehabilitated sexual offenders will show recidivism within a short period of time. D. Fikelhor, p. 340, ABA study, supra.

Myth: Children are protected by a guardian ad litem who ensures that their best interests are upheld when there are allegations of sexual abuse.

Fact: Family law specialists have concluded that "generally there are no standards, no certification, no requirement of neutrality, and no guarantee that it is the child's best interests that is being represented. J. Pennington and L. Woods, National Center on Women an Family Law, "Legal Issues and Legal Options in Civil Child Sexual Abuse Cases, Representing the Protective Parent" (1990) p.16. (emphasis supplied)

Myth: The domestic relations and family courts protect the constitutional rights of parents making charges of sexual abuse.

Fact: The National Center for Protective Parents, in a recent study titled, "The Hardest Case: Custody and Incest, "has concluded that these cases nearly all involve constitutional issues…" (Feb. 1993:21). (see Reno memo for a full explication of the myriad violations of due process rights of protective parents) "ACAA" The American Coalition for Abuse Awareness, is represented by the Washington, D.C. law firm of Verner, Lipfert, Bernhard, Mcpherson and Hand. Memo to Janet Reno for protective parents.

APPENDIX C

Educational Tools

Many custody/parenting time cases include allegations of "parental alienation" or "parental alienation syndrome" (PAS), a term coined by Richard Gardner, M.D. that is unsubstantiated in the research literature (Fink, 2010). This discredited and debunked "syndrome" by the American Psychological and American Psychiatric Associations, continues to be used to remove children from custody/parenting time with their protective parent (primarily mothers). The end result is children are abuse emotionally, physically, and sexually by their custodial parent (Stark, 2010). These cases span decades in the family court as bias by judges, uninformed custody evaluators (Saunders, et. al., 2011), and other court-related personnel continue to put children in harm's way with their abusive parent (Mclean, 2012). The protective parent does everything possible to rescue the children from this situation while being mistreated and misrepresented by the players in family court (Goldstein & Hannah, 2010; Goldstein & Liu, 2013). The outcome for these children is an adult life filled with psychotherapy to overcome the trauma of their childhood (Perry, 2005; Shonkoff, et.al., 2012), and the physical impacts that haunt them throughout their lifetime (Felitti & Anda, 1998). The trauma for the protective parent includes lifelong impacts as well (Rivera, Sullivan, Cris, & Zeoli, 2012).

ACE STUDY and RESEARCH

ACE Research Requires Custody Court Reform

The research about the enormous harm caused by childhood exposure to trauma could be a discouraging and depressing finding. It demonstrates that the failure of our society to prevent these traumas ruins and shortens many lives and inevitably takes so much of the pleasure out of the lives of a significant portion of the population. At the same time, this information is exciting because we can use it to change our responses. We have the ability to make our society enormously wealthier and happier if we can speak openly about these problems, take them seriously and create the reforms necessary to significantly reduce the trauma. In order for any treatment to work, it is critical that the child suffer no further exposure to DV, direct abuse, or other trauma. This means that ordering the child to live with the abuser or have unsupervised visitation is especially dangerous. In many cases abusive fathers use the visitation exchanges to continue harassing or even assaulting the mother. Even if the father never abuses the mother again and does not commit child abuse, it is likely he will abuse future partners. DV is caused by the abuser's belief system and there is no reason to expect the end of one relationship will change his beliefs. Accordingly it is likely the child would be exposed to further DV. This will interfere with the healing and greatly increase the child's health risks. This is one of many good reasons DV experts recommend supervised visitation for abusers. The Saunders' study found that the courts were not requiring supervised visitation for alleged abusers as often as they should. The ACE research makes it even more vital that custody courts change this risky practice.

The ACE Study also raises serious concerns about another common response by custody courts to allegations of child abuse and DV. The often flawed practices lead courts to disbelieve true allegations and then they punish mothers (which really punish the children) by severely restricting the children's access to the mother. This is usually based on a claim of alienation. In most of these cases the mother is the primary attachment figure. Denying children a meaningful relationship with their primary parent increases the risk of depression, low self-esteem, and suicide when older. All of these consequences overlap with the risks of other traumas; indeed, losing contact with a parent is one of the traumas included in the ACE Study. When this extreme decision is not based on a genuine safety issue, and alienation is not connected with safety issues, the risk to children's health is unacceptable. This finding supports a recommendation in the Saunders' study that courts avoid what Saunders referred to as "harmful outcome" cases.

Family Courts are required to make custody and visitation decisions based on the best interests of the children. Each state has legislation or case law that provides judges with the factors they need to consider in determining children's best interest. Most of the factors do not involve safety issues and we have seen many cases in which courts minimize safety risks to focus on far less consequential issues.

The ACE research should change the way courts respond to DV and child abuse. Children exposed to DV, direct abuse and other traumas will suffer many more illnesses and injuries throughout their lives and are likely to have shorter lives----UNLESS THE COURTS DO SOMETHING EFFECTIVE TO PROTECT THEM. It is hard to imagine any consideration that goes more directly to the meaning of the best interests of children. Aside from a factor that would raise immediate safety concerns, nothing else comes close to the importance of shielding children from the short and long-term harms caused by DV and child abuse.

> There is a strong connection between DV and child abuse. Fathers who abuse the mother are much more likely to also hurt the children. Indeed given the enormous harm to children of witnessing DV, it should be treated as a serious form of child abuse. The ACE research counts each type of trauma as one point. Thus children often face their father's abuse of their mother as well as direct physical, emotional, and sexual abuse.

Psychiatric Association have ethical guidelines that suggest professionals without the necessary expertise in a relevant subject area consult with someone who is an expert. Unfortunately this requirement is voluntary. Do the ACE findings demand that these professional associations make such consultations mandatory?

These considerations when applied to professionals who are supposed to be neutral such as GALs or evaluators seem much clearer. The very purpose of their involvement is to best protect the children. They cannot serve in these roles without the needed expertise and familiarity with current research. There must be some method of accountability if their ignorance or negligence places children in jeopardy.

The catastrophic risks to children's health revealed in the ACE Study means that custody courts must undertake reforms that make sure children are protected. If the courts are unwilling to create a new system in which all professionals have a responsibility to safeguard children from health risks, the courts must create practices to make sure they can protect the children in DV and child abuse cases. At a minimum this would include:

1. Making safety the first priority.
2. Create specialized courts for DV and child abuse custody cases.
3. Use a multi-disciplinary approach that includes DV experts
4. Look to current valid scientific research to inform decisions.
5. Require training and retraining of court professionals regarding DV.
6. Stop relying on bogus research and professionals who are part of the cottage industry.

Child Sexual Abuse in Custody and Visitation Litigation: Representation on Behalf of Victims

by Sharon R. Lowenstein

Three factors influence American courts in their victimization of children involved in custody and visitation litigation where child sexual abuse allegation.

The molesting parent acts secretly whereas the protecting parent acts publicly.

Our courts presume that the best interest of the child requires contact with both parents, and this "friendly parent" presumption is applied equally to children who are not at risk of parental abuse.

Our courts commonly interpret best interest of the child in terms of parental rights, and parental rights generally mean paternal rights.

Victimization of children occurs in three ways in American courts.

A mother who seeks to protect her child from sexual molestation by the father generally must prove by "clear and convincing" evidence both that the abuse occurred and that the father is the one who did it. If she fails to meet this difficult standard of proof that he did it our courts are likely to treat the child as if the abuse did not occur.

Once the allegation against the father is not proven and the issue of sexual abuse is treated as a non-issue, the court is likely to shift its attention to the mother. She is seen as emotionally abusive for raising the allegation and for being an "unfriendly parent," i.e., interfering in the relationship between the child and the father.

When this occurs, courts commonly interpret "best interest of the child" not in terms of the quality of bonding between the child and each parent and not in terms of the trauma that the child will suffer by being taken from the custodial, i.e., maternal, home, but in terms of the presumption the child should be "awarded" to the "friendly" parent. The child is then taken from the mother as punishment for raising the allegation and given to the father as an award for appearing the most cooperative in the eyes of the court.vii

On Trial:
Judge Charles B. Schudson and Billie Wright Dziech

If a respectable, reasonable adult is accused of perverse, assaultive behavior by an uncertain, emotionally distraught child, most adults who hear the accusation will fault the child. Disbelief and rejection by potential adult caretakers increase the helplessness, hopelessness, isolation, and self-blame that makes up the most damaging aspects of child sexual victimization… Since the majority of adults who molest children occupy a kinship or trusted relationship… the child is put on the defensive for attacking the credibility of the trusted adult, and for creating a crisis of loyalty which defies comfortable resolution. (Chapter 1, p.4) Ibid., pp. 178-

The system is always more concerned with the wellbeing of the criminals than of the victims. When children are the victims, surely change can be made. (L.G. Arthur, "Child Sexual Abuse: Improving the System's Response," Juvenile and Family Court Journal 37, 2 (1986).

Legal traditions from the Declaration of Independence to the Constitutional Convention to the countless Supreme Court decisions remind us—indeed, require us—to reexamine our laws to assure they provide justice for all. We cannot forsake that history; if in our passion to protect one individual's rights, we ignore those of another, especially those of a child, we cannot claim to be a just society. (pp. 20) Research shows that in family courts, false allegations remain rare. The allegations of sexual abuse occur in approximately 2 percent of custody and visitation disputes, and most of those are substantiated. (pp. 204) N. Thoennes and J. Pearson, "Allegation of Sexual Abuse in Custody and Visitation Cases: Family court judges may fail to understand evidence essential to correct decision making. The tragic result may be that incorrect family court decisions will "have extremely damaging effects either by subjecting the child to continued abuse or by depriving the child of a relationship with a non-abusive parent. Ignorance and indifference to the problem, acceptance of the status quo, are comfortable and undemanding. If the public doesn't realize how pervasive the problem is, it can abandon the legal system to police, attorneys, judges, and legislators who have little motivation to question it. Sgroi, whose Handbook of Clinical Intervention in Child Sexual Abuse is a classic in its field. Sgroi reminds us that "we tolerate sexual abuse of children in our society because we continue to process cases through an adversary system that is overwhelmingly weighted against the child victim at every level.

The Child Sexual Abuse Accomodation
by Rolland C. Summit. M.D.

The syndrome includes five categories:

1. Secrecy
2. Helplessness
3. Entrapment and accommodation
4. Delayed, conflicted and unconvincing disclosure
5. Retraction

The prevailing reality for most frequent victim of child sexual abuse is not a street or school ground experience and not some mutual vulnerability, but an unprecedented, relentlessly progressive intrusion of sexual acts by an overpowering adult in a one-sided victim-perpetrator relationship. The fact that the perpetrator is often and in apparently loving position only increases the imbalance of power and underscores the helplessness of the child. (pp. 81-82) A caring father would not logically act as the child describes; if nothing else, it seems incredible that he would take such flamboyant risks. That logical analysis contains at least two naïve assumptions: (1) the molestations thoughtful and (2) that it is risky. Molestation of a child is not a thoughtful gesture of caring, but a desperate, compulsive search for acceptance and submission [54].

If the child did not seek or did not receive immediate protective intervention, there is no further option to stop the abuse. The only healthy option left is to learn to accept the situation and to survive. There is no way out. The healthy, normal, emotionally resilient child will learn to accommodate to the reality of the continuing sexual abuse. [84]

If the very parent who abuses and is experienced as bad must be turned to for relief of the distress that parent has caused, the child must, out of desperate need, register the parent—delusionally—good. She may discover altered states of consciousness to shut off pain or to dissociate from her body. [84]

PROPOSED FEDERAL LEGISLATION (7/22/03)
AS AMENDED ON 8/18/03
Conceived and Drafted by:
Richard Ducote, Esq.
731 Fern Street
New Orleans,LA 70118
504.314.8400
Ducotelaw@aol.com

42 United States Code § 5105a. Protective Parent Reform Act

(a) This Act shall be known as the "Protective Parent Reform Act." The purpose of this Act is to correct the trend in child custody and visitation cases wherein abused or neglected children, and children in homes where domestic violence exists, are placed by courts in the custody of the abusive, neglectful, or violent parent with the protective parent's custody, visitation, and contact with the child limited.

(b) For any State or public agency to receive any assistance under the provisions of §§5106, 5106a, 5106(c), or 5116, for fiscal year 2005 and any year thereafter, the State or the State in which the public agency applicant is situated must demonstrate that effective June 1, 2005, the following safeguards have been effected and implemented either by statutory enactment or court rule promulgated by the highest court in the State, with such enactment or court rule applicable statewide in every court having jurisdiction over child custody, parental visitation, parenting time, parenting plans, conservatorship of children, or any other issue involving the residence of a child and the contact between the child and his or her parents, incidental to or following separation or divorce, or in connection with a paternity case where the parents have were not married, to ensure that a parent who reasonably believes that his or her child is threatened by child abuse, child neglect, or domestic violence, perpetrated or allowed by the other parent is not punished by the court, or otherwise penalized by loss or limitation of custody, contact, or visitation with his or her child, or the child denied the custody and contact with that parent, for that parent's having such reasonable belief and for acting lawfully in accordance with such belief:

(1) The prohibition against *ex parte* contacts with the judge hearing a child custody or child visitation case, as defined and controlled by state law, shall be specifically made applicable to child custody and child visitation cases, and shall, in addition to the general applicability of the prohibition, specifically include contacts between judges and guardians *ad litem*, minor's counsel, custody evaluators, mental health professionals, mediators, screeners, and other such persons traditionally participating in child custody and visitation cases.

(2) The roles of guardians *ad litem*, minors' counsel, and children's attorneys shall be limited to advocating for the wishes of the child at issue, and to participating in the court proceedings by presentation of evidence and argument in the same manner as a parent's attorney. Such persons shall be prohibited from substituting their own opinions and judgments for the wishes of the child, submitting evidence which would be excluded under the applicable evidence law if tendered by any other party, and in no case shall such person be deemed a quasi-judicial officer or be granted any fact-finding role. This provision shall not require a State to mandate an attorney to represent any child in custody or visitation cases, but shall only be interpreted to the limit the role of such person when provided.

(3) Parents shall be provided full and timely access to all custody and mental health evaluations and reports which are to be considered in any custody or visitation proceeding, including all underlying data for such evaluations and reports, and shall be afforded the opportunity to depose prior to the trial and to cross examine at trial any and all mental health or custody evaluators who will testify in a custody or visitation proceeding.

(4) No expert opinion or expert evidence attempting to discredit a parent's motivation for asserting that his or her child is abused, neglected, or at risk of the effects of domestic violence committed by the other parent, or attempting to discredit a child's report of such abuse, neglect or violence, shall be allowed in a custody or visitation case unless that opinion or evidence is based on concepts and theories generally accepted by the scientific community and supported by credible and admissible evidence of facts which can be established independently of that expert's opinion.

(5) Due process shall be afforded all parents in such custody and visitation cases, and such custody and visitation decisions removing custody, visitation, or contact from a parent who believes or asserts that his or her child is the victim of abuse, neglect, or the effects of domestic violence perpetrated by the other parent shall not be made on the basis of written declarations or affidavits, or without adequate written advance notice and the opportunity to be heard as defined by state and federal constitutional law, even on a purportedly emergency basis, simply because that parent holds that belief. Furthermore, no such parent shall lose custody, visitation, or contact with a child based only on the opinion of a mental health professional that such parent is at risk of unlawfully fleeing with the child, unless credible and admissible evidence independent of the professional's opinion establishes that parent's plan or intent to flee.

(6) Court sponsored mediation, conciliation, and intake screening programs shall not make recommendations or fact-finding reports to the judge regarding child custody, visitation, or contact unless all parties freely agree in advance of the transmittal of such report, and any parent shall have the right to contest the report.

(7) No findings by any child protection agency shall be considered *res judicata* or collateral estoppel, and shall not be considered by the court unless all parents are afforded the opportunity to challenge any such determination.

(8) Whenever child abuse, child neglect, or domestic violence is an issue in a child custody or visitation case, no mental health professional or child custody evaluator who lacks specialized training and experience in child abuse, child neglect, or domestic violence relevant to the specific allegations shall be appointed by the court to conduct any evaluation in the case.

(9) Admissible evidence of child abuse, child neglect, or domestic violence shall be considered in any child custody or visitation case.

(10) No parent shall be deprived of custody, visitation, or contact with his or her child, nor restricted in such custody, visitation, or contact, nor shall such a child be placed in foster care, simply because that parent reasonably believes that his or her child is the victim of child abuse, child neglect, or the effects of domestic violence, and acts lawfully in response to such reasonable belief to protect the child or to obtain treatment for the child.

(11) No valid final order of protection or domestic violence restraining order rendered pursuant to the State's domestic violence or family violence protection statutes and filed with the State's protective order registry shall be violated by the award of custody or visitation to the perpetrator of domestic violence where such is prohibited by the domestic violence order of protection then in effect.

The Hardest Case by H. Joan Pennington

Before The U.S. House of Representatives Judicial Committee, August 6, 1992.

If judges still refuse to recognize spouse abuse after twenty years of public outcry, it must be evident to you that child sexual abuse does not exist for judges in civil courts today, and their decisions reflect this. Sexually abused children cannot wait another twenty years to be heard in court. Judicial training is crucial to the safety of thousands of children (now 40 years later).

Because judges refuse to acknowledge that fathers rape children, protective parents are losing their battle to protect the child, and they are being punished from raising the child's claim of abuse by losing custody of the child. The legal system has failed to protect these children from sexual abuse, and has failed miserably.

I am here today to testify on behalf of parents who are being denied equal access to justice in our legal system. This access is denied when judges refuse to acknowledge the existence of incest in our society and in their courtrooms. Legislation is necessary and appropriations are required to implement mandatory training for all judges who hear domestic violence cases, bearing in mind, that spouse abuse is only one form of domestic abuse. Studies show a high correlation between spouse abuse, child abuse and incest.

Many times, before these cases go into court, the protective parent has been told by medical or mental health professionals that their child has probably been sexually abused by the other parent. The child has disclosed the abuse naming the other parent and exhibits the behaviors associated with children who have been sexually abused. At some point, usually after protracted litigation, the protective parent determines that the legal system cannot or will not protect the child. In most of these cases the protective parent loses custody and the molester is awarded permanent custody. The child is denied access to the only person who believed in them and tried to protect them, and their life of terror continues.

Exclusion of legally admissible evidence denies a litigant the means by which to prove they have been harmed. (62) See, Estes v. Dick Smith Ford, Inc., 856 F.2d 1097 (8th Cir. 1988) Suppression or destruction of evidence, interference with one's right to institute legal action, or impeding the appellate process, violates an individual's right of access to the courts. Access to the courts must be "adequate, effective and meaningful. Denial of a hearing also denies the child the opportunity to cross-examine those evaluators and clinicians who face no other accountability for false or misleading statements and conclusions that sentence a child victim to live with her rapist. (64) The constitutional right access to the courts derives from the first amendment right to petition, and the Fifth and Fourteenth Amendment right to due process. Chrissy F., supra. (pp. 25) The Hardest Case: Custody and Incest.

The Incest Case—Now, we bring in the incest charge. It is so easy for this judge, with no training in incest to believe that this mother is brainwashing the child, and therefore, it is in the child's best interest to be removed from this emotionally disturbed woman, and custody is awarded to the father. If the mother promises three or four years down the road not to bring up the incest, she may get an hour or two of supervised visitation. If hearings are held, the evidence needed to prove the abuse is very often excluded by the court, as are witnesses for the protective parent. Another problem is evident in the fact that judges are rarely required to attend any type of training. Without the proper training, judges act upon their own background in judging cases. This means the judge may be acting on information which is totally inappropriate to proper adjudication of these cases. (pp. 18-19)

Dr. Richard Gardner: A Review of his Theories and Opinions on Atypical Sexuality, Pedophilia, and Treatment Issues
by Stephanie J. Dallam

a. "PAS in a child is a form of emotional abuse. In a way, it may be even more detrimental than physically and /or sexually abusing a child." Addendum 1 (June 1999) Parental Alienation Syndrome (2nd Edition)
b. He presented himself as a professor of psychiatry at Columbia University. He was never on staff. All his books were self published and never subjected to peer review. His theory is overused and misused, and is not based on any science. Under the relevant evidentiary standards, the courts should not accept this testimony.

c. Pedophilia has been considered the norm by the vast majority of individuals in the history of the world. (1992, p. 593)
d. He strongly recommends that we abolish the mandated reporting of sexual abuse and that the fathers need to be helped to appreciate that there is a certain amount of pedophilia in all of us.
e. His suicide was violent and he stabbed himself 7 times in the heart and chest.

If a child feels guilt about participating in the sexual activities with adults, Gardner (1992, p. 549) recommends that the child be told that in other societies such behavior is considered normal and that our society has an exaggerated, punitive and moralistic attitude about adult-child sexual encounters.

As part of his theory, Gardner (1992, pp. 24-5) proposes that pedophilia serves procreative purposes. ("There is a certain amount of pedophilia in all of us") (Gardner 1992, pp. 592-593)[viii]

The Evidentiary Admissibility of Parental Alienation Syndrome: Science, Law, and Policy

by Jennifer Hoult, J.D.

Professional affiliation represents achievement, standing, and recognition in the relevant field and is thus relevant to expert certification and credibility. (280) Gardner claimed that he was a full professor at Colombia University's College of Physicians and Surgeons, and he described as such in his cited peer- reviewed articles, in legal decisions, and in law reviews. (283) While this title may have led judges to believe that Gardner was a paid and tenure professor bolstering his bid for expert testimony in some 400 cases, Gardner was neither paid, tenured nor a full time professor at Columbia. He was an unpaid volunteer. (288)

A Review of his Theories and Opinions on Atypical Sexuality, Pedophilia, and Treatment Issues by Stephanie J. Dallam, RN, MSN, FNP, January—

February 1998-Vol 8, No 1) In addition to feeling sorry for his own misfortune, the father should be helped to feel pity for the child for having been "a victim in a society that considers his behavior a heinous crime or a mortal sin" (Gardner (1992, p. 594)

PAS as a hypothetical "proposed syndrome" without supporting any empirical evidence, remains "unsupported speculation" (304) Lacking scientific foundation, PAS cannot logically or scientifically qualify as a medical syndrome. In jurisdictions throughout the United States, courts have severed maternal contact with children based on expert testimony diagnosing mothers with a novel psychological syndrome called Parental Alienation Syndrome ("PAS") that purportedly results in the alienation of children from their fathers. DDC diagnose women with PAS primarily when they exercise their legal rights. They do not examine the father's conduct, his psychiatric history, violent conduct, and his exercise of legal rights are not construed as symptoms of pathology. PAS underlying theory and functional use in court demonstrate that its admissibility violates public policy with regards to women's and children's legal rights and well-being. (403) Vol. 26, No. 1, Spring 2006)

All his self-published works with no scientific proof have done insurmountable damage to families in our courts.) He claimed that pedophilia and incest are not child abuse. He committed suicide May 25, 2003. Gardner's lack of qualifications, and his abolished theory is still out there being used by the non-educated judges, lawyers, therapist, court appointed evaluators, GALs, and social workers.

How Many Children Are Court-Ordered Into Unsupervised Contact With an Abusive Parent After Divorce?

By Joyanna Silberg, PhD.

According to a conservative estimate by experts at the Leadership Council on Child Abuse and Interpersonal Violence (LC), more than 58,000 children a year are ordered into unsupervised contact with physically or sexually abusive parents following divorce in the United States. This is over twice the yearly rate of new cases of childhood cancer.

Experts at the LC consider the crisis in our family courts to constitute a public health crisis. Once placed with an abusive parent or forced to visit, children will continue to be exposed to parental violence and abuse until they reach 18. Thus, we estimate that half a million children will be affected in the US at any point of time. Many of these children will suffer physical and psychological damage which may take a lifetime to heal. The Leadership Council urges citizens to work with legislators and agencies in their communities to examine this problem, review state agency policies and procedures, and develop legislative and policy solutions that help ensure safety from violence for children following divorce.

Are "Good Enough" Parents Losing Custody to Abusive Ex-Partners?

By Stephanie Dallam, the Leadership Council

High conflict families are disproportionately represented among the population of those contesting custody and visitation. These cases commonly involve domestic violence, child abuse, and substance abuse. Research indicates that that custody litigation can become a vehicle whereby batterers and child abusers attempt to extend or maintain their control and authority over their victims after separation.

Although, research has not found a higher incidence of false allegations of child abuse and domestic violence in the context of custody/visitation, officers of the court tend to be unreasonably suspicious of such claims and that too often custody decisions are based on bad science, misinterpretation of fact, and evaluator bias. As a result, many abused women and their children find themselves re-victimized by the justice system after separation.

Naming the Judicial Terrorists: An Expose of an Abuser's Successful Use of a Judicial Proceeding for Continued Domestic Violence

by Donna J. King

Many abusive men, previously involved in intimate relationships, utilize the United States' judicial system to continuously torture their victims long after separation and divorce with 'institutionally entrenched... judicial strategies' that subordinate and subjugate abused women. Protracted judicial proceedings cause the United States' judicial system to become the ideal weapon for abusers to indefinitely deploy coercive control against their victims.

The Tactics and Plots of Psychopath Aggressors in the Family Law System

by Charles Pragnall, National Council for Children Post-Separation

"In the twenty years I have been advising parents, children, and their legal advisers in several hundred cases, I have often been asked, "Why is it that children are so often ordered to have contact with, and even into the custody of, parents who have abused them and have perpetrated violence against their partners."

The answer to this question is not simple and involves an examination of the requirements of Family Laws which stress the importance of children having both parents in their lives after parental separation, the dynamics of legal processes, and the often very clear gender biases of the principals involved in judicial processes.

But one of the most outstanding and consistent features of proceedings involving the care of children post-separation are the conduct and behaviours which can be identified as clearly fitting the definitions of psychopathy/sociopathy.

The major personality traits of the psychopath are supremacy and narcissism. The afflicted individual must be in complete control of their environment and all persons who are a part of that environment or can serve the psychopaths purposes in maintaining control.

The psychopath is capable of using both aggressive anger and passive anger with cunning and guile, to achieve their goals of exerting control. Examples of such contrary behaviours are the aggressive violence against an intimate partner, with the frequent inherent abuse of children, and to groom friends, relatives, and professionals into believing they are harmless and indeed a very stable and friendly person. If thwarted in attaining these goals however, the passive can quickly turn into the aggressive.

Such professionals now refer to such cases as 'High Conflict' cases when it is clear that they are situations of a violent Aggressor/Tormentor/Persecutor and their victims. It is easy to see how the cases in Austria and America where young girls were imprisoned for many years by controlling individuals and regularly abused in several ways were undetected, when the aggressors/persecutors/tormentors were able to convince their family members, relatives, and associates that they were reasonable, normal people. The same often occurs in other cases of violence and murder where neighbours report that the accused murderer is a 'nice and friendly neighbour'. They do not recognise the Jekyll and Hyde aspects of the psychopath's ploys and tactics and those they have effectively groomed in their beliefs.

It is not difficult to see therefore how the psychopath is able to readily gain the sympathy and support of some of the professionals engaged in the Family Law system and for them to abandon and forfeit their professional objectivity and impartiality in such circumstances. In 'Blaming others' the psychopath will allege the former partner is mentally ill and in some cases the former partner may be suffering a Complex Post Traumatic Disorder after suffering years of physical, mental, and sexual abuse and violence. This is often misinterpreted and misdiagnoses a Borderline Personality Disorder or similar psychiatric term. In effect it is a classic

'Blame the victim' scenario.

The groomed professionals then enable the psychopath to achieve their primary objective which is to maintain power and control over their victims, their former partner and children. It is an act of vengeance and spite but mostly it is to maintain the power and control and feelings of supremacism and narcissism. "I am faultless and flawless and in control of my whole environment" are the unvoiced cravings of the psychopath, and "I can continue to inflict my tortures on my victims with impunity" are the psychopaths continuing behaviours."

Department of Justice Report Demands

Custody Court Reforms
by Barry Goldstein

The United States Department of Justice provided a grant to support a major study by Dr. Daniel Saunders of the University of Michigan to determine how well court professionals and particularly evaluators are responding to domestic violence cases.

Many court professionals have been taught these are 'high conflict' cases and unintentionally use responses that help abusers, but the vast majority of these cases are actually domestic violence cases in which a father who often had little involvement in caring for the children during the relationship seeks custody as a tactic to pressure the mother to return or punish her for leaving. The Saunders' study confirms other research that most of these cases involve domestic violence. We repeatedly see cases in which the father allowed or often required the mother to provide all or most of the child care and then seek to convince the court that she suddenly became unfit when she left him or made complaints about his abuse. The Saunders' report demonstrates how evaluators with inadequate training or beliefs hostile to battered mothers help these abusers gain custody.

The Saunders' study supports earlier findings of substantial gender bias against women litigants. At least forty states and many judicial districts established court-sponsored gender bias committees that demonstrated the bias against women. The connection found by Saunders between beliefs in male dominance and patriarchy with inadequate dv training, belief in the myth that women frequently make false allegations and approaches that minimize or deny valid complaints about domestic violence, demonstrate how evaluators and other court professionals contribute to this gender bias.

For many years, protective mothers and professionals supporting them have been criticizing the practices used by custody courts in domestic violence cases.

The Saunders' study demonstrates the courts are getting a high percentage of their cases wrong and these mistakes are inevitable as long as they continue relying on evaluators and other professionals with inadequate domestic violence training, widespread belief in the myth that women frequently make false allegations of abuse.

APPENDIX D

Reports

Reports the courts had before the Court Order of Judge Leopold June 5, 1990, December 17, 18, 19, 1990 and February 5 and 6, 1991. Order signed February 27, 1991.

- Divorce letter
- Initial Police Report
- L. Baker, Psy.D., Clinical Psychologist 9/14/1989
- Dr. Jones Letter to Truhlar
- Detective Perry Police Department Report 11/08/90
- Guardian Ad Litem
- Guardian's Closing Argument Dated 2/19/ 1991
- Payment to Dr. Richard Gardner
- Judge Leopold Order

STANLEY G. LIPKIN
ATTORNEY AT LAW
ONE CIVIC CENTER PLAZA
1560 BROADWAY, SUITE 680
DENVER, COLORADO 80202

(303) 861-5800

February 1, 1988

Ms. Maralee McLean
3571 S. Uravan
Aurora, Colorado 80013

Re: Marriage of McLean and [redacted]
Case No. [redacted]

Dear Maralee:

Enclosed please find a letter I received on January 29, 1988 from [redacted] attorney, Robert J. Beattie. In an earlier telephone conversation, Mr. Beattie indicated that [redacted] would settle for "nothing less than joint custody." I informed Mr. Beattie that joint custody was the furthest thing from your mind at this time and that I also considered such an agreement an impossibility based upon the conflict between you and [redacted]. I urged Mr. Beattie to calm [redacted] down and to stop him from harassing you if he ever hoped to have a better working relationship with you. I also called Mr. Beattie again on January 29, 1988 to inform him that [redacted] was in specific violation of the Temporary Orders through telephone harassment. Mr. Beattie indicated he would immediately contact [redacted] to ask him to stop.

In a telephone conversation I had with Dr. Margolis on January 29, 1988, we discussed two issues. First of all, Dr. Margolis expressed her concern as to whether or not it would be appropriate to have a restraining order entered to protect you. I explained to her that there was an automatic restraining order upon the filing of the action which prohibits the harassment that is going on. I also informed her of the Referee's orders limiting contact between you and [redacted]. Therefore, what we have is not the need for a restraining order but a question of enforcement. I know Andrea discussed this with you last week. My feeling is that if the harassment does not stop immediately, we should go into court on contempt to ask that [redacted] be sanctioned for violating the previous orders of court. I think it is most appropriate to let [redacted] know very early that you will not put up with his harassment. If we do not enforce the orders of court at the outset, we will probably be encouraging [redacted] to continue the same behavior. While restraining orders and

Page Two
Ms. Maralee Mclean
February 1, 1988

contempt are aggressive proceedings, there is often a greater danger by foregoing enforcement. Therefore, I would advise you that if [redacted] harassment has not stopped after my conversation with his attorney last week, we should haul him into court without further delay.

The other area discussed with Dr. Margolis is the question of [redacted] psychological well-being. She indicated that she had some concerns based upon the reports she had received from you and the journals. She asked whether we could have a psychological or psychiatric evaluation done of [redacted] to determine his mental status. Basically, there are two ways we can accomplish this. There would be a psychological evaluation within any custody evaluation. Mr. Beattie indicated that it was [redacted] desire to have a custody investigation done and asked if you would be willing to split the costs. Since these costs would likely be in the nature of $1,000 and the statute requires the party requesting the evaluation to advance the initial costs, I told Mr. Beattie that if [redacted] wanted the investigation he would have to front the costs. The other way we could approach the issue would be to simply ask for an evaluation of [redacted] which would be performed at your expense. This is a simpler approach than a custody investigation which also involves an evaluation of yourself, of [redacted], and an investigation of the marital history with recommendations made as to custody and visitation. You could expect a psychological or psychiatric evaluation to cost in the neighborhood of several hundred dollars. If you can afford this expense, I would be happy to file a motion with the court to require the individual evaluation. It is possible that [redacted] counsel could respond by asking for the custody investigation which would then require [redacted] to advance additional costs.

Please let me know what your thoughts are on the areas I have discussed and how you would like to proceed. Please also let us know promptly if [redacted] gets out of compliance with the financial orders in your case.

Sincerely,

Stanley G. Lipkin

SGL/ac

City of Aurora
POLICE DEPARTMENT ORIGI .L

89-1602976

Sexual Assault on a Child	[redacted]	07-20-89	11-14-89

UCR Disposition Change To: ☐ Arrest ☐ Exceptionally Cleared ☐ Unfounded ☒ Inactive

☐ Prosecute For Lesser Charge ☐ Juvenile ☐ Victim Failure To Prosecute ☐ Declined By DA ☐ Duplicate Charges ☐ Suspect Incarcerated ☐ Suspect Death ☐ Other Jurisdiction

PROPERTY

Property	Currency	Jewelry	Clothing	Vehicle (Local)	Office Equipment	Radio TV Cameras	Fire Arms	House Hold Goods	Consumables	Live Stock	Misc	Total
Stolen	$	$	$	$	$	$	$	$	$	$	$	$
Recovery	$	$	$	$	$	$	$	$	$	$	$	$

IF PROPERTY ITEMIZATION, USE THE FOLLOWING FORMAT

CONTINUATION FOLLOW UP SHEET
NARRATIVE

07-21-89 This detective received and reviewed this case.

I also noted that at this time, as shown on the original offense report, the victim's name is not listed, the location of occurrence is not listed, the date and time of occurrence is not listed and only the [RP] Maralee McLean is listed. The body of the report advised that McLean would not give Officer Genaro, who completed the offense report, any further information. I later received a message from McLean advising that she wanted me to call her back.

I contacted Ms. McLean, whereupon she advised that she wanted to, at this time, give all the information involving the alleged sexual assault. McLean advised that she feels that the suspect [redacted], would kill her when he finds out about the report. Ms. McLean advised that she wanted police protection. I advised Ms. McLean that [redacted] would be notified to stay away from her and the child but as far as the availability of an officer to personally protect her, that would not be possible.

I contacted dispatch and requested that they send out an officer for a supplemental report.

I contacted Arapahoe County Social Services and learned that Jennifer Floyd had been assigned to the case.

After I received the supplemental report listing the allegations, I contacted Jennifer Floyd and advised her of the information. Jennifer Floyd advised that she would suspend visitation by the father, [redacted], until the investigation had been completed.

I also talked to Officer B. Maul, who completed the supplemental report, and he advised that McLean told him that she didn't give the full information earlier because she was afraid that [redacted] would hurt her or the child. According to Officer Maul, McLean advised that she had an independent witness who had heard the victim, [redacted] make statements about the sexual assault.

I contacted Ms. McLean by telephone and advised her of the steps that would be taken.

Det. F.H. Parker ehh 10298 11-28-89 Page 1 of 4

Methods of Assessment (continued)

Phone contacts with:
Dr. Matthew Back, Maralee's psychologist
Jennifer Floyd
Dee Brodbeck
Ruth Gibbens, [redacted] babysitter

Discussion of Results

The clinical interview with Maralee furnished the examiner with information regarding her daughter's development, a history of her marriage to [redacted] and her observations of [redacted] behavior related to the allegations of sexual abuse. During the clinical interview with Maralee she appeared considerably upset and anxious. She appeared to be a woman who has been under a great deal of stress.

According to Merlee her 10-year marriage to [redacted] was fairly happy until she became pregnant with their only child, [redacted] Maralee filed for divorce when [redacted] was 8 months old. Maralee believed that [redacted] rejected her when she was pregnant. She reported a great deal of arguing and incidents of physical abuse toward the end of their marriage.

Joint custody was awarded to the parents with Maralee named as the primary residential custodian. [redacted] visits with Julie occurred on Tuesdays, Thursdays and Saturdays. Maralee stated that [redacted] visitations with [redacted] were regular and that he "never missed a visitation."

In July, according to Maralee, after a visitation with [redacted], [redacted] complained that her vagina hurt. Maralee took off [redacted] pants and [redacted] then spread her legs and stated, "Mommy, I have an ow-ee. Daddy hurt me." The next morning Maralee stated that [redacted] persisted in her claim that "Daddy hurt me." Maralee took [redacted] to her pediatrician, Dr. Stan Rosenberg. He found no physical evidence of sexual abuse.

Two days later, after another visitation with her father, [redacted] demonstrated digital penetration of her vagina in front of Maralee. According to Maralee [redacted] spread her legs and placed her fingers slightly inside her vagina and stated "Daddy touches me there." Also, Maralee stated that [redacted] talked about this "incident" in front of a number of Maralee's friends. She called the pediatrician again and he contacted Social Services. Maralee also claimed that [redacted] began to thrust her tongue out and flicked up and down when describing what her daddy did to her.

Initially, Maralee claimed that she did not ask [redacted] leading questions such as "What did Daddy do to you?" Instead, Maralee asked [redacted], "What happened." Maralee stated that she was in a "state of shock" because she didn't believe [redacted] would do "such a thing." Yet as time went on and [redacted] persisted in her claims, Maralee began to believe what her daughter was allegedly saying.

The police were notified and [redacted] adamantly denied the charges. Since that time Maralee has felt unsupported in her attempts to get help for her daughter. She continues to feel unsupported by the professionals who initially dealt with the case and believes that it is she "who is on trial" instead of her ex-husband. Maralee firmly believes her daughter's accusations and is significantly frustrated in that

Dr. L Baker
Child Physchologist
Age: 2.5

According to Dr. Back, he had professional contact with Maralee for approximately one year around the time of her separation and divorce from [redacted]. He believes Maralee to be credible and feels that her concerns about [redacted] are well founded. He stated that Maralee was fearful of [redacted] yet initially made excuses for his behavior. Her concerns at the time involved [redacted] infidelity, emotional abuse, and his financial irresponsibility. Through treatment she was able to gain sufficient distance to justify her concerns about [redacted] and take appropriate action to protect herself.

Ruth Gibbens, [redacted] babysitter for the past year, was contacted by phone. Ruth runs a licensed day care service in her home. She stated that during the spring and summer of 1989 [redacted] behavior began to noticeably change. She began removing her clothes and fondling herself in front of the other children. According to Ruth, [redacted] had previously been a "happy-go-lucky" child. However, in the spring of '89 [redacted] began to fight with other children. She occasionally bit other children and would whine a great deal. On one occasion while Ruth was bathing [redacted] she began fondling her genitals and stated that "Daddy hurt me." She also on one occasion claimed that her "pee pee" hurt and she coudn't go to the bathroom. She continued to demonstrate digital penetration of her vagina to Ruth while stating, "Daddy did that." She also wiggled her tongue in and out of her mouth while she placed her fingers inside the opening of her vagina. According to Ruth, [redacted] also told the other children at the daycare what her "daddy did." Occasionally, [redacted] would spend the night at Ruth's home since Maralee is a flight attendant and her schedule at times calls for overnight duty. Ruth noted that [redacted] began to have nightmares and cried a great deal during the afternoon naps and at nighttime. [redacted] needed a considerable amount of consoling before she could settle back down to sleep. Again, this behavior was a marked change from her previous patterns of sleep.

[redacted] became observably nervous when examining the genital areas on the anatomically correct dolls. Initially she undressed the dolls one by one and began to examine the genital areas of all the dolls. She placed her index finger inside the girl doll's vagina. She then looked at the examiner and asked where "her mommy" was. She wanted to go out in the waiting room and get her mother.

[redacted] did not display any spontaneous behaviors that would indicate sexual abuse by her father. However, upon direct questioning: "What did Daddy do to [redacted]?" she responded by spreading the little girl doll's legs and stuck out her tongue and flicked it up and down. She then got up and went over to play with other toys. Her play with the doll house demonstrated warmth and affection with both mother and father dolls.

There appears to be sufficient evidence in [redacted] behaviors during the clinical interview and the observations of her behaviors by Maralee, the babysitter, and the clinician that [redacted] has either been sexually abused or has been exposed to sexual stimuli. The nervousness, agitation and anxiety [redacted] demonstrated while examining the dolls' genitalia, her anger at the "daddy doll," and her repeated demonstrations of digital penetration are congruent with a child who has been exposed to sexual abuse. The marked change in [redacted]s behavior along with her allegations to her mother, the babysitter and various other friends of Maralee that "Daddy hurt me" are significant in that they also indicate exposure to sexual abuse.

JONES AND CHAO, P.C.
Clinical Psychologists
4770 East Iliff Avenue, Suite 233
Denver, Colorado 80222

Arthur C. Jones, Ph.D.
Christine M. Chao, Ph.D.

(303) 753-9738

February 24, 1990

Doris B. Truhlar
Truhlar and Truhlar
1901 West Littleton Boulevard
Littleton, Colorado 80120

Re: [redacted] and Maralee McClean

Dear Ms. Truhlar:

As you know, I have been seeing [redacted] and Maralee McClean for separation counseling over the last few months. This letter is to report on the progress of those meetings and offer my recommendations concerning the case at this point.

I met with [redacted] and Maralee for a total of five sessions (12/5, 12/12, & 12/19/89; 1/9 & 1/30/90). Despite the obvious tension between the two of them, both were cooperative in scheduling appointments and participating in the sessions. However, from the first session it was clear that it would be very difficult to establish a common working agenda. [redacted] expressed a strong desire to meet to get beyond hostilities and establish some co-parenting communication with Maralee. Maralee expressed her feeling that her main agenda was her hope that [redacted] would admit that he had abused his daughter and be open to getting help with his underlying emotional problems. The process in each session was repetitive, with [redacted] raising issues (e.g., visitation arrangements, insurance for [redacted] other practical issues) and Maralee insisting that he was avoiding the real issue, which for her was the fact that he had abused [redacted]. After the first three sessions, I suggested spacing our appointments, hoping that the passage of time would help to allow discussion of issues of common concern for [redacted] and Maralee and some healing of wounds from their painful divorce. However, even after some time had passed it was very difficult to proceed. This process was exacerbated by Maralee's report that after several weeks of not talking about it, [redacted] began to re-initiate discussions about "Daddy touching me down there." This culminated in a report by [redacted] babysitter to Social Services concerning her (the babysitter's) feeling that abuse of [redacted] is continuing. At this point I do not think that continued conjoint sessions with [redacted] and Maralee will be productive and I have therefore suspended scheduling any new appointments for now. I'm open to beginning the counseling again if both parties indicate they feel there is a chance for progress.

The facts in this case continue to be elusive, but I must share my impression that [redacted] consistently cooperative and open stance in my dealings with him have

FORM 520-510

City of Aurora
P('CE DEPARTMENT ORIGINA!

2. Original Case Record Number [redacted]

1. Initial Offense Classification	15. Victim	13. Date Original Report	72. Date This Report
Sexual Assault	[redacted]	07-20-89	12-10-90
111. RI Entry Number	112. PY Entry Number	113. TYP Codes	

8. UCR Disposition-Change To
☐ Arrest ☐ Exceptionally Cleared
☐ Unfounded ☐ Inactive

8A. Exceptional Clearance Category
☐ Victim Failure To Prosecute
☐ Prosecute For Lesser Charge ☐ Juvenile ☐ Declined By DA ☐ Duplicate Charges
☐ Suspect Incarcerated ☐ Suspect Death ☐ Other Jurisdiction

114. PROPERTY	A. CURRENCY	B. JEWELRY	C. CLOTHING	D. VEHICLE (LOCAL)	E. OFFICE EQUIPMENT	F. RADIO, TV, CAMERAS	G. FIRE-ARMS	H. HOUSE-HOLD GOODS	I. CON-SUMABLES	J. LIVE-STOCK	K. MISC.	L. TOTAL
STOLEN	$	$	$	$	$	$	$	$	$	$	$	$
RECOVERY	$	$	$	$	$	$	$	$	$	$	$	$

IF PROPERTY ITEMIZATION, USE THE FOLLOWING FORMAT:

115. Item No.	116. Quantity	117. Brand Name	118. Property Description	119. Serial #	120. Stolen	121. Rec.	122. UCR Property Type
					$	$	

I showed [redacted] an anatomical drawing of a white preschool age female child. I had her identify parts of the body on the drawing. She correctly identified the head, eyes, nose, mouth, arms, fingers, legs, and toes. She identified the vagina as "pee pee," and the buttocks as "bottom."

I talked to [redacted] about the concept of good touch, bad touch. I asked her if anyone ever talked to her about this. [redacted] told me that her mommy had. I asked [redacted] what her mommy had told her about good touch, bad touch. She said, "Mommy touched me here," and was pointing at her knee. [redacted] told me that that was a good touch. [redacted] then pointed to her genital area and said that daddy had touched her there and said that was a bad touch. [redacted] made this statement without any questioning on my part, other than the question about good touch and bad touch.

I gave [redacted] some examples of the concept of good touch, bad touch, and asked her to identify the example as either a good touch or a bad touch. The first example I gave [redacted] was a hug. She identified this as a good touch because it would make her feel good. The second example I gave her was a punch in the nose. She identified this as a bad touch because it would hurt. The third example I gave her was a doctor's examination where the doctor might have to check her "pee pee" to see if she was okay. [redacted] identified this as a bad touch because it would hurt. She stated that it would be a good touch if it was done to make her well, however, it had to be a doctor and only if it was to make her well. The next example I gave her was changing the diaper on a baby. She identified this as a good touch. She said it would be a good touch because it was done to make the baby clean.

I asked [redacted] if anyone had ever touched her in a way that she would call a bad touch, or in a way that made her feel funny or comfortable. [redacted] told me, "Daddy did." I asked [redacted] where he had touched her and she said, "My pee pee." [redacted] was pointing to her genital area when she said this. I then asked [redacted] what she had been touched with and she said, "It's red and it's hard and it hurt." At this time, I showed [redacted] the anatomical drawing of the white preschool age female child and I provided her with a red pen. I asked [redacted] to mark on the drawing, where she had been touched. [redacted] colored the genital area and the buttocks on this drawing.

I then showed [redacted] an anatomical drawing of a white adult male. I asked her what that was a picture of and she stated, "A daddy." I then asked [redacted] if she could show me if there was anything on the drawing that she had been touched with. At this time, [redacted] pointed to the penis on the

109. Event Number	110. Operation I.D.	Yes ☐ No ☐

69. Officer Signature	IB Number	70. Supervisor Initials and Date	71.
Det. D.E. Perry, #10312 ehh	WFP	SLM 12-28-90	Page 3 of 14

FORM 520-510

City of Aurora
P(CE DEPARTMENT ORIGINAL

2. Original Case Report Number [redacted]

Offense	Victim	Date Report	Date This Report
Sexual Assault	[redacted]	07-20-89	12-10-90

☐ Arrest ☐ Exceptionally Cleared ☐ Unfounded ☐ Inactive

☐ Victim Failure To Prosecute ☐ Prosecute For Lesser Charge ☐ Juvenile ☐ Declined By DA ☐ Duplicate Charges ☐ Suspect Incarcerated ☐ Suspect Death ☐ Other Jurisdiction

PROPERTY	CURRENCY	JEWELRY	CLOTHING	VEHICLE & LOCALS	OFFICE EQUIPMENT	RADIO, TV, CAMERAS	FIREARMS	HOUSEHOLD GOODS	CONSUMABLES	LIVESTOCK	MISC.	TOTAL
STOLEN	$	$	$	$	$	$	$	$	$	$	$	$
RECOVERY	$	$	$	$	$	$	$	$	$	$	$	$

IF PROPERTY ITEMIZATION, USE THE FOLLOWING FORMAT:

NARRATIVE

drawing. I asked [redacted] what she called that and she stated, "a peanut." I then asked [redacted] to take the red pen again and mark on the drawing what she been touched with. At this point, [redacted] colored the penis on the drawing.

I asked [redacted] what color her daddy's "peanut" was. She stated that it was red and it was hard. I asked [redacted] where she was touched with his "peanut," and she said, "my pee pee and bottom." [redacted] was pointing to her vaginal area and buttocks when she said this. I asked [redacted] where this had happened. She told me, "at daddy's house, downstairs." I asked [redacted] when it happened and she said, "lasterday." I tried to establish a timeframe for the word "lasterday" but was unable to do so.

I asked [redacted] if anyone had told her to tell me this and she stated, no. I also asked [redacted] if her father had said anything to her about telling anyone what he had done to her and again she said, no. I also asked [redacted] if anyone else had ever touched her in those places and again she told me, no. [redacted] could not provide me with any other information and I concluded my interview with her.

I reviewed the deposition of Ruth Gibbens. She is [redacted] babysitter. The deposition cites numerous incidents where Ruth Gibbens has observed [redacted] involved in what she felt was excessive masterbation and also making statements that her daddy had hurt her, and when she made that statement, she was pointing to her vagina. She also made other statements, such as: daddy touches me here, or, daddy does this, and she would show Ms. Gibbens what had been happening. Ms. Gibbens also said that she would have to watch [redacted] closely and not leave her alone with other children for whom she was providing daycare because when she did, [redacted] would take her clothes off and show other children her body and also ask them to touch her. Ms. Gibbens advised that she did contact social services at this time. (See Ruth Gibbens' deposition for further information.)

11-09-90

Event Number — Operation I.D. Yes ☐ No ☐

Det. D.E. Perry, #10312 ehh NEP SLM 12-28-90 Page 4 of 14

FORM 520-510

City of Aurora
P CE DEPARTMENT ORIGINA!

2. Original Case Report Number: [redacted]

1. Initial Offense Classification: Sexual Assault
15. Victim: [redacted]
13. Date Original Report: 07-20-89
72. Date This Report: 12-10-90

111. PI Entry Number
112. PY Entry Number
113. TYP Codes

8. UCR Disposition Change To: ☐ Arrest ☐ Exceptionally Cleared ☐ Unfounded ☐ Inactive

8A. Exceptional Clearance Category: ☐ Victim Failure To Prosecute ☐ Prosecute For Lesser Charge ☐ Juvenile ☐ Declined By DA ☐ Duplicate Charges ☐ Suspect Incarcerated ☐ Suspect Death ☐ Other Jurisdiction

PROPERTY

114. PROPERTY	A. CURRENCY	B. JEWELRY	C. CLOTHING	D. VEHICLE (LOCAL)	E. OFFICE EQUIPMENT	F. RADIO, TV, CAMERAS	G. FIRE-ARMS	H. HOUSE-HOLD GOODS	I. CON-SUMABLES	J. LIVE-STOCK	K. MISC.	L. TOTAL
STOLEN	$	$	$	$	$	$	$	$	$	$	$	$
RECOVERY	$	$	$	$	$	$	$	$	$	$	$	$

IF PROPERTY ITEMIZATION, USE THE FOLLOWING FORMAT:

115. Item No.	116. Quantity	117. Brand Name	118. Property Description	119. Serial #	120. Stolen	121. Rec.	122. UCR Property Type
					$	$	

NARRATIVE

11-26-90

I was contacted by Dr. Susan Reichert, who advised me that she is on staff with the Child Protection Team at Children's Hospital. Dr. Reichert advised me that Merelee McLean had brought her three year old daughter, [redacted], to Children's Hospital for a medical examination. Dr. Reichert stated that after performing a medical examination on [redacted] she found no signs of sexual abuse. Dr. Reichert stated that she could not confirm or rule out the possibility of sexual abuse. Dr. Reichert said that given [redacted] story (that she had provided to me) she was very concerned that something may have happened to [redacted] and felt that this issue should be taken very seriously even though no medical evidence of sexual abuse was found.

I received a report from Dr. Reichert on the medical examination that she had performed on [redacted] on 11-20-90. I noted that Dr. Reichert had conducted her physical examination, and when she reached [redacted] genital area, [redacted] made the comment that her daddy had also hurt her in her private parts and on her stomach and in the buttocks area. Dr. Reichert asked [redacted] what she had been touched with and she always responded, paper or paper towel. Dr. Reichert stated that [redacted] answered these questions in a very automatic way, as though she had it in her mind that that was what she was going to state no matter what the question was. Dr. Reichert noted that [redacted] seemed very anxious about her responses.

While Dr. Reichert was talking to [redacted], she made the following spontaneous comment: "I can't go back home to my dad." Dr. Reichert asked her why and [redacted] said, "I don't like to go to my dad's." When Dr. Reichert asked her why, she said, "He touches me," and when she said this, [redacted] was pointing to her "vulva." Dr. Reichert stated that she asked [redacted] what she had been touched with and she said, "a bottle." Dr. Reichert again asked [redacted] what color the bottle was and she said, "pink." Dr. Reichert also asked [redacted] what was in the bottle and she said, "milk."

108. Event Number
110. Operation I.D. Yes ☐ No ☐

69. Officer Signature: Det.D.E.Perry,#10312 ehh
ID Number: 3/9P
70. Supervisor Initials and Date: SVM 12-28-90
71. Page 11 of 14

DISTRICT COURT, COUNTY OF ARAPAHOE, STATE OF COLORADO

Case No. [redacted] Division 11

MARALEE MCLEAN'S RESPONSE TO GUARDIAN AD LITEM'S MOTION FOR FORTHWITH HEARING CONCERNING VISITATION

The People of the State of Colorado in the Interest of:

[redacted] a Child, and Concerning

MARALEE McLEAN and [redacted], Respondents, and

RUTH GIBBONS, Special Respondent.

Maralee McLean objects to the relief requested by the guardian ad litem for the following reasons:

1. Guardian ad litem has misrepresented to the Court the position of Detective Perry in paragraph 3. of her motion. Refer to annexed Exhibit "A" containing the handwritten responses of Detective Perry with respect to guardian ad litem's allegations in paragraph 3. wherein he emphasizes that the investigation is still open, pending the decision of the Kempe Center to review this case, that all reports will be forwarded to the Arapahoe County District Attorney's office for review and that in his opinion there may have been some type of contact between Peter and the child but that it is unclear if that contact was for the purpose of sexual abuse or some other type of inappropriate contact which has proven to be upsetting to [redacted]

2. Guardian ad litem has misrepresented the position of caseworker Kirsten Jensen in paragraph 5. of her motion. Refer to annexed Exhibit "B" which is a handwritten letter from caseworker to Maralee McLean dated Monday, December 3, 1990, wherein she expresses frustration over the filing of guardian ad litem's motion, a plan for visitation which included total supervision by the caseworker, a willingness to have the Kempe Center involved and a concern for the safety of [redacted].

3. Maralee McLean believes that the best interests of [redacted] would be served by permitting Detective Perry to continue his investigation to its logical conclusion, allow him to submit the data gathered to the Arapahoe County District Attorney's office, secure the involvement of the Kempe Center, allow the caseworker to continue her planned assessment of the situation and, if guardian ad litem continues to misrepresent the opinions and positions of the professionals in this case to have her removed from that position.

DATED: December 4, 1990

DISTRICT COURT, COUNTY OF ARAPAHOE, STATE OF COLORADO

Case No. [redacted], Division 5

MARALEE'S CLOSING ARGUMENT

The People of the State of Colorado in the Interest of:

[redacted] a Child,

and Concerning

MARALEE McLEAN and [redacted],

Respondents.

Maralee argues as follows:

I. The existing custodial arrangement should remain in effect with appropriate modifications with respect to [redacted] visitation with [redacted] or, in the alternative, Maralee should be granted sole custody of [redacted] and [redacted] rights of reasonable visitation with [redacted].

[redacted] failed to demonstrate an advantage to changing the primary residence of [redacted] from Maralee and to eliminating the decision making process for [redacted] upbringing set forth in the original custodial arrangement. This failure on [redacted] part is especially salient when you take into consideration the parties' pattern of involvement with [redacted] since her birth and through the final days of the hearing in February.

Since her birth and for over four years without interruption, Maralee has been the primary parent for [redacted], providing a stable environment through consistent employment since graduation from college and raising the child virtually by herself. Maralee's constant involvement in [redacted] life has created a close bond between the two, giving Maralee greater insight into [redacted] emotional, intellectual and physical needs. [redacted] extended family of maternal grandparents, five aunts and uncles and neices and nephews interact on a regular basis with Maralee and [redacted] providing even more stability.

[redacted] involvement in [redacted] life was non-existent for the eight months following her birth and then there was only minimal measured contact with temporary orders through the entry of the Decree and thereafter. But Maralee encouraged [redacted] to participate in [redacted] life by voluntarily expanding the amount of Court ordered visitation and included over-nights. In the fall of 1989 increased contact occurred only under the direction and control of the Department of Social Services.

II. The guardian ad litem's recommendation with respect to sole custody should be disregarded or viewed with great suspicion by the Court.

The guardian ad litem's obvious lack of objectivity and bias toward [redacted] taints her opinion on the issue of custody.

As an officer of the Court and as the guardian ad litem, she stated under oath that she had not formulated an opinion on the issue of custody and would not do so until all of the evidence had been presented. However, prior to the conclusion of the case, including Maralee's testimony, and less than twenty-four hours after she made the statement, she tendered a detailed Recommendation to this Court.

The Recommendation's inconsistencies dictate that her opinion had been formulated even as early as December of 1990. The Recommendation refers to [redacted] as being three and one-half years old when at the time the Recommendation was tendered to the Court she was four years old. In addition, paragraph 7. of the Recommendation addresses visitation during Christmas of 1990 which occurred two months before the February hearing.

From her appointment in the fall of 1989, the guardian ad litem has attempted to orchestrate the entire proceedings, has demonstrated a dominance over both representatives of the Department of Social Services and the other professionals involved, and created the appearance of successfully influencing the professionals' attitudes and opinions in favor of [redacted] and against Maralee. Her open and notorious fraternization with [redacted], his counsel, the Department of Social Services, and certain other professionals augmented the appearance, if not the reality, of lack of objectivity to Maralee and the public, putting in question the validity of her opinions.

III. Maralee's initial reaction to possible abuse was reasonable and appropriate. No one questioned the truthfulness of her reportings. That concern was perpetuated with information provided by Ruth Gibbens, a professional daycare provider, [redacted] repeated behavior, the observations and opinions of Dr. Baker, Dr. Adams and Detective Perry, experts in the area of abuse, the confirmation of Kim Fowler, a woman who had been abused as a child, and observations of others.

While Maralee remains unconvinced that [redacted] did not abuse [redacted] at some point in the past, she did state under oath that she felt capable of setting aside her concerns provided there was no renewed behavior that would prompt her to again take protective measures to assure [redacted] safety. But, should such behavior occur Maralee stated that she understood, accepted and would follow the recommendations of the professionals in this case as to the procedure for dealing with that renewed behavior.

DATED: February 19, 1991

THEODORE P. KAPLYSH,
a professional corporation

By *Theodore P. Kaplysh*
Theodore P. Kaplysh, #819
Attorney for Respondent
Maralee McLean
The Penthouse
1776 South Jackson Street
Denver, Colorado 80210
Telephone: 758-8981

CERTIFICATE OF SERVICE

I certify that a true copy of the foregoing was mailed to the following parties and/or attorneys of record pursuant to Rule 5, C.R.C.P. this *19th* day of *February*, 1991:

Lynn Graves
Arapahoe County Attorney
Arapahoe County Department
of Social Services
1400 West Littleton Blvd.
Littleton, Colorado 80120

Stephen P. Calder, Esq.
Market Tower Two, Suite 821
3025 South Parker Road
Aurora, Colorado 80014

Doris B. Truhlar
Attorney at Law
1901 West Littleton Boulevard
Littleton, Colorado 80120

By *[signature]*

DR2.39

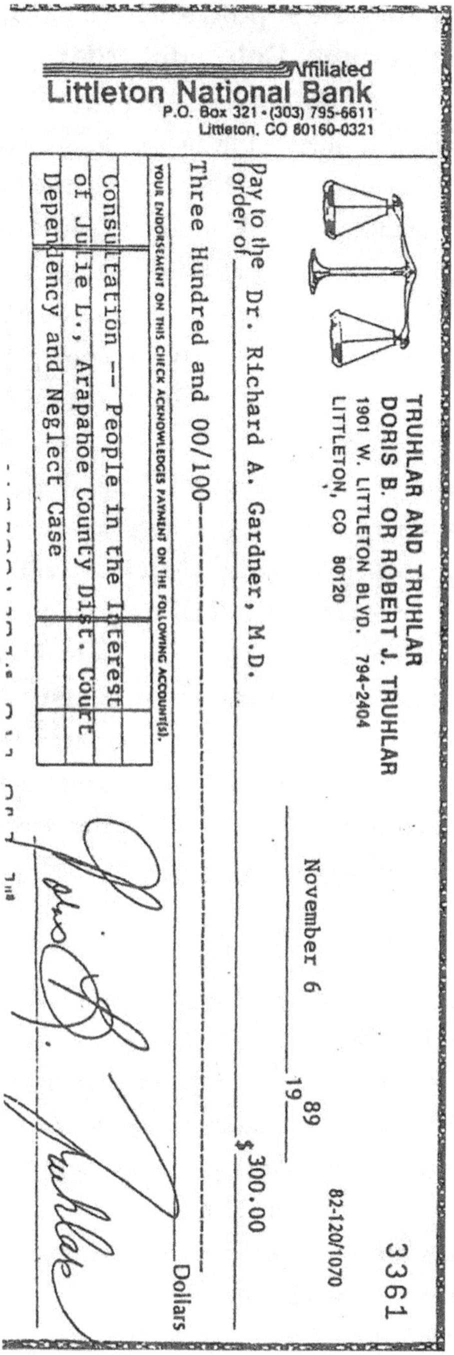

Affiliated
Littleton National Bank
P.O. Box 321 • (303) 795-6611
Littleton, CO 80160-0321

TRUHLAR AND TRUHLAR
DORIS B. OR ROBERT J. TRUHLAR
1901 W. LITTLETON BLVD. 794-2404
LITTLETON, CO 80120

3361

82-120/1070

November 6 19 89

Pay to the order of Dr. Richard A. Gardner, M.D. $ 300.00

Three Hundred and 00/100———————— Dollars

YOUR ENDORSEMENT ON THIS CHECK ACKNOWLEDGES PAYMENT ON THE FOLLOWING ACCOUNT(S).

Consultation -- People in the Interest
of Julie L., Arapahoe County Dist. Court
Dependency and Neglect Case

Excerpts from Judge Leopold's District Court Arapahoe County Colorado Order

February 27, 1991

"The conduct of the guardian ad litem was the subject of in chambers meeting of counsel on February 6, 1991 and is referenced in Ms. McLean's closing argument. As to this issue, the court specifically finds as follows:"

On Feb. 5, 1991 the GAL testified under oath that she had not formed an opinion for a recommendation to the Court and would not do so until all the evidence had been presented. On Feb. 6, 1991 and particularly before Ms. McLean had completed her testimony, the GAL filed a written recommendation favoring the respondent.

The Court's file contains several pleadings filed by the GAL which, when read in the context of her actions of Feb. 6, 1991 suggest that she was predisposed in favor of the respondent well before Feb. 6, 1991. However the guardian ad litem's testimony and premature recommendations create an impression of bias which certainly causes Ms. Mclean and her supporters, if not others familiar with this case, to question the integrity of the adjudicative process herein.

Accordingly, the Court strikes the GAL's written recommendation filed Feb. 6 1991 and give it no weight. All the GAL's examination and the responses thereto are disregarded by the Court before the matter is returned to division 9."

"Ms. McLean first suspected that respondent had sexually assaulted the child in July, 1989. Although the court can conclude that Ms. McLean's initial response was appropriate, the overwhelmingly evidence indicates that her subsequent conduct was totally inappropriate. Ms. McLean spent more than two years in unceasing efforts to validate her beliefs. She subjected the child to tape recording of conversations, repeated examinations and evaluations and interrogation. Although Ms. McLean has testified that she has put this issue behind her because she cannot develop credible corroborative evidence, her statements lack conviction and credibility.

Dr. Gail Adams Adams, an expert in clinical psychology, recommends a set schedule for each parent. The child should have a consistent day care provider. That person should not be Ruth Gibbens because Gibbens gave too much credence to the sexual abuse allegations. Dr. Adams believes that the respondent's ability to promote the child's relationship with Ms. Mclean is much more consistent than is Ms. Mclean's ability to promote the child's relationship with the respondent. Kimberly Fowler is a friend of Ms. McLean. Ms. Fowler and Ruth Gibbens are suspicious of the respondent. Both apparently believe that the respondent sexually abused the child. Ms. Gibbens is concerned with the respondent to set limits. Ms. Fowler believes that respondent stages his behavior for observers.

Respondent appears to have followed most of the court orders. Ms. McLean has admitted to violating a court order. When asked about her future attitude toward Court Orders Ms. Mclean was equivocal.

Reports the courts had prior to Court Order of Judge Michael Bieda.

July 29, 1992, October 6 and 7, 1992.
"Interim Orders" entered October 7, 1992.

- Kaiser Report, Dr. Marion 6/6/91 no response from social service or the new g.a.l.
- Humana Hospital Report, Dr. Greer 9/20/91 police noti- fied, child to be seen by experts at Children's Hospital immediately
- Police Report officer Tim King, per dispatch to Humana Hospital report of sexual assault on 4-year-old girl, social services notified 9/20/91
- Children's Hospital Report from Child Advocacy and Protection Team sexual abuse experts dated October 19, 1991
- Forthwith Hearing
- Witness list sent to Kopetski and Purcell by my attor- ney's which enclosed 21 documents, and 19 witnesses of which 11 were professionals as Doctors or police party to this case and never contacted with phone # provided 16 of the witnesses.
- "Emergency Order" that was entered March 23, 1992 by Judge Deanna Hickman.

- Letter to Judge Michael Bieda regarding sexual abuse urging the Judge to contact Children's Hospital Child Advocacy and Protection team of Doctors concerning the sexual abuse of child in this case, March 11, 1993
- University of Colorado Health Center or Kempe National Center for Prevention and Treatment of Child Abuse and Neglect. March 27, 1992
- Respondents letter to stop professionals from looking at the abuse.
- Law Week Colorado November 2, 2012 "1994: Arapahoe District Judge Michael Bieda booted after receiving "do not retain" recomendations. Bieda's reviewing commission accused him of sexism, temper issues, deficient legal knowledge and a lack of compassion."
- Judge Bieda's order.

KAISER PERMANENTE
Colorado Permanente Medical Group, P.C.

NAME: [redacted]
I.D. NO. [redacted] C

CLINIC PROGRESS RECORD

DATE/SERVICE | TREATMENT

Date 6-6-91 | S: c/o itching vagina
Time 1445 | "my dad touches me."
Doctor [illegible] | [illegible]
Age 4½ | [illegible]
Home phone [redacted] | Called Child Protection agency c info
Work phone " | left message w/ CB to 6/10. [illegible] 6-6-91
TPR 98.4
B/P
WT 43#
Allergies NKA
Meds Ø

[redacted]

06-06-91

SUBJECTIVE: [redacted] is here with her mom because [redacted] believes that her father has been touching her in her private places. Mom says that this has been an ongoing problem, or at least she has held the strong suspicion of this, for at least a year and a half. She has no objective evidence, but this very strong conviction that this has been taking place. Says that [redacted] has difficulty sleeping at night, cries out. She describes her father as putting his fingers inside of her. He puts his "peanut" beside her and sometimes she see white stuff at the end of the penis. She was recently at her father's house.

She is here today, stating that there has been some yellow vaginal discharge, which mom has noticed on the panties for the past two to three days. Doesn't feel that there is any burning or itch. Denies frequency, as well.

OBJECTIVE: This is an alert, bright little girl, who appears well. A vaginal exam today externally, shows some crusting on the superior aspects of both labia majora. There is a small amount present. The hymenal ring, for the most part, appears intact, although the vaginal opening is somewhat larger than expected and the vaginal vault, at least the first centimeter of it, is visible, appears erythematous. There is no odor noted. Wet prep swab was taken from the vaginal vault. Chlamydia and GC were likewise done from this area, although yield from these is likely to be low.

ASSESSMENT:
1. Possible sexual abuse.

PLAN:
1. Wet prep results are unremarkable. Will await GC and chlamydia.

16023 (7-87)

CLINIC PROGRESS RECORD

DATE SERVICE — TREATMENT

[redacted]

06-06-91
Page 2

2. If vaginal discharge continues, I would consider treating her.
3. Will have to discuss this with child protection agency per Arapahoe County.
4. Will arrange further follow up pending lab results.

Joe Marion, M.D.

JM/pcn/cm

KAISER PERMANENTE

7

6-21-91

Dear Pamela

As you know I've seen [redacted] in my office for possible sexual abuse. I have spoken with [redacted] mom on the phone several times since the initial visit and she voices concerns that [redacted] is not being protected from her father. I have also spoken with Dr Carol Jenny from Childrens Hospital.

I feel at this point that further examination of [redacted] is warranted and furthermore this should be accomplished by Dr Jennings. I have conveyed this to [redacted] mom. Thank You

Sincerely

J. M.

RECEIVED JUN 2 6 1991

Kaiser Foundation Health Plan of Colorado • Colorado Permanente Medical Group, P.C.
Kaiser Foundation Hospitals
[illegible] East [illegible] Avenue • Aurora, Colorado [illegible]

HUMANA HOSPITAL AURORA

1501 S. POTOMAC • AURORA, COLORADO 80012 • TELEPHONE (303) 695-2600

TIENT'S IAME [redacted] PATIENT #: [redacted]

ENDING YSICIAN DREW GEER, M.D. ADMISSION DATE: 9-20-91

REFERRAL PHYSICIAN:

SUBJECTIVE: This is a 4-year-old female who was brought in by her mother for evaluation of a vaginal discharge. Mother reports that the child has complained of a vaginal discharge that has been intermittently present for three days. She describes it as thick and yellow. The child has not been ill. She has no fevers or chills. No abdominal pain. She has been having normal bowel movements. She denies any problems with urination. Mother reports a similar episode happened a number of months ago. She was evaluated at that time at Kaiser, had cultures done that were subsequently negative. Throughout this evaluation there has been a question of sexual child abuse. Mother states that the child is being sexually abused by the child's father. The mother and father are separated, however, the father does have visiting rights and has had custody of the child at times. This has been involved in a lengthy court battle. It is not clear from the history that the mother gives what the outcome is at this time. The father did have custody of the child four days prior to this presentation and also on the night of presentation. The child did state to me that the father put his fingers in her vagina. She does state that it was fingers only, and reports that no other sexual contact. Per the mother's history the child said that the father put his fingers in the vagina and rectum, and also put "white stuff" on her. The mother states that this has been going on for a year. She states that she has filed a report and has been evaluated by physicians before. It had been recommended for her to see an expert in sexual abuse, but the mother states that this has been stopped by a court order.

OBJECTIVE: The child is alert and quite cheerful in no distress. Her CHEST is clear. Her ABDOMEN is soft and nontender. Examination of her EXTERNAL GENITALIA reveals a crusty yellowish discharge in the perivulvar region. She is erythematous and tender to touch over both vulva. There is approximately a 1 mm. vertical laceration on the posterior forchette. Cultures were taken for GC and Chlamydia of the discharge just at the vaginal introitus. Speculum examination was not done and cervical cultures were not taken. Wet prep and gram stain were also done. The gram stain showed only rare white blood cells and a small number of mixed flora. The wet prep showed no yeast or fungi, no Trichomonas. The remainder of the cultures were pending at the time of discharge. Aurora Police Department was notified. They came and interviewed the mother. Holding order was placed against the father so he will not have visitation rights until the situation can be sorted out by social services and the court system. Social services will contact the mother in the morning.

Continued...

HUMANA HOSPITAL AURORA

501 S. POTOMAC • AURORA, COLORADO 80012 TELEPHONE (303) 695-2600

[redacted] PATIENT #: [redacted]

DREW GEER, M.D. ADMISSION DATE: 9-20-91

Continued Page -2-

ASSESSMENT:
1. Alleged sexual abuse.
2. Vaginal discharge.

PLAN: The patient was discharged home in care of her mother. They were to call back for culture results. Again, they were recommended to see an expert in sexual abuse. Social services will be involved with the case in the morning.

Drew Geer, M.D.
DG/CSI#307
D: 9-20-91
T: 9-21-91

FORM 520-SCS

City of Aurora
POLICE DEPARTMEN

OFFENSE REPORT

1. Offense: SEX ASSAULT ON A CHILD
2. Case Report No. [redacted]

3. CCL: 17X | 4. Off: 3601 | 5. CLS: X | 6. STT: 0 | 7. Premise Code | 8A. ☒ Suspect ☐ Juvenile ☒ Adult ☐ Unknown

8. Disposition: ☐ Unfounded SIC/Y ☐ Cleared By Arrest ☒ Open ☐ Exceptionally Cleared

9. Location of Occurrence: [redacted] | 10. GEO Code: 14 | 11. Connecting Case Numbers

12. Date/Time Occurred: on or between — Month 09, Day 19, Year 91, Time UNK; 09, 20, 91, 19:15
13. Date/Time Reported: on or between — Month 09, Day 20, Year 91, Time 19:19
14. How Received: ☒ Dispatch ☐ Citizen ☐ On View ☐ Supervisor

CODES: V-Victim R/P-Reporting Party W-Witness S-Suspect

15. Code	16. Name (Last, First, Middle) / 22. Residence / 26. Business	17. Sex	18. Race	19. Age	20. Date of Birth	21. Occupation
V-1	[redacted]	F	CAU	4	01/22/87	
	23. City: AURORA				24. Zip Code: 80013	25. Telephone: [redacted] X = Day ☐
PG-1	MCLEAN, MARALEE	F	CAU	37	05/18/54	FLIGHT ATTENDANT
	[redacted] 23. City: AURORA				24. Zip Code: 80013	25. Telephone: [redacted] X = Day ☐
	26. Business					[redacted] ☐

A. WAS THERE A WITNESS TO THIS CRIME? YES ☒ IF NO, PLACE X →

CANVAS

27. Residence/Business Checked	28. Person Contacted	29. Age	30. Home Phone	31. Business Phone

WITNESSES

32. Code	33. Name / 39. Residence / 43. Business	34. Sex	35. Race	36. Age	37. Date of Birth	38. Occupation
[redacted]		F	HSP			[redacted]
Contacted? Yes ☒ No ☐	40. City				41. Zip Code	42. Telephone X = Day ☐
	[redacted]					☐
[redacted]		34. Sex	35. Race	36. Age	37. Date of Birth	38. Occupation
Contacted? Yes ☒ No ☐	39. Residence 40. City				41. Zip Code	42. Telephone X = Day ☐
	[redacted]					☐

B. CAN A SUSPECT BE NAMED? YES ☒ IF NO, PLACE X →

C. CAN A SUSPECT BE DESCRIBED OR IDENTIFIED? YES ☒ IF NO, PLACE X →

SUSPECTS

44. Code	45. Name	46. Address	47. Telephone
S-1	[redacted]	UNK	[redacted]
Description	[redacted] 52. Weight 53. Height 54. Build		58. Glasses ☐ Yes ☐ No
	56. Clothing		
44. Code	45. Name	46. Address	47. Telephone
Description	48. Date of Birth 49. Sex 50. Race 51. Age To 52. Weight 53. Height 54. Build 55. Hair		
	56. Clothing 57. Eyes		58. Glasses ☐ Yes ☐ No

D. CAN A SUSPECT VEHICLE BE IDENTIFIED? YES ☐ IF NOT, PLACE X — ☒

59. Make	60. Model	61. Style	62. Color(s)	63. License No. & State	64. Vin

E. IS STOLEN PROPERTY IDENTIFIABLE? IF YES, DESCRIBE ON SUPPLEMENTARY FORM IF NO, PLACE X → ☒

F. IS A SIGNIFICANT M.O. PRESENT? IF YES, DESCRIBE ON M.O. SHEET IF NO, PLACE X → ☒

G. IS PHYSICAL EVIDENCE FOUND? IF YES, DESCRIBE IN NARRATIVE IF NOT, PLACE X →

H. PRELIMINARY INVESTIGATION COMPLETED? YES ☒ IF NO, PLACE X →

65. Reason Not Completed

66. CSI Requested Yes ☐ No ☒ If No, Reason: NOT NEEDED

68. Victim(s) - R/P Signature | Date | TR-SUPP YES ☐

69. Officer Signature | ID Number | 70. Supervisor Initials and Date

City of Aurora
POLICE DEPARTMENT

[redacted]

1. Initial Offense Classification: SEX ASSAULT ON A CHILD
15. Victim: [redacted]
13. Date Original Report: 09/20/91 | 12. Date This Report: 09/20/91
11. RI Entry Number: 5516364 EMC EM
112. PT Entry Number
113. PIP Codes
8. UCR Disposition-Change To: ☐ Arrest ☐ Exceptionally Cleared ☐ Unfounded ☐ Inactive
8A. Exceptional Clearance Category: ☐ Victim Failure To Prosecute ☐ Prosecute For Lesser Charge ☐ Juvenile ☐ Declined By DA ☐ Duplicate Charge ☐ Suspect Incarcerated ☐ Suspect Death ☐ Other Jurisdiction

PROPERTY

114 PROPERTY	A. CURRENCY	B. JEWELRY	C. CLOTHING	D. VEHICLE (LOCAL)	E. OFFICE EQUIPMENT	F. RADIO, TV, CAMERAS	G. FIRE-ARMS	H. HOUSE-HOLD GOODS	I. CON-SUMABLES	J. LIVE-STOCK	K. MISC	L. TOTAL
STOLEN	$	$	$	$	$	$	$	$	$	$	$	$
RECOVERY	$	$	$	$	$	$	$	$	$	$	$	$

IF PROPERTY ITEMIZATION, USE THE FOLLOWING FORMAT

115. Item No.	116. Quantity	117. Brand Name	118. Property Description	119. Serial #	120. Stolen	121. Rec.	122. UCR Property Type
					$	$	

CONTINUATION FOLLOW UP SHEET
NARRATIVE

09/20/91 FRI 20:05 hrs

Per dispatch I went to Humana Hospital at [redacted] on a report of a sexual assault on a four year old girl.

Upon arrival at the emergency room I was contacted by the ER nurse W-1 [redacted] who related the following:

W-1 [redacted] said around 18:15 hrs PG MCLEAN MARALEE brought her daughter (V-1 [redacted]) into the emergency room on a complaint that her daughter (V-1) was "discharging."

W-1 [redacted] told me that she contacted V-1 [redacted] and (V-1 SAID) that her father touched her on her "bottom." W-1 [redacted] said that PG MCLEAN told her that V-1 [redacted] had a "discharging" problem three months ago.

I then went and contacted PG MCLEAN + V-1 [redacted] in the exam room.

When I first contacted V-1 [redacted] she could tell me how old she was and when I asked her mother for their home telephone number PG MCLEAN started to give me some other number by accident and V-1 [redacted] spoke up and said "It's [redacted]"

I then asked V-[redacted] if she knew the difference between telling a lie and telling the truth. V-1 [redacted] said that

109. Event Number | 110. Operation I.D. | Yes ☐ No
69. Officer Signature: [signature] KING | ID Number: 13169 | 70. Supervisor Initials and Date: [initials] 09/20/91 | Page 2 of 17

FORM 520-510

City of Aurora
POLICE DEPARTMENT

Original Case No. [redacted]

1. Initial Offense Classification: SEX ASSAULT ON CHILD
15. Victim: [redacted]
111. AI Entry Number
112. PY Entry Number
12. Date Original Report: 08/30/81 | 72. Date This Report: 08/30/81
113. TYP Codes

8. UCR Disposition-Charge To: ☐ Arrest ☐ Exceptionally Cleared ☐ Unfounded ☐ Inactive

8A. Exceptional Clearance Category: ☐ Victim Failure To Prosecute ☐ Prosecute For Lesser Charge ☐ Juvenile ☐ Declined By DA ☐ Duplicate Charge ☐ Suspect Incarcerated ☐ Suspect Death ☐ Other Jurisdiction

PROPERTY

114. PROPERTY	A. CURRENCY	B. JEWELRY	C. CLOTHING	D. VEHICLE (LOCAL)	E. OFFICE EQUIPMENT	F. RADIO, TV, CAMERAS	G. FIRE-ARMS	H. HOUSE-HOLD GOODS	I. CON-SUMABLES	J. LIVE-STOCK	K. MISC	L. TOTAL
STOLEN	$	$	$	$	$	$	$	$	$	$	$	$
RECOVERY	$	$	$	$	$	$	$	$	$	$	$	$

IF PROPERTY ITEMIZATION, USE THE FOLLOWING FORMAT

115. Item No.	116. Quantity	117. Brand Name	118. Property Description	119. Serial #	120. Stolen	121. Rec.	122. UCR Property Type
					$	$	

CONTINUATION FOLLOW UP SHEET

NARRATIVE

she knew the difference I then asked V-1 [redacted] if she told me she was 10 if that would be a lie or would that be the truth V-1 [redacted] then told me it would be a lie.

I then asked V-1 [redacted] if she remembered what she told the nurse when she arrived at the hospital V-1 [redacted] then smiled at me and she tried to hide her face behind her mother. PG McLEAN then told her daughter that it was ok to talk to me.

I then asked V-1 [redacted] if someone had touched her. V-1 [redacted] then stated "My dad did"

I then asked V-1 [redacted] "where did you touch you at"? V-1 [redacted] then pointed at her vagina. I then asked V-1 [redacted] what she called that and she stated "PEE P

I then held out my notebook in front of V-1 [redacted] and I moved my hand across the notebook and I asked if she was touched in this manner V-1 [redacted] then stated "He put his fingers in

I then asked V-1 [redacted] how many times did he "put his fingers in" and V-1 [redacted] lifted up her hand showing five fingers. I asked V-1 [redacted] with the "fingers in" did it hurt. V-1 [redacted] stated "yeah."

109. Event Number | 110. Operation I.D. | Yes ☐
ID Number | 70. Supervisor Initials and Date | Page 3

City of Aurora
POLICE DEPARTMENT

2. Original Case Report Number: [redacted]

1. Initial Offense Classification: SEX ASSAULT ON A CHILD
15. Victim: [redacted]
13. Date Original Report: 09/20/91
72. Date This Report: 09/20/91
111. AI Entry Number
112. FY Entry Number
113. TYP Codes

8. UCR Disposition Change To: ☐ Arrest ☐ Exceptionally Cleared ☐ Unfounded ☐ Inactive

8A. Exceptional Clearance Category: ☐ Victim Failure To Prosecute ☐ Prosecute For Lesser Charge ☐ Juvenile ☐ Declined By DA ☐ Duplicate Charges ☐ Suspect Incarcerated ☐ Suspect Death ☐ Other Jurisdiction

PROPERTY

114 PROPERTY	A. CURRENCY	B. JEWELRY	C. CLOTHING	D. VEHICLE (LOCAL)	E. OFFICE EQUIPMENT	F. RADIO TV, CAMERAS	G. FIRE-ARMS	H. HOUSE-HOLD GOODS	I. CON-SUMABLES	J. LIVE-STOCK	K. MISC.	L. TOTAL
STOLEN	$	$	$	$	$	$	$	$	$	$	$	$
RECOVERY	$	$	$	$	$	$	$	$	$	$	$	$

IF PROPERTY ITEMIZATION, USE THE FOLLOWING FORMAT:

115. Item No.	116. Quantity	117. Brand Name	118. Property Description	119. Serial #	120. Stolen	121. Rec.	122. UCR Property Type
					$	$	

CONTINUATION FOLLOW UP SHEET
NARRATIVE

at this time Sgt Crooks was in the exam room and he asked V-1 [redacted] where the above incident took place at.

V-1 [redacted] said in her "dads car." Sgt Crooks then asked her where her dad was seating and where she was seating

V-1 [redacted] said her dad was in the "big seat" and she was in the "little seat"

I then asked V-1 [redacted] if she could remember if it was light or dark out when the above occurred and she state light

I then asked V-1 [redacted] if her dad always did this to her but I could not get an answer from her

I then contacted PG-1 MCLEAN stated that her ex-husband is S [redacted] and they have been divorce for four years PG-1 MCLEAN said that her and her ex-husband equal custody of V-1 [redacted]

PG MCLEAN said that her ex-husband exchanges their just about every other day

PG MCLEAN told me that S-1 [redacted] got V-1 [redacted] on 09/17/91 (TUES) and he return on 09/18/91 (WED) S-1 [redacted] then got V-1 [redacted] on 09/19/91 (THURS) and she was return to PG MCLEAN 09/20/91 (FRI)

109. Event Number: 17
110. Operation I.D.
ID Number
70. Supervisor Initials and Date: [illegible]
Yes ☐
Page 4

Caseworker: Paula Comfort

Subjective:

This four-year, ten-month old female was brought to Ambulatory Care Clinic and the Child Advocacy and Protection Team for a medical evaluation of possible sexual abuse. She was accompanied to clinic by her mother, Maralee McLean, and mother's attorney, Mary Jane Cox. By mother's report, this child was seen 9/20/91 in Humana Hospital in Aurora. At that time, the child was noted to have a 1 mm. vertical laceration on the posterior fourchette and cultures were taken for gonorrhea and chlamydia. Speculum examinations were not done and cervical cultures were not obtained. A wet-prep and gram stain were also done which were negative for any abnormal flora. It was requested that this child have an examination by a "sexual abuse expert" which was the reason for her being brought to the CAPT clinic.

At this examiner's request, mother reviewed the child's extensive history. Mother related that this child saw Dr. Dee Brodbeck between 7/89 and 8/89 and also seen by Dr. Lee Baker, a psychotherapist. Currently the child is seeing therapist, Gail Adams. Reportedly, there have been numerous concerns about abuse issues with this child, and the child has had several interviews with Arapahoe County Department of Social Services. Mother also notes that the child was placed in foster care in October 1989 for approximately six weeks.

Past Medical History:

Mother states that there have been no major illnesses, accidents or injuries with this child. Primary medical care was obtained by Dr. Stan Rosenberg until recently, and currently, now that custodial

Affiliated with
University of Colorado Health Sciences Center

changes have been made, the child is being seen at Kaiser.

Behavioral Symptoms:

Mother relates that approximately one-year ago, this child had a lot of masturbation and she currently has intermittent masturbation. Mother states that she seems to have some nightmares and is very clingy. Mother is unsure whether or not that is due to abuse issues or this child's frequent changes in environment.

Social History:

Mother works for an airlines, and I am unsure of father's occupation. Mother relates that the divorce was when [redacted] was approximately six months old, and they have had joint custody until last February when father was awarded primary custody and mother has visitation rights.

Interview with Child:

[redacted] was interviewed alone in the room without mother or mother's attorney present. In the room was this examiner and a medical student, Linda Chaudron. The child was asked why she was here today, and she answered, "because of my discharge" (child pointed to her vaginal area). We went through all the body parts and the child was able to name all body parts. She calls her vaginal area "pee-pee" and her rectal area "bottom." I then asked [redacted] what she meant by having a discharge, and she said, "you know, it's some stuff that comes out down there" (pointing to her vaginal area). I then asked her a little bit about what happens when she has that discharge, and she said, "well, sometimes it hurts when I go potty, otherwise, I'm okay." We began by talking about some non-threatening subjects, and I asked [redacted] where she lived. She replied, "I have two houses." I asked her who lives in each of her houses, and she stated that in her first house, "my mom lives and Connie and Benna" (question spelling). [redacted] went on to say that Benna was a "real bunny." [redacted] stated that at her other house her dad lived and "Hussle", her daddy's dog. I then asked [redacted] why her mother and father do not live in the same house, and [redacted] said "cause my mommy and daddy don't get along very well - they don't like each other." I then asked [redacted] what she thought about that, and she said, "I think they should get married again." It was at this point that [redacted] changed topics rather quickly and asked me if I had ever seen the movie "Annie". I replied that I had not seen the movie. [redacted] then replied, "You should see that movie, it's a lot like me - it's real sad." It should be noted that at this point, [redacted] affect changed remarkably, and she became very sad, somewhat withdrawn and looked down at her hands and would not make eye contact with this examiner. This was in marked contrast to her playful interaction in the beginning of our interview. I then asked her if she could tell me some of the nice things she does at her mother's and father's houses, and she replied "well, at mommy's house, we get up and make breakfast and we have fun doing that, and I think that's nice." I then asked her about her father, and she said, "I don't know. . . daddy doesn't do anything nice."

I then asked [redacted] to tell me about some of the "not so nice things" that happened at either her mother's or father's house, or things that happened to her when she felt that she was bad or had misbehaved. [redacted] then replied, "Well, sometimes my mommy spanks me if I'm bad. I don't know about my dad's house, because I try not to be bad there." I asked her about anything that happened that was not so nice, and she said, "well, at my daddy's house. he touches me down there, and I don't think that's so nice." I asked her what she meant by "down there", and what she called that area, and she said, as she was pointing to her vaginal area, "that's my pee-pee." I asked her what her daddy touched her with, and she pointed to her own hands, and I asked her the name of what she was pointing to, and she said, "his hand." I asked her if it was his whole hand or part of his hand, and she pointed to her fingers. I asked her where she was when this happened, and she said, "at my daddy's house." I asked her what part of the house she was in, and she said, "in my bedroom." She went on to relate that this had happened during the daytime and that her father had his clothes on. When asked what she had on, she stated that she had her clothes on, but "he pulls them down, and he shouldn't do that." She states that it hurts when her daddy does that, and she tells him "stop it, daddy." I then asked her to tell me whether or not she really lived in two houses - or maybe she was making that up, and she said, "no, I really live in two houses." I then asked her whether or not she really had a dog named "Hustle" or maybe she was making that up, and she said, "no, I really do have a dog named Hustle." I then asked her whether or not her father touching her had really happened, or maybe she was making it up - or someone else may have told her to say that, and she said, "no, it really happened." It should be noted once again that she was very serious during this aspect of the interview which again was in contrast to her playful, interactive nature at the beginning of our talk. I then asked her whether or not she could live anywhere she wanted, where she would want to live. She said, "I would like to live with my grandma and grandpa, I don't want to live here." I said to [redacted], "Let's pretend that you could live with your mommy or daddy, and you could spend as much time with either one as you would like, what do you think you would do?" [redacted] replied, "Well, I would like to spend a little time with my daddy, but I think I would like to spend more time with my mommy." I then asked her why she felt this way, and she said, "Well, I like my daddy but I like to do lots of things with mommy and she talks to me a lot." At this time, we decided to go over the rest of her body and talk to her about her body parts and ask her if she had any questions or worries about any of her body parts, and the only concern she had was when we came to talking about her nose and she said that sometimes her nose gets "stuffy." When we got to her genital area, she again repeated that her concerns were "when my daddy touches me there, it hurts."

Objective:

Temperature: 36.5. Pulse: 88. Respiratory Rate: 20. Weight 21.5 kg. Generally, [redacted] appeared to be a well-developed, well-nourished, child who was in no apparent distress. She appeared to have good language skills and was developmentally appropriate for age. Her HEENT exam was within normal limits. Her neck had full and equal range of movement. Lungs were clear to auscultation with easy excursion. Her cardiac exam revealed normal sinus rhythm of her heart, and no murmurs were heard. Her abdomen was soft, non-tender and without hepatosplenomegaly. Her GU exam was done with the aid of a colposcope in the frog-leg and knee-chest position. The child was noted to have a tear-drop shaped hymenal opening, and an 8 mm. horizontal diameter with gentle anterior traction on the labia. There is an abraded noted from 3 to 5 o'clock. The remainder of the hymenal edge was noted to be thin and velamentous. The posterior fourchette was noted to have normal and equal vascularity, and the anus had normal tone and was without fissures or abrasions. There was no discharge or bruising throughout the perineum.

Assessment:

This child has a generous vaginal opening with an abraded area from 3 to 5 o'clock that could be considered a normal variant. This child gave a history of touching to her genital area by father, and this history appeared to be elicited in a spontaneous manner and her answers did not appear to be rehearsed or rote in nature.

After completion of the examination, I was able to read the old file on this child and Dr. Reichert's assessment. It appears that this child's examination has changed within the past year. It is worrisome that this child's genital examination has undergone marked changes in one year.

Because of the changes in the child's genital exam, the abraded area from 3-5 o'clock, and the absence of discharge at this visit, it is recommended that this child be seen for a follow-up examination in three to five weeks' time. It would be helpful if the child could return to clinic when the discharge is present.

Plan:

1. Findings to be related to caseworker and all appropriate attorneys.

2. Based on the extensive nature of this case, I would highly recommend that this family undergo an extensive interactional evaluation.

3. Return to CAPT clinic for follow-up appointment.

Donna Nelligan, C.H.A. PA-C

Donna Nelligan, C.H.A., PA-C

DISTRICT COURT, COUNTY OF ARAPAHOE, STATE OF COLORADO

Case No. [redacted], Division 10

MOTION FORTHWITH TELEPHONE HEARING RE: EVALUATION BY THE KEMPE NATIONAL CENTER FOR PREVENTION AND TREATMENT OF CHILD ABUSE

In re the Marriage of:

MARALEE McLEAN, Petitioner,

and

[redacted] Respondent.

COMES NOW the Petitioner, Maralee McLean, by and through her attorney of record, Cox and Mustain-Wood, and moves this Honorable Court to enter an Order compelling the parties of this action, above-named, and the minor child, [redacted] to participate in an evaluation to be performed by a team at the Kempe National Center for Prevention and Treatment of Child Abuse on August 26, 1991 and September 3, 1991 and to further order that each party pay one-half of said evaluation, and

AS GROUNDS THEREFOR DOTH STATE

1. That Petitioner had earlier filed a Motion for the Appointment of a Mental Health Professional to determine if a custody evaluation would be appropriate in this case.

2. This Motion is currently set for hearing in Division 10 on October 18, 1991.

3. The Guardian <u>ad Litem</u> filed her Response to this Motion on or about May 2, 1991 and supported the Petitioner's Motion and requested the Court to enter said Motion.

4. On or about May 17, 1991, the minor child complained to her mother that her "pee-pee" hurt and on several occasions prior to that reported to her mother that her father was still inappropriately touching her in the vaginal area.

5. The Petitioner attempted to take the minor child to see the child's long-time pediatrician, Dr. Stan Rosenberg, who could not see the child because the Respondent/Father, who now has sole custody, moved all of the child's medical records to Kaiser Permanente.

1

6. The minor child continued to complain that her 'pee-pee" hurt and on June 6, 1991 the Petitioner took the child to see Dr. Joseph Marion, M.D. at Kaiser Permanente. The report of Dr. Marin is attached hereto and incorporated herein. The minor child, on that date, stated at the examination that "my dad touches me".

7. The assessment of Dr. Marion was that there had been possible sexual abuse and his report indicates he would have to discuss the issue with the child protection agency at Arapahoe County.

8. Dr. Marion, on June 21, 1991 sent a letter to Petitioner's counsel, Randall Mustain-Wood, indicating that after he had conferred with Dr. Carol Jennings at Children's Hospital and Dr. Marion concluded that further examination of [redacted] was warranted.

9. On or about June 5, 1991, [redacted] told her therapist, Dr. Gail Adams, that "my daddy hurts me! He puts his fingers in me. I never sleep at my dad's. I only slept there once. My daddy puts white stuff in my pee pee".

10. As this information for Dr. Marion was shared with all counsel and Dr. Gail Adams, it was the understanding of Petitioner and her counsel that all counsel and Dr. Adams agreed that an evaluation of the two parents and the Kempe Center was appropriate at this time.

11. An evaluation was scheduled for August 5th and 6th, 1991. Unfortunately, due to the Guardian ad Litem and Dr. Adams' request for further explanation of the procedure to be used by the Kempe Center and due to Respondent's counsel not receiving timely notice of the appointment times, no stipulation was reached in time to utilize the August 5th and 6th dates. A copy of the letter from Diane Baird describing the procedures to be followed in the attached hereto and incorporated herein.

12. Appointments with the Kempe Center are difficult to obtain.

13. Counsel for Petitioner has been informed that the Kempe Center can evaluate the minor child, [redacted], and her parents on August 26, 1991 and September 3, 1991.

14. To further delay this evaluation is not in the best interest of the minor child.

15. The Cost of said evaluation will be, approximately, $3,500.00 and Petitioner proposes that the evaluation be paid for

2

equally by the parties. A retainer of $1,000.00 must be paid by each party prior to the evaluation commencing.

WHEREFORE, Petitioner respectfully requests this Honorable Court enter an Order compelling the parties of this action, above-named, and the minor child, [redacted], to participate in an evaluation to be performed by a team at the Kempe National Center for Prevention and Treatment of Child Abuse on August 26, 1991 and September 3, 1991 and that the cost of said evaluation of approximately $3,500.00 will be paid for equally by the parties and that a retainer of $1,000.00 will be paid by each party prior to the evaluation commencing.

Respectfully submitted this 14 day of August, 1991.

COX AND MUSTAIN-WOOD

Mary Jane Truesdell Cox, #7768
Attorneys for Petitioner
6601 S. University Blvd., #200
Littleton, Colorado 80121
Telephone: (303) 730-0067

VERIFICATION

I, Maralee McLean, the Petitioner herein, being first duly sworn upon oath, declare and allege that I have read the above and foregoing Motion for Forthwith Telephone Hearing Re: Evaluation by the Kempe National Center for Prevention and Treatment of Child Abuse, know the contents therein, and that the same is true and correct to the best of my knowledge and belief.

Maralee McLean, Petitioner

STATE OF COLORADO)
) ss
COUNTY OF ARAPAHOE)

SUBSCRIBED AND SWORN TO me this 14th day of August, 1991, by Maralee McLean.

Notary Public

My commission expires:
(S E A L)

NOTARY PUBLIC STATE OF COLORADO
MY COMMISSION EXP. OCT 21,1991

LAW OFFICES OF
COX AND MUSTAIN-WOOD
PRACTICE LIMITED TO FAMILY LAW
6601 SO. UNIVERSITY BLVD., SUITE—200
LITTLETON, COLORADO 80121

OFC.# (303) 730-0067
FAX.# (303) 730-0344

MARY JANE TRUESDELL COX
JAMES C. SCHUMACHER

RANDALL C. MUSTAIN-WOOD

TIMOTHY B. WALKER, P.C.
OF COUNSEL*
*FELLOW AMERICAN ACADEMY OF MATRIMONIAL LAWYERS
*FELLOW INTERNATIONAL ACADEMY OF MATRIMONIAL LAWYERS

January 9, 1992

Leona Kopetski
1735 Lafayette
Denver, Colorado 80218

Re: McLean/[redacted]

Dear Leona:

Maralee indicated to me that you had requested that both parties give information as to areas that they would like to have you investigate in doing your evaluation. I view this as an extremely important evaluation. I'm sure as far as [redacted] is concerned this is probably going to be the last time for a long time that there will be any investigation of the allegations that [redacted] is making regarding the current situation with her parents. Therefore I feel, as I'm sure I recall you testifying, that a very thorough evaluation is needed in this case.

From what I've been hearing from my client as well, I'm concerned because there seems to be a rather drastic change in [redacted] behavior over this last year. Also according to my client she is concerned that [redacted] has lost her confidence in Gail Adams and so, at this time, [redacted] effectively is not in a therapeutic relationship which she needs. As you will recall, there was some question at the time of the hearing as to whether or not Dr. Adams should continue as the therapist for [redacted] since she has been, unfortunately, placed in the role of an evaluator in the past. I have enclosed a signed copy of the Order for you which does address the fact that you are to make the decision as to who the ongoing therapist should be for [redacted], if one is needed.

Ms. McLean informs me that she'll be meeting with you today, January 9, 1992, and therefore I wanted to have the enclosed exhibits available for you so that she might address them and explain to you what the exhibits are and why she feels they're important for you to review. It is also my understanding that you have only had an opportunity to meet with her once and that there are more times that will be scheduled. I'm concerned that she has sufficient time to explain to you what [redacted] has been experiencing and telling her about recent sexual abuse over this last year.

If there is any other additional information you feel would be helpful, please do not hesitate to contact me. I'm sure Mr. Calder will also be more than willing to provide any information that you may need. I am intending to file a motion to allow me to review the exhibits that were submitted into evidence at the time of the juvenile hearing. At this time, the file is closed but there may or may not be documents there that would be helpful in your making a recommendation and I feel you should have a right to see those if they, in fact, are on file with the Court.

For your information enclosed please find the following documents:

1. Stipulated Order naming you as the evaluator in this case.

2. Handwritten statement written by Maralee on January 22, 1980 regarding her observations of her husband at that time, [redacted].

3. Letter from Laurie Margolis written September 20, 1988.

4. Western Union Mailagram from [redacted] to Maralee Mclean dated April 29, 1987.

5. Response to the previous Guardian ad Litem, Doris Truhlar's, Motion for Forthwith Hearing on Visitation which includes attachments by Detective Ken Perry and Kirsten Jensen, the previous social worker.

6. Letter dated June 2, 1990 from one of [redacted] previous child care providers.

7. Log showing each parent's involvement with [redacted]. Mrs. McLean will have to inform you as to the author and date of this diary contemporaneous.

8. Note written by Maralee on a date she will have to provide you regarding statements of [redacted] regarding sexual abuse.

9. Copy of a Motion entitled Motion for Forthwith Telephone Hearing Re: Evaluation of the Kempe National Center for Prevention and Treatment of Child Support to which is attached a letter from Dr. Joseph Marion of Kaiser documenting his examination of [redacted] on June 6, 1991.

10. Reports from the Aurora Police Department dated July 20, 1989 through December 12, 1990 prepared by various officers, but primarily detective David Perry.

11. Report by Dee Brodbeck who evaluated [redacted] on October 5, 1989.

12. Report of Dr. Leigh M. Baker dated October 1, 1989.

13. Copy of the Psychological Evaluation of [redacted] and Maralee McLean by Dr. Arthur Jones.

14. Report of the Arapahoe County Department of Social Services dated February 27, 1990.

15. Report of Donna Nelligan from Children's Hospital who is a member of the child advocacy and protection team there dated October 18, 1991.

16. Letter from Dr. Arthur Jones to Doris Truhlar the previous Guardian ad Litem dated February 24, 1990.

17. Report from the Aurora Police Department prepared by Officer Tim King dated September 19, 1991.

18. Letter from the Department of Social Services dated October 20, 1989 written to the Honorable Bradley Yoder.

19. The Order entered by Judge Leopold which is the current Order regarding custody and visitation dated February 27, 1991.

20. A box containing the journal written by [redacted]. Leona, this is the only copy I have of this journal and therefore it is crucial that it remains intact and that it can be returned to me at some point in time. If there is any copying you need to do from it, please feel free to do so but I do need to have the original returned to me.

21. Next listed are all of the witnesses that we would request that you talk to. If you have any questions about how these people are relevant, please talk Maralee. I would appreciate your contacting each of these people because I think it is important to get the overall picture. Their phone numbers are provided for your convenience.

Witnesses:

Donna Nelligan
Children's Hospital
861-6919

Dr. Carole Jenny
Children's Hospital
861-6919

Dr Marguerite White
University Hospital
270-7924

Officer Tim King
Aurora Police Department
341-8300

Detective David Perry
Aurora Police Department
341-8300

Dr. Joe Marion
Kaiser, Aurora
699-6000

Dr. Drew Geer
Aurora Humana Hospital
695-2628

Kim Fowler
Personal friend
Work: 421-2424
Home: 750-5517

Ruth Gibbons
Julie's previous babysitter
693-1829

Dr. Leigh Baker
790-5585

Elizabeth Deal
Personal friend
690-2778

Kelly Stewart
New Hope Pre-School
693-3490

Connie Poetiray
Roommate-renter
693-9907

Bud & Donna McLean
Grandparents
406-245-6581

Leslie Dumody
Sister (nurse)
New # to be provided

Dennis Brachfield
Friend
777-7475
Beeper: 266-7984

Ellen Kessler
Previous babysitter
Spokane, Washington
Home: 509-690-3691
Work: 509-320-2490

Laurie Margolis, Ph.d.
773-9966

Dr. Stan Rosenberg
Pediatrician for first 4 years of [redacted] life
690-8660

Happy New Year to you. Thank you again for being willing to become involved in this case.

Sincerely,

Mary Jane Truesdell Cox

MJTC/llp
enclosures

cc: Maralee McLean
Paula Tomko
Stephen Calder

DISTRICT COURT, COUNTY OF ARAPAHOE, STATE OF COLORADO

[redacted] AND [redacted] Division 10

TEMPORARY ORDERS

In re the marriage of:

MARALEE MCLEAN,

Petitioner,

and

[redacted]

Respondent.

THIS MATTER having come on for telephone conference hearing this 25th day of March, 1992, at the hour of 1:30 p.m., presided over by the Honorable Deanna Hickman, District Court Judge, the Court having heard statements of counsel concerning the issues of temporary visitation between the minor child, [redacted] and her mother, Ms. McLean, the Petitioner, and the Court having reviewed the file, as well as the report and recommendations of Dr. Purcell and Ms. Kopetski, and now being fully advised in the premises, enter the following Temporary Orders:

1. The visits between Ms. McLean and [redacted] which were the subject of the Emergency Orders entered March 23, 1992, shall be supervised by Bridges and shall take place each Thursday, beginning March 26, 1992, and shall last for one hour in duration. Counsel for the parties shall endeavor to work out between them, and on behalf of their parties, a mutually agreeable time and place for the visitations.

2. The Petitioner, Maralee McLean, shall be responsible for the payment of any and all costs associated with said supervised visitations.

3. With respect to telephone contact between the minor child and her mother, Ms. McLean shall be permitted to call [redacted] one time per week, which call shall take place between the hour of 6:00 and 7:00 p.m. on Monday, unless Ms. McLean is out of town working on Monday, in which event the call shall take place on Wednesday between the same hours. Said telephone calls shall be of no more than 30 minutes duration.

4. In accordance with the recommendations of the Kopetski/Purcell report found on page 74, [redacted] may call her mother if and when consultation between [redacted] and her father results in a decision that a phone call from [redacted] to her mother is appropriate.

5. Inasmuch as this case is assigned to Judge Bieda in Division 10, upon his return from vacation the case and further proceedings thereon shall be returned to Division 10 for further proceedings.

DONE AND SIGNED IN OPEN COURT this 27th day of March, 1992, nunc pro tunc March 25, 1992, at the hour of 1:52 p.m.

BY THE COURT:

DEANNA E. HICKMAN
DISTRICT JUDGE

THE HONORABLE DEANNA HICKMAN
DISTRICT COURT JUDGE

The Children's Hospital

Filed in the Div.
MAR 11 1993
District Court
Arapahoe County, Colo

March 11, 1993

1056 East 19th Avenue
Denver, Colorado 80218

(303) 861-8888

Child Advocacy and Protection Team

(303) 861-6919

Carole Jenny, MD
Director
Associate Professor of Pediatrics

Judge Bieda
Arapahoe County District Court

Re: Case #87DR1524
Maralee McLean, Petitioner
[redacted] Respondent
Concerning the Minor Child
[redacted]

Dear Judge Bieda:

Our Child Advocacy and Protection Team has been involved in an extensive medical evaluation of [redacted]. In my opinion, the medical examination of this child is concerning for sexual abuse. I had been subpoenaed on this case once but was not called and never had an opportunity to enter my medical findings in expert witness testimony. I hope you will consider my findings and evaluation before you render a final opinion in this case. I would be happy to furnish any information, records or testimony that would be helpful in the resolution of this case.

Sincerely,

Donna Nelligan CHA PA-C
Donna Nelligan, C.H.A.
Physician's Assistant
Child Advocacy and
Protection Team

S Reichert MD
Susan K. Reichert, M.D.
Assistant Professor of
Pediatrics

Reviewed by Carole Jenny, M.D., Associate Professor of Pediatrics, Director, Child Advocacy and Protection Team

R/A

Affiliated with
University of Colorado Health Sciences Center

University of Colorado Health Sciences Center

Department of Pediatrics
The C. Henry Kempe National Center for the Prevention and Treatment of Child Abuse and Neglect
"Providing Hope for the Children"

1205 Oneida Street
Denver, Colorado 80220-2944
[illegible] 321-3963

University Hospital
School of Medicine

School of Nursing
School of Dentistry

DATE: March 27, 1992

TO: Distribution

FROM: Child Advocacy and Protection Team
The Children's Hospital

Diane Baird, MSW
Kempe National Center

RE: [redacted], DOB 1-22-87

We have been peripherally and directly involved as this case has unfolded over the last two years. Although it now appears that the matter is decided, we remain concerned that the physical findings consistent with sexual abuse have not received due consideration or explanation. We would welcome and encourage your help at a staffing to share professional perspectives about [redacted] and her parents, and perhaps the issues raised by this and similar cases.

The staffing will be held Monday, April 6, from 1 to 3 p.m. in the Rehabilitation Conference Room on the 5th floor of Children's. Parking is available on the fifth floor of the parking gararge. Take the connecting hallway from the garage to Children's. The Rehabilitation Conference Room is at the end of the hallway just before the large waiting room, on the right hand side. For further directions, please call 861-6919.

Distribution: Richard Krugman, MD
Paula Tomko, Esquire
Gail Adams, PhD
Claire Purcell, PhD
Leona Kopetski
Joseph Marion, MD
Kim Campbell, MD
D. D. Harvey
Tim King
Drew Geer, MD
Dave Perry
Mary Jane Cox, Esquire

RECE[illegible] 3 0 1992

ANDERSON, CALDER & SANDMAN
A PROFESSIONAL CORPORATION
ATTORNEYS AND COUNSELORS AT LAW
PAVILION TOWER I, SUITE 1200
2831 SOUTH PARKER ROAD
AURORA, COLORADO 80014-3065
TELEPHONE 303-751-9444
TELECOPIER 303-751-[illegible]

GRANT A. ANDERSON
STEPHEN P. CALDER
JEFFREY L. SANDMAN

OF COUNSEL
EDWARD C. DAY

April 1, 1992

Mary Jane Cox
6601 South University, #200
Littleton, Colorado 80121

Re: [redacted]

Dear Mary Jane:

A rather disquieting development in the [redacted] case has recently been brought to my attention. I am refering to the letter of March 27, 1992 from the Child Advocacy and Protection Team of the Children's Hospital, and also to the "staffing" which Diane Baird and the Kempe National Center apparently intend to hold on April 6th from 1:00-3:00 p.m. with respect to [redacted]

I am trying desparately to mask my outrage at this unilateral and extrajudicial interferance in on going judicial proceedings which this letter and the "staffing" represent. I am utterly insensed by the fact that these people think it is necessary and appropriate to send a letter such as the March 27th letter, and include in the "distribution" yourself, Paula Tomko, etc., while excluding me! It makes me wonder about their objectivity as well as anyone who would consider participating.

Just a friendly word of advice; on February 27, 1991, Judge Leopold entered Permanent Orders in this case which remain in full force and effect. Paragraph 15 reads:

> "The prior orders of the Court concerning examinations of the child regarding sexual abuse remain in full force and effect."

One of the "prior orders" to which Judge Leopold refered is that which was dated December 19, 1990 (the "Interum Temporary Orders) which provide:

> "There shall be no examinations or <u>evaluations</u> of [redacted] with respect to the issue of sexual abuse without first obtaining an order of this court." (emphasise added) (paragraph 5)

On June 5, 1990 Judge Leopold entered the following order, which remains in effect:

"No further evaluations or examinations on child by a new or different professional shall occur without the requesting party filing a Motion for Ruling pursuant to C.R.C.P 121." [emphasise added]

If I find out that Maralee McLean had anything to do with bringing about this "staffing", she and anyone advising her will be the subject of a contempt citation.

My client and I both seriously question whether it is ethical for any of the attorneys listed on the "distribution" to attend and participate in such a staffing. The Court orders make it quite clear that further "evaluations" of [redacted] case are not to be made without prior order of Court. As we all know, the Court has entered orders appointing certain specified mental health professionals to conduct evaluations and to provide treatment. The Kempe Center is not among them, and with the exception of a single narrowly defined order allowing Children's Hospital to conduct one physical examination, Children's Hospital is not among them either.

C.R.S. 14-10-127 contains two particularily relavent provisions to this situation. First, it provides that reports and evaluations connected with custody cases are "confidential." The people on this "distribution" have not received an authorization from the sole custodian of [redacted], [redacted], to share in or be privy to the types of information which would be divulged and discussed in this "staffing." Furthermore, [redacted] has not authorized the release of the Kopetsky/Purcell report, dispite your apparent request that this report be made available to the "staffing." Secondly, the referenced statute provides that only Court appointed mental health professionals are to be engaged in the evaluation and report process. As I have already indicated, the Kempe Center and Children's Hospital have not been so appointed.

It appears, from the fact that you have requested permission of Ms. Kopetsky to release her report to this "staffing", that you are intending to participate in it. Though I wholheartedly disagree with the propriety, and even the ethics, of such a decision. If that is your decision, I feel I owe it to you to state my position in case you might want to reconsider. It is my intent to send a similar letter to the Kempe Center and Children's Hospital who, as you know, are under different ethical and legal constraints and, though they are not bound by the court orders issued in this case, are subject to civil litigation for intrusive conduct of this nature.

I am sorry this had to come to this.

Very truly yours,

ANDERSON, CALDER & SANDMAN
a Professional Corporation

Stephen P. Calder

SPC/trp

P.S. [redacted], as sole custodian for [redacted] and with the authority of C.R.S. 14-10-130 (1) vested in him, hereby advises that you, your agents or employees, and your client, Meralee McLean, are not authorized to divulge any medical or related information what so ever about [redacted] to any person or entity, specifically the Kempe National Center, Children's Hospital, Diane Baird, D.D. Harvey or his organization.

Excerpts from Judge Bieda's Order

March 16, 1993

"Based upon the evidence presented, the Court found that the mother suffers from hysterical personality disorder. The court also found the mother has developed an obsession regarding the alleged sexual abuse. It found that the child had been "severely damaged by the allegation and action of the mother, and as consequence the child will need long term therapy."

At that time the Court granted sole custody of the child to the father and allowed visitation with the mother. Implicit in the Court's order is a finding that no sexual abuse occurred.

The mother violated the court order to subject the child without an order on November 17, 1990.

Again, the mother violated the order in June of 1991, taking the child for another vaginal exam without a court order.

March 1992 Judge Deanna Hickman entered an order, which immediately limited visitation by the mother with the child to supervised visits only. The order required the mother's visitation to be conducted at and supervised by Children's Hospital.

The Court found:

The recommendations, findings, and concern especially by Ms. Kopetske and Dr. Purcell in the report of March 23, 1992, are sufficiently alarming to warrant imposition of immediate emergency orders as set forth herein due to the potential for immediate and irreparable harm to minor child if such order were not so implemented.

During the present proceedings, this Court advised counsel and the parties that the sexual abuse issue had been previously tried by a different judge, that the findings had been made adverse to the mother and that the Court had found, implicitly in its order that no sexual abuse had occurred. This court advised the parties that this Court was not sitting as an appellate court and that the sexual abuse issues previously raised by the mother had already been determined. In essence, this Court ruled that a new judge had been assigned to the case did not mean that the case went back to "square one," but rather, the parties were bound by the previous rulings made by the Court.

During the trial of the issues now before the Court, the mother offered no new credible evidence that would require the Court to reconsider the previous custody determination, nor did the mother request the Court to revisit the previous custody determination in her motion. The bulk of the mother's case, however, was to use the hearing as yet another forum to validate her accusations against the father. A minor part of her presentation was an attempt to justify her previous conduct which had violated the express orders of the Court, and to deny or explain the findings set forth in the report of Ms. Kopetski and Ms. Purcell.

In its Conclusions and Recommendations, the report stated: In their evaluation, as in every evaluation before it, enormous pressure by (the mother) to validate her conviction the (father) is sexually abusing (the child). It is very clear that for (the mother) the only purpose of having an evaluation is to gain another opportunity to state her conviction (that the child) must be protected from her father in hopes of finding an ally.

The report concluded: ...we reviewed the information gathered from others and in our own evaluation to see if there was evidence that (the father) is abusing (the child). Our conclusion is consistent with the conclusions of every other professional clinician we called. The concern about sexual abuse was taken very seriously. There is considerable and convincing evidence which supports a conclusion that she (the child) is definitely not being abused sexually, physically or emotionally by (the father). Though children may not verbalize any complaint, their physical and/or emotional pain and a disturbance in their relationship between (the child) and her mother, we would have been concerned.

It is inconceivable that (the child) could have had the perverse experiences and physical injury by her father that her mother describes and still behave toward him and with him as (the child) does.

The report also opines about the mother's personality:

The mother's personality characteristics are consistent with descriptions given by Wakefield and Underwager about parents who make false accusations of sexual abuse during custody disputes. They are also consistent with *parental alienation syndrome,as defined by *Gardner and as developed from experience by this team. (Id. p.69)

Visits with (the child) and her mother should be supervised. We are concerned that (the mother) has the resources and may be able to rationalize or justify to herself a plan to disappear with (the child). We are also concerned she may take her case to the media where (the child) would be exposed to publicity and to the exploitation of people who are interested in the social cause of sexual abuse.

In the event that any further investigations regarding sexual abuse are required they should consider (the mother), and her parents, relatives, friends, etc. as possible perpetrators… It is very important that the mother be held responsible for the effects of her actions. We recommend that she be responsible for all cost of evaluations, legal procedures, or therapies related to allegations of sexual abuse or related to custody and visitation questions. Obviously, (the mother) should pay child support.

The court, after considering their testimony and the report in its entirety, finds their investigation to be very thorough, accurate, credible, and professionally well done. It was an in-depth review of the history and evidence available.

Accordingly, the court will give the report and their testimony considerable weight in its decision.

Kopetski recommended that supervised visitations between the mother and the child must continue until the mother receives the therapy she desperately needs to put this matter behind her.

Ms. Kopetski testified that she had reviewed all of the various reports, evaluations, therapist reports, social worker reports, medical reports, and so forth and that it was her opinion the child had not been sexually abused by her father. She testified that because of the mother's obsession with the sexual abuse she was concerned that the mother may abduct the child if given the opportunity. She stated that she did not rule out the possibility of sexual abuse from another source, including the mother, and that the focus "on her genitals could be a form of sexual abuse."

During the course of the trial, the Court had the opportunity to observe the demeanor of the mother. The Court found her to be very dramatic and constantly trying to attract the attention of the Court. She testified at one point that the interactional report and evaluation, "makes me sick to my stomach."

When asked by her own counsel if she would continue with having the child examined if she had the opportunity, her answer was not a "no, I will not," but instead a long tirade on the history of the case. She could not or would not give a direct answer to this question. The mother also admitted to violating the Court's previous orders prohibiting her from having the child examined. She blamed the police detective whom she had contacted for suggesting she have the child examined; however she did not tell him of the Court's order.

In light for the overwhelming evidence that indicates that visitation would be harmful to the child, and that there is a risk that the mother will flee with the child.

Court concludes:

The mother and her counsel have admitted no credible evidence in this proceeding to show the father is now abusing the child or had ever abused his daughter sexually or otherwise. In fact, the overwhelming evidence is quite to the contrary.

Therefore, the court concludes, as did Judge Leopold two years ago, the father has not abused his daughter. The mother has emotionally abused the child by subjecting her to repeated exams, without court approval: by insisting she tell anyone who will listen that her father is abusing her, and by subjecting the child to intense media exposure and scrutiny.

The court finds that non-supervised visitation by the mother in this case would endanger the child's physical health and impair her emotional development, and it is in the best interest of the child that visitations with the mother be supervised. The supervised visits shall continue indefinitely, until such time as the mother can demonstrate to the court's satisfaction that she is no longer a danger to the child and that she recognizes the harm that she has done to the child and the damage and expense she has caused the father."

Of note: Kopetski and Purcell quoted Dr. Ralph Underwager and Dr. Holida Wakefield which was referenced in the above statements in Judge Bieda's order.

**I think it is important for the reader and for educational knowledge to be advised of the PAIDIKA, Winter 1993, Volume 3, Number 1 issue 9: The Journal of Pedophilia "Pedophiles can boldly and courageously affirm what they choose. They can say that what they want is to find the best way to love. Underwager states that pedophiles spend a lot of time and energy defending their choice. I don't think they need to do that, Pedophiles can boldly and courageously affirm what they choose. Pedophiles can make the assertion that the pursuit of intimacy and love is what they choose. With boldness they can say "I believe this is in fact part of God's will."

The problem is that the United States pedophilia is viewed so negatively that it would be very difficult for a pedophile, even with the most idealistic of motives and aspirations to make his relationship actually work. The solution he suggests is that pedophiles become much more positive. They should directly attack the concept, the image, the picture of the pedophile as an evil, wicked, and reprehensible exploiter of children.

**Dr. Holida Wakefield

"Given the schizophrenia and these hysterical attitudes about childhood sexuality, it's going to be difficult for pedophiles to appear more positive, to start saying they're not exploiters of children, that they love children, the sexual part included,even if it's a minor part. The goal is that the experience be positive, at the very least not negative, for their partner and partner's family. Even if it were a good relationship with the boy, if the boy was not harmed and perhaps even benefitted, if it tore the family of the boy apart, that would be negative."

Dr. Richard Gardner refer: Appendix C

APPENDIX E

References, Informational Articles and Books

Maralee Mclean "Mother Seeks Courtroom Reform for Sexually Abused Children and Protective Parents" ABA Child Law Practices, Claire Chiamulera, Vol.32 no. 6, June 6, 2013

Sarah Barness. "Mom Goes Public With Her Harrowing Story To Prevent More Children From Being Victimized" A Plus Media. Jan, 25 (2018)

Sheila Weller. "Mothers On the Run." US NEWS. June 13, 1988.

"America's Most Sexist Judges," Redbook. Dec, 1994 andFeb, 1994.

"California Family Courts Helping Pedophiles, Batterers get Child Custody, by Derek Jamison, Wed, March 2, 2011.

"Please Daddy, No" O, The Oprah Magazine by Jan Goodwin. "Parental Alienation" by Jana Bommersbach, Phoenix Magazine, May 2006

"Mom termed 'Parental Alienator' wins rare vindication in courts," L.A. Daily News, June 18, 2006

"How Many Children Are Court ordered into unsupervised visits or contact with the abusive parent after divorce?" by Joyanna Silberg, The leadership Council, September 22, 2008, http://leadershipcouncil.org/1med/PR3.html

"Courts Must Open Eyes and Ears to Abused Children" Women E- News by Maralee Mclean, Janurary 10, 2014

Meier, J. S. (2003). "Domestic Violence, Child Custody, and Child Protection: Understanding Judicial Resistance and Imagining the Solutions." American University Journal of Gender, Social Policy, and Law, 11, 657-731.

Meier, J.S, and Dickinson, S George Washington Law School, 35 Law & Ineq. 311 2017) Mapping Gender: Shedding Empirical Light on Family Courts' Treatment of Cases Involving Abuse and Alienation. Journal of Theory and Practice, Vol. 35, Issue 2

Ira Daniel Turkat, Ph.D., Harmful Effects of Child-Custody Evaluations on Children. Court Review, Vol. 52 pages (152-158)

Lears Magazine, Februaray 1992, INCEST by Heidi Vanderbuilt are substantiated. Incest a Chilling Report, Feb 1992 pp. 42-64

National Center For Prosecution of Child Abuse Vol 16, Number 6, 2003 * Parental Alientation Syndrome what Professionals need to know Part 1 by Erica Ragland, 2 Hope Fields

Revolution Feministe, Dec 13, (2016) Sporenda, F. Under the Law of the Father

ACE STUDY

Adverse Childhood Experiences

The initial ACES study was conducted in San Diego and led by Dr. Vincent Felitti at Kaiser Permanente and Dr. Robert Anda from the CDC. www.cdc.gov/violenceprevention/acestudy

NEWS MEDIA

CNN PRESENTS, Parental Alienation by Judy Woodruff and Cathy Slabogin (1997)

Sacrificing Mothers and Children: Family Courts Be- hind an Epidemic of Pedophilia Abuse by Keith Harmon Show (2012)

No Way Out But One: Documentary, by Garland Waller

APPENDIX F

Helpful Books for Parents, Attorneys, Judges, and Professionals

Judith Lewis Herman, Father-Daughter Incest, Harvard Universtiy Press, May 05,(2000)

Judith L. Herman, Trauma and Recovery: The Aftermath of Violence—From Domestic Abuse to Political Terror, Publisher Basic Books, July 07, (2015)

Judge Charles B. Schudson, and Billie Wright Dziech. ON TRIAL: America's Courts and Their Treatment of Sexually Abused Children. Beacon Press, 2010.

-A must read for all judges, lawyers, therapist, social workers, court appointed evaluators.

Kleinman Toby, J.D. and Daniel Pollack, "Domestic Abuse, Child Custody and Visitation" (Winning in Family Court) Oxford University Press, 2017

Lowenstein, S. R. (1991). Child sexual abuse in custody and visitation litigation: Representation for the benefit of victims. UMKC Law Review, 60, 227-82.

Lundy Bancrofts, Why Does He Do That. Berkley Trade Publishing, 2003.

Lundy Bancrofts, The Batterer as the Parent. Sage Publishing, 2002.

Mclean Maralee, "Prosecuted But Not Silenced" (Courtroom Reform for Sexually Abused Children) Morgan James Publishing, 2018

Mo Theresa Hannah, Ph.D and Barry Goldstein, J.D., Domestic Violence, Abuse, and Child Custody: Legal Strategies. Robert D. Reed Publisher, 2002. Civic Research Institute, Inc. April, (2010)

-Important book for judges, lawyers, therapist, social workers and more for pertinent education.

Myers, John E.B. A Mothers Nightmare—Incest: The legal guide for parents and professionals. Thousand Oaks, California Sage Publishing, 1997.

-Myers a distinguished professor and scholar. He is one of the country's foremost authorities on child abuse.

Many custody/parenting time cases include allegations of "parental alienation" or "parental alienation syndrome" (PAS), a term coined by Richard Gardner, M.D. that is unsubstantiated in the research literature (Fink, 2010). This discredited and debunked "syndrome" by the American Psychological and American Psychiatric Associations, continues to be used to remove children from custody/ parenting time with their protective parent (primarily mothers).The end result is children are abused emotionally, physically, and sexually by their custodial parent (Stark, 2010). These cases span decades in the family court as bias by judges, uninformed custody evaluators (Saunders, et. al., 2011), and other court-related personnel continue to put children in harm's way with their abusive parent (Mclean, 2012). The protective parent does everything possible to rescue the children from this situation while being mistreated and misrepresented by the players in family court (Goldstein & Hannah, 2010; Goldstein & Liu, 2013). The outcome for these children is an adult life filled with psychotherapy to overcome the trauma of their childhood (Perry, 2005; Shonkoff, et.al., 2012), and the physical impacts that haunt them throughout their lifetime (Felitti & Anda, 1998). The trauma for the protective parent includes lifelong impacts as well (Rivera, Sullivan, Cris, & Zeoli, 2012).

Geffner Robert, Ph.D, (Editor) et al. Domestic Violence Offenders: Current Interventions, Research, and Implications for Policies and Standards. Haworth Press, 2002.

Geffner Robert, Ph.D, (Editor) et al. Violence and Sexual Abuse at Home: Current issues in Spousal Battering and Child Maltreatment. Hawthworth Press, 1997.

Goldstein, Seth, J.D. The Failure of Family Courts to Protect Children from Abuse in Custody Disputes; a Resource Book for Lawmakers, Judges, Attorneys and Mental Health Professionals (pp. 105-112). FBI LAW ENFORCEMENT BULLETINE Seth L. Goldstein and R.D. Tyler

Putman Frank, PhD., MD. Dissociation in Children and Adolescents. Guilford Press, 1997.

Silberg Joyanna, PhD. The Dissociative Child: Diagnosis, Treatment and Management. Sidran Press, 1998.

Spiegel David, MD. Repressed Memories (Editor) et al.American Psychiatric Press, 1994.

Armstrong, L. Kiss Daddy Goodnight. New York: Hawthorne Books, 1978

Freyd, Jennifer. Betrayal and Trauma. Blockage of the information is functional. The logic of forgetting childhood sexual abuse. 1997.

-Pierce Janet Award for Excellence in Scientific writing, International society for Study of Dissociation

Bross, D.C. Multidisciplinary Advocacy for Mistreated Children. Denver: National Association of Counsel for Children, 1984.

Finch, S. M. "Adult Seduction of the Child." Medical Aspects of Human Sexuality

Hare, Robert D. Without Conscience: The disturbing world of psychopaths among us.

Kempe, R. S., and C. H. Kempe. Child Abuse. Cambridge, Mass.: Harvard University Press, 1978

Myers, J. E. B. Child Witnesses: Law and Practice. New York: Wiley Law Publications, 1987.

Chesler Phyllis, Ph. D. Mothers On Trial, The battle of Children and Custody, 1986

Carner Talia, Carner, Puppet Child, 2002

Neustein Amy, M.D., and Michael Lesher, J.D. Madness to Mutiny

Sgori, M., ed. Handbook of clinical Intervention in child sexual abuse cases. Lexington, Mass. Lexington Books, 1982.

Paidika. Brief The Journal of the Pedophilia, Vol. 3, Number 1, Issue 9 Winter 1993.

Saunders, Daniel, M.D. "When Battered Women Lose Custody."

Dr. Dan B. Allender, PhD. A Wounded Heart (pp. 32).

-Dr. Allender believes the process of "blocking memories" arises out of confusion, horror, shame, and sorrow. Put simply, it is more than pain that causes "blockage." It is a sense of one's world dissolving without the help we desire: order being replaced by chaos; relationship shattered by betrayal; and joy and happiness surmounted by despair. However gentle or menacing the intimidation may be, the secrecy is both the source of the fear and the promise of safety: "Everything will be all right if you don't tell." "This is our secret; nobody else will understand." It is clear to the child that this is something dangerous and bad.

Gail Goodman and Bette Bottoms (Editors). Child Victims and Witnesses. (pp. 96 and 97).

-In the most thorough study to date, Jones and McGraw (1987) studied 576 reports of sexual abuse received by the Denver Department of Social Services during 1983. Although the agency labeled 47 percent of the cases "unfounded," the researchers believed that less than 8% of the allegations were actually false. Most disturbing is the fact false allegations seem to be increasing in the context of custody and visitations disputes. While less than 2% of contested custody and visitation cases involve sexual abuse allegations.

Leora N. Rosen, PhD. Beyond The Hostage Child. Towards Empowering Protective Parents. August 2014 and "The Hostage Child" Sexual Abuse Allegations in Custody Disputes (Indiana University Press, 1996

Sam Vaknin, Ph.D. Malignant Self Love, (Narcissism Revisted) Prague & Skopje, 2006

DOMESTIC VIOLENCE & CHILD ABUSE RESOURCES

- American Bar Association Child Custody and Support
- Battered Mothers Custody Conference
- Battered Women's Justice Project (BWJP)
- Children Against Court Ordered Child Abuse
- Darkness to Light
- Fightback Foundation
- The Institute on Violence, Abuse and Trauma (IVAT)

- The Leadership Council on Child Abuse & Interpersonal Violence
- Legal Momentum
- Mothers of Lost Children
- National Coalition Against Domestic Violence
- National Family Court Watch Project
- National Organization for Men Against Sexism
- NPEIV National Partnership to End Interpersonal Violence
- Protective Mothers Alliance International
- PublicHealth.org
- Stop Abuse Campaign

ENDNOTES

i. An article I found on Ted Bundy years later fits this profile: "The psychopath's hot sexual exterior and stone- cold interior create a combustible mix that is irresistible to women as fire is to a pyromaniac. They are men who use, abuse, and manipulate others for the sheer pleasure of it. In fact most psychopaths would sooner murder your soul than your body. Sociologist Jose Sanchez, of Kean College in Union, New Jersey, describes them as sophisticated affluent types who blend and for many women are the most dangerous men in the world. The mask of sanity makes the psychopath so dangerous and terrifying. He is intelligent and has irresistible charm. They are masters at manipulating others for their personal gain their charm is legendary. He is so charming, so capable of sounding sincere, that the woman is mesmerized, especially if she wants romance. Psychopaths are incapable of feeling concern or remorse for the consequences of their actions. They can calmly rationalize the most heinous crimes. Experts at faking emotions, they may live quite normally for a while and then suddenly commit a brutal, stupid, or irresponsible act. They are undeniably narcissistic. They may express love but are incapable of feeling it. They see everything in terms of their own happiness, their own wants and desires." People Magazine 1977.

ii. Parent Alienation Syndrome by Richard Gardner p 24-5

iii. Gardner, (24-5)

iv. UMKC LAW REVIEW VOL, No. 2 pg 248. Gardner pages

v. Parent Alienation Syndrome by Richard Gardner 250-251

vi. Elizabeth Parsons Ware Packard, 1864

vii. Sharon R. Lowenstein, "Child Sexual Abuse in Custody and Visitation Litigation: Representation on Behalf of Victims, "UMKC Law Review, Vol. 60, No. 2, 1991.

viii. Dr. Richard Gardner: A Review of his Theories and Opinions on Atypical Sexuality, Pedophilia, and Treatment Issues by Stephanie J. Dallam, RN, MSN, FNP, Jan-Feb 1998, Vol 8, No 1

www.ingramcontent.com/pod-product-compliance
Lightning Source LLC
LaVergne TN
LVHW090433230725
816804LV00022B/839